LAN Basics with
Hands-On Software
3.11/3.12

Patricia Harris

Mesa Community College
Mesa, Arizona

McGraw-Hill

New York St. Louis San Francisco Auckland Bogotá Caracas
Lisbon London Madrid Mexico Milan Montreal New Delhi
Paris San Juan Singapore Sydney Tokyo Toronto

McGRAW-HILL
San Francisco, California

**LAN Basics
with Hands-On NetWare 3.11/3.12**

1 2 3 4 5 6 7 8 9 0 FGR FGR 9 0 9 8 7 6 5 4

ISBN 0-07-026915-7

Sponsoring Editor: Frank Ruggirello
Editorial Assistant: Debra Yohannan
Technical Reviewer: Craig Bodkin
Production Supervisor: Richard DeVitto
Project Manager: Shepherd, Inc.
Interior Design: Rick Hecker
Cover Designer: Janet Bollow
Compositor: Shepherd, Inc.
Printer: R. R. Donnelley & Sons

Library of Congress Catalog Card Number 94-78767

Table of Contents

Dedication

I wish to dedicate this text to my loving husband of 20 years, Jack, and my two fantastic girls, Lindsay and Nicole. I appreciate their understanding of my occasional late nights and letting me sleep in the next day during the times I was absorbed in the writing process. Thanks for understanding and working together to accomplish both the mission and vision. I love you three with all my heart.

I wish to acknowledge and also thank Rich Klein for coaxing me into signing with McGraw-Hill as an author and for his encouragement to share the accumulation of my classroom and personal professional works.

What would writing be without the whip cracker, Frank Ruggirello. With pride and joy, I appreciate the opportunity and friendship nurtured through this venture.

There is no question that this text benefitted from the reviewer's comments and I wish to personally thank them for their comments which only made this work flow better—thanks to their thoughtful attention.

Last, but not least, thanks and appreciation go to Rick Hecker and Debra Yohannan. Without both of them, working behind the scenes, none of us could have moved forward.

Patricia Harris

Preface

Learning NetWare just got easier. The skills and concepts presented in *LAN Basics with Hands-On NetWare 3.11/3.12* provide basic survival skills for anyone working on a NetWare Local Area Computer.

Designed for the LAN novice, this book provides basic vocabulary and skill-building. The reader will be able to distinguish protocol from topology, and obtain skills to differentiate NetWare commands from comparable DOS commands as well as gain new experience in accessing resources located on another computer.

Step-by-step, hands-on, easy-to-read instructions and a seamless integration of screen shots, reference charts, and key related points throughout this highly visual book provide a powerful teaching tool. This book networks the information and empowers the learner to offer an interactive learning experience.

This LAN is also a ready-reference guide with its use of key related points, margin terms, and at least one screen shot for each exercise. Designed to ease the learning of LAN and NetWare concepts while building skills through hands-on exercises, the use of the **NOTE:** sections and troubleshooting tips help overcome common distractions.

The text lends itself best to a hands-on lab setting, but can easily be adapted to a lecture with the lab as an independent component to the course. Each chapter is a building-block to the next one. With the exception of a few exercises, most are written to a low-security, high-proficiency end-user rather than freely allocating or proliferating the network supervisory level of security. This text can also supplement the main text in any course, in any discipline, using a NetWare network. When the instructor wants to be freed from the housekeeping chores of teaching the network or computer skills, *LAN Basics with NetWare 3.11/3.12* will address the needs of the novice LAN user.

Key Organization Elements

A **Brief Introduction to each Exercise** prepares the reader to begin the exercise for the first time or to repeat a particular exercise out of the regular sequenced progression.

A **Running Glossary** contains technical terms defined in the margins as they appear throughout the text.

Hands-On Exercises are indicated by a computer icon at the first step. Each exercise section provides numbered steps, citing the illustrations, tables, or figures as the reader performs the steps.

Key Related Points provide a check-point review of each hands-on exercise.

In Your Own Words sections provide critical thinking exercises.

Instructor Support

A comprehensive Instructor's Manual includes:

Answers to all end-of-chapter material as well as helpful hints on reviewing the concepts and leading a discussion using the In Your Own Words section.

An outline of the suggested time requirements for completing the chapters as well as advance preparation necessary and helpful strategies for administering the select chapters where student account access security privileges need to be increased.

Overhead transparency masters, chapter outline, matching terms, extra projects and extra fill-in the blank, true/false, and multiple choice tests and review material.

Networking–NetWare and LAN Concepts

OBJECTIVES

- Define a network and compare network types.

- Compare mainframe and minicomputer networks to client-server and peer-to-peer LANs.

- Define the purpose of the LAN operating system, server, client, network interface card, cabling system and connectors.

- Examine LAN topologies, protocols, and standards.

- Examine LAN cabling access methods and transport subsystems.

- Compare bandwidth to transmission speed.

- Define Novell's NetWare Operating System.

- Compare LANs to WANs and MANs.

CHAPTER INTRODUCTION

This chapter will address the purpose of a Local Area Network (LAN), the components of a LAN and define the LAN as a tool for the efficient distribution and sharing of resources. As companies downsize their computer networks from mainframes and minicomputers to interconnected desktop PC networks, a LAN is used to link workgroups together. It is the goal of this chapter to discuss the migration from the proprietary networks owned by the manufacturers of the mainframes and minicomputers to the privately owned and operated local area networks (LANs) where computers are networked within a close geographic area, usually within a department, building or group of buildings.

The Typical Pre-Network Office Setting

Inside a small office, Alexia asks Marsha for a copy of the report she has been working on. Marsha retrieves a floppy disk from her drawer, inserts it into her computer, saves the file to the disk, and passes the disk to Alexia. Alexia starts working on the report, but gets sidetracked on another matter. Meanwhile, Marsha gets some new figures to integrate into the report, but instead of updating Alexia's file, she works on her own document file. Then Alexia finishes her changes to the document. There are now two different versions of the same report, thus someone has to waste valuable time combining all the changes into one document file.

The morale of the story is: Today's smallest office has given way to a proliferation of computer technology, focused on meeting its particular needs. Nothing beats the flexibility and power of a local area network for sharing information and resources.

NETWORK: A TOOL FOR THE EFFICIENT USE OF SHARED RESOURCES

Network
Interconnection of computers and devices using various media. Typically established to share and distribute information to computing resources using a high-speed data communication medium.

A **network** is a system that transfers information. Electronic mail, data files, and programs are just a few examples of information transferred in a networked environment.

In the traditional mainframe or minicomputer systems, a single computer stores all the data and makes all of the calculations. With the PC-based systems of today, each unit is equipped to store data and perform calculations individually. Because of the internal hardware components and the design of the individual (personal) computer systems, such as the hard disks, microprocessors, and random-access memory contained in each personal computer system, the actual computing power which once went on only inside the central mainframe or minicomputer is now available within each personal, desktop computer system.

Downsizing
The redesign of mainframe generation computing to interconnected, desktop PCs (local area networks).

Upsizing
Matching the application requirements to the capabilities of the available hardware and software.

Peers
Computers acting as either a client and/or server simultaneously.

Peer-to-Peer
A network architecture where two or more nodes communicate directly without the need of an intermediate device. A node can be both a client and/or a server.

Node
Computing device capable of communicating on a network. With NetWare, a workstation is often called a node.

The networking trends of the 90's are driving network growth. The term **downsizing** comes to networking as companies move away from mainframes and minicomputers to a network of interconnected desktop PCs. **Upsizing** is finding new uses for the network today where small workgroups expand their individual desktop PCs to take advantage of moving information through the entire company's organization. More sophisticated software applications require faster computers to run them and faster networks to transmit data. The very act of sharing data creates more data, creating a need for larger more dependable hard drives and computer systems. The growing complexity of networks is forcing large and small companies alike to weigh the benefits against the costs.

Computer networks provide rapid access to various sources of information. The network is a tool for facilitating employee communications and conducting business in a timely fashion through the access and sharing of programs and data files, and through the use of electronic mail. It is not unlikely to see today's network users sending and receiving messages electronically, without ever printing them to paper.

Networks decrease resource redundancy. They allow every workstation to use the same program from wherever they are located on the network, without installing the program on each workstation's hard disk. With a network, the savings is substantial, not only on software, but on printers and disk storage devices as well.

The concept of file and print sharing enables a user to sit down at any PC, anywhere they have access to log in to the network, and access their files or print their data to any printer on the network.

Network Types: Distributed or Centralized (Peer-to-Peer or Client-Server LANs)

When network nodes perform the same function, they are referred to as **peers**. Communication between such nodes is usually referred to as **peer-to-peer**. The term **node** is used here to refer to computers on the network, whether they act as a server or a workstation.

The peer-to-peer LAN is classified as a **distributed network.** PCs on a peer-to-peer network can be configured (1) exclusively as a server to share its data and application files, (2) solely as a client to obtain resources from other computers (acting as servers) or (3) as both a client and a server. In the latter case, the server can also be used as an individual, stand-alone computer.

Distributed networks are less powerful and often times slower than server-based LANs, especially when many people access the same database. Historically, a peer-to-peer LAN is less expensive per unit than centralized, or **client-server networks**. Distributed networks are thought to be easier to install, but more difficult to maintain than

Distributed Network
A computer network in which processing is performed by several separate computers linked by a communication medium. The processing unit, referred to as the server, completes the task independently and reports the results when completed. (See page 3).

Client-Server Network
A network architecture where clients request resources from the servers. Servers store data and programs, and coordinate network-wide services to clients. Client-server architecture exploits the power of the network server. (See page 3).

Centralized Network
A computer network in which a single, extremely powerful computer coordinates network-wide services to clients.

client-server networks because of the many separate servers, all with hard disks requiring back-ups and on-going regular maintenance.

Client-server networks offer centralized access to services, applications, and/or devices. The client-server, or server-based LAN is classified as a **centralized network.** Data is processed at individual networked PCs **(workstations)** but stored on a central, or dedicated file server, where shared resources are consolidated. Distributed processing takes place at the individual workstations as the data is downloaded to the workstation's memory. These networks are typically larger, more powerful, and historically more expensive per unit than distributed, peer-to-peer, networks. The current trend is away from peer-to-peer LAN and toward client-server networks.

Network Trends: Client-Server LANs

While large companies may still use a mainframe or a minicomputer for network services, the personal computers have grown powerful enough to operate as servers in many, if not most, networks. The trend toward larger client-server networks sharing software has created a demand for multiprocessor servers, which use two or more microprocessor chips. The most audible trend in networking is the migration to client-server networks, which are a cross between traditional mainframe computing and simpler peer-to-peer networks.

With traditional mainframe or minicomputer systems, a single computer stores all the data and makes all the calculations. Each device is classified by its hardware capabilities and individual processing potential. A **terminal** is a device with no internal microprocessor, and serves as a screen display unit to handle screen output and keyboard input. A **PC** is another type of device which can be adapted for use on a mainframe or minicomputer network system by the use of terminal emulation software, rendering the PC's microprocessor useless as it relys upon the processing capabilities of the mainframe or minicomputer. With either a terminal or PC emulating a terminal, the processing takes place on the central or main computer, not distributed to the device accessing the mainframe or minicomputer.

At the other end of the networking continuum, peer-to-peer networks link desktop PCs so they each can access files, programs, and peripherals (especially printers) found on other networked PCs. Peer networks tend to scatter data across the network, which makes it difficult if not impossible to find data. When the user of a peer PC can find and utilize a program or file from another peer, the data is simply downloading and processed at the user's individual PC.

Both the mainframe and minicomputing environments as well as the peer network environments have their limitations. Mainframe and mini-

Workstation
Any personal computer (other than the network server) attached to the network. This term also can refer to high-performance computers optimized for scientific or graphic applications. Workstations, in this book, take on the former, rather than the latter, definition. (See page 4).

Terminal
Combination keyboard and display devices that do not have distributed processing capability, commonly referred to as dumb terminals. (See page 4).

PC
Personal Computer. With networks, any personal computer can be called a node. (See page 4).

Network Operating System
Software which is installed and configured to coordinate the many functions of computer-to-computer communication. With client-server networks, the NOS is installed and runs on the network server.

computers are expensive to maintain and upgrade. The **network operating system** of the mainframe or minicomputer is proprietary, owned and controlled by the manufacturer of the hardware, and can operate on a priority basis where users may have to wait their turn until jobs with higher priority are serviced first.

Client-server networks constitute a compromise between the traditional mainframe/minicomputer and peer network environments. The client-server network divvies up computing chores between client and server. Like a mainframe or minicomputer, the network's most important files and programs are stored on a single computer called a server. Like a peer network, users of the client-server network download information to their client PCs, where the actual computing/processing occurs.

LANS

Local area networks, (LANs) could be thought of as pockets of coordinated computing within a small geographic area. A LAN could be networked with many servers. If the LAN holds many servers, the servers are likely to be in place to segment the LAN to meet demand, as a way to divide and balance the network traffic. When workstations attached to different servers want to communicate, the servers act to control and route communications. Thus, the server balances the load within their segment, and facilitate client workstation communication between network segments.

The Network Server

The **network server** looks no different than the client workstation from the outside, but inside the server is usually configured with a very fast microprocessor, such as the Intel 80486 or Pentium microprocessor chip. The server contains as much as four times the amount of RAM as the client workstation, and is typically equipped with large hard disk storage capacity, sometimes arranged in an array of hard disks. Network servers typically handle the coordination of various functions, including hard disk storage and printing tasks. The network server is usually called the *file server* or *server,* which refers to the computer (or computers) that run the network.

Usually, most network servers are designed to function and serve as a remote hard drive for any networked PCs attached to it. The workstations use the server's resources but can also share their own devices with other workstations on the network; this is usually in coordination with the network server which handles the routing of jobs to other network devices.

Local Area Network (LAN)
A group of computers and peripheral devices located in a close geographic region and connected by a communications medium. The medium is typically coaxial, twisted-pair or fiber optic cabling and responsible for carrying the communications along the connecting path. (See page 5).

Network Server
A computer that coordinates access to files, printing, communications, and other resources available on the network. A server typically has a more advanced processor, more memory, and larger disk storage capacity than client workstations. (See page 5).

DOS
Acronym for Disk Operating System. An operating system typically found on client workstations, known as DOS clients, originally developed by Microsoft for the IBM PC. Novell markets Novell DOS, originally developed by Digital Research and called DR-DOS.

NetWare
Multi-task network operating systems developed by Novell, Inc.

The server is where the *Network Operating System (NOS)* is installed. The server controls the network operating system, not the local client workstation operating systems. Each client workstation uses its own operating system **(DOS)** to boot-up (start-up). Next, the client will load the client portion of the network operating system and then use its network interface card to communicate over the cabling system and attach to the network's operating system controlled by the server.

The Purpose of the Network Operating System

NetWare is classified as one type of Network Operating System (NOS). NetWare works with the local operating systems, such as DOS, OS/2 or Unix, to expand the resources of an individual LAN client workstation. The server contains the network operating system which is dedicated to granting requests for clients. The network interface card is the physical component inside the server which interconnects the network operating system to all the other physical network devices. The server is orchestrating communication between itself and other servers, the attached clients and shared resources, such as printers.

Novell's Network Operating System

Novell's operating system is called **NetWare** and is a very popular choice to run the network today. NetWare comes in versions, such as 3.x and 4.x. These versions of Novell's NOS software provide the intelligence that passes information from the server to the NIC inside each workstation. NetWare allows companies to set up logical connections to the server(s) on the network so they can utilize and share their resources. NetWare keeps track of the users on the LAN, and provides other capabilities, such as electronic messaging, resource monitoring, and security.

The Novell 3.12 Server

This book focuses upon Novell's version 3.12 of the NetWare family of operating systems. Once installed on the LAN server, NetWare 3.12 can address up to 32TB (terabytes or trillion bytes) of disk storage and can handle a total of 2,048 hard disks per server. The total addressable RAM and the largest file size for a NetWare 3.12 server is 4GB (gigabytes).

Other Servers on the NetWare LAN: Print Servers

To utilize a printer attached to the file server, a logical connection between the workstation and the print server's printer is established.

With NetWare, printing does not have to be centralized on the file server. Workstations can share their locally attached printers. PCs can be dedicated as print servers or separate devices can also be installed to alleviate the file server from having to carry and manage the printing load alone.

Booting to the LAN: The Physical and Logical Connections

The *physical connections* between network nodes are made by the NICs and cabling; however, the *logical connections* are also a factor to consider in networking. When a workstation wants to connect to the server, NetWare sets up the logical connection. For example, if the workstation wanted to use the hard disk of a network server, drive F: could actually be accessing/switching to the server's hard disk across the network. This would appear as if drive F: were located directly on the workstation. Logical connections are made between the workstation booting to the network and the user logging in. Logical connections are typically drives F: through Z: on the workstation.

The Network Client

Client
A PC directly attached (physically attached) to the LAN cabling system installed and running client software to activate its network connection.

The term **client** refers to computers connected to the server. As previously stated, the term server refers to the computer (or computers) that run, operate and manage the network. The client initiates requests where the server processes, manages, and controls these requests. As mentioned earlier, the client will first run its own, local operating system (such as DOS) and then load and run the client program(s) to configure the workstation to be seen as a network client by the server.

Stand-Alone Applications
Programs typically installed on the stand-alone PC. Some stand-alone applications can be adopted for multi-use on a network server, while others cannot.

Shared Applications: Pure network (or network-aware programs) compared to stand-alone (or single-user programs)

Most **stand-alone applications** (or single-user applications) can be installed on a network server, but are smart enough to detect that you are trying to run them on a network. Some single-user software simply has technical incompatibilities with some networks and may subtly, or not so subtly, malfunction in the presence of a network. If single-user software does allow you to let two or more users have simultaneous access, then there's questionable legal and ethical ground to consider.

Pure Network Applications
Programs that must be installed on the network as they are reliant upon simultaneous access, or the connections the network avails.

On the other hand, **pure network applications** (or network-aware programs) are created to utilize networks and easily allow for simultaneous access. Each program has a separate and distinct user interface which you must learn before these applications can be used effectively. One example of pure applications is electronic mail, which is perhaps the most common network-aware application. Electronic mail allows users on local workstations to send messages to others on the network. It represents one way that networks can improve communication.

Another example of a pure network application is file transfer utilities. File transfer is an essential application in nearly all networks because it moves files from one computer to another, such as a PC to a mainframe. In some cases, this requires translation of the file from the data format of one computer to that of another.

Terminal Emulation
A method of operation or software which turns a PC or networked workstation into a terminal, usually for the purpose of communicating with a mainframe or minicomputer.

Terminal emulation was the first pure network application. As explained earlier, prior to what is known today as "the age of networking," people used terminals to access application programs on the mainframe and minicomputers. Terminal emulation software performs this function to allow microcomputers to act as if they were a terminal.

Groupware
Software specifically designed to be used by a group working on the same project and needing to share or coordinate data.

Groupware, a common term used today, refers to an application that allows users to electronically coordinate calendars, meetings, phone calls, and other appointments. Mainly known for providing administrative services, groupware is designed to increase productivity and cooperation among groups of coworkers. The intent of groupware is to seamlessly integrate application program functions.

Examples of stand-alone (or single-user) applications adapted to run in a client-server environment include: word processing, spreadsheet, databases, presentation graphics, and project management. Stand-alone applications adapted to run on a network are typical examples of file sharing, where software must be adapted for the network or "multi-user certified."

When the stand-alone application packages are adapted for client-server (or multi-user) computing, they are broken down into two parts: the client and the server. The client runs the application's user interface and related processing, while the server usually houses the CPU-intensive operations, such as database lookups or application-dependent processing.

Stand-alone (or single-user) applications are adapted to client-server (or multi-user) computing because of (1) ease of use, (2) file sharing, (3) resource limitations, (4) set-up and maintenance, and (5) economies of scale.

NetWare's Security and System Administration Features

Almost all network operating systems provide some way of keeping track of users. NetWare keeps track of the users through usernames (or user accounts), set up in its system configuration menu utility, Syscon.

NetWare file servers are designed to be able to handle a very important connectivity feature, system security. Upon logging in to the network server for the first time, you must know your valid username and password, initially set and assigned by the System Administrator. If you forget your password, the System Administrator can reset it, enabling you to log in.

Security options on the network range from being able to hide or restrict access to improving resource allocations. Print server operators and user account managers help the System Administrator with various security and bottleneck areas of the network.

With NetWare 3.11 and earlier versions of NetWare, electronic mail (messaging) was an additional feature often purchased separately. Beginning with NetWare's 3.12 version, electronic mail has been bundled as part of the operating system purchase. Electronic mail message administration is separate from the network's system administration.

LANs, MANs, AND WANs

As mentioned earlier, the direct, physical attachment of all the computers to the centralized cabling (*backbone*) establishes a network classified as a local area network. The cabling on a LAN could run within and between buildings. LANs are typified by their direct cabling attachment (physical connection) to the backbone as well as by the close proximity of the computers within a small geographic area. LANs are not usually larger than a college campus and can be described as a single location (e.g., a building, a campus, or several buildings on campus) of connected computers and peripherals to data and peripheral-sharing groups. LANs are distinguished by high data transfer rates, low error rates, and inexpensive media. Most LANs are privately owned and maintained.

Metropolitan Area Network (MAN) A high-speed, geographically dispersed network that typically connects LANs across a metropolitan city.

A **metropolitan area network (MAN)** is usually spread across a city. MANs use the bounded media (physically attached cabling) connect to nodes within a LAN as well as connect to other nodes at other geographic sites within a metropolitan city using unbounded media (e.g., microwave and laser) to communicate. MANs could also use modems and phone lines to interconnect.

MANs have much in common with LANs, but are, in many ways, more sophisticated. In addition to data and voice, MANs transmit video and other types of audio. They are designed to handle greater distances than LANs and can be used to tie several LANs together for high-speed, integrated network systems.

Wide Area Network (WAN) A network dispersed across a large geographic area, often crossing boundaries of cities and states.

A **wide area network (WAN)** is usually spread across states. With a WAN, leased telephone lines and high-speed modems are primarily used to communicate data. Common communications carriers like MCI, Sprint, or AT&T could be used to offer similar services. Communication takes place over telephone lines, satellites, or terrestrial microwave systems. WANs are often created by connecting LANs and MANs and often involve a conglomeration of different technologies. Compared to LANs and MANs, WANs are slower and more error prone. An example of a WAN is the Internet.

CHARACTERISTICS OF NETWORK COMMUNICATIONS

As defined earlier, a network is a system that transfers information. Electronic mail, data files and programs are examples of information transferred in a networked environment.

Computer networks include all the hardware and software required to connect the computers as well as other shared devices used to communicate along a channel (cabling system or other type of medium), so that resources and information can be shared simultaneously. This interconnection of devices enables and facilitates the transfer of information.

Medium
Used to interconnect computers on a network. Bounded (cabling) medium is more common than unbounded (microwave, laser, etc.).

Networks are characterized as systems that host data communications. To clarify, data communication is comprised of four components: the sender, receiver, medium, and message. The sender could be one PC communicating to another, the receiver. A networked computer sends a message to another computer through a **medium** (usually a cabling system). Cable is the most popular way today to connect the computers together. There is also a newer technology, the wireless network medium, which is making impressive progress though in the developmental stages as of this writing.

To network PCs you need some kind of electronic communications system. The sending and receiving of a single bit of information, using electronic signaling, is the way networks function. This means that over the network, a voltage change will take place so many times per second. The rate at which the voltage can change on a given piece of wire is dependent on the material and its construction, hence the importance of the properties of the medium. Various effects, such as resistance (the cable's tendency to oppose the flow of electricity) and impedance (much like resistance, although this comes into play when the electrical signal is changing rather than when it's constant), limit how fast and how far you can send electrical signals.

Getting back to the four components of data communication (sender, receiver, medium, message), the coordination of the electrical signals between network interface cards is the essence of data transmission. You must know whether the signal is the transmission from one level to another or whether the signal is when a particular voltage is reached. Then, you must know how to tell if the signals have been corrupted in transmission. You will need to have a set of rules (standards) that determine when you can or cannot send data.

Devices that communicate with other devices on a network are called nodes, stations, or network devices. The signaling medium and network interface cards are designed to specify the transmission. The faster the rate of signaling (more or less equal to the rate of transition from one voltage level to another), the harder it becomes to send clean signals over long distances. Problems arise that could affect the signal include attenuation (diminishing electrical signals) and EMI, electromagnetic interference (or noise). The specific type of network interface cards vary by manufacturer, and must be factored into the equation when measuring the efficiency of network communication's systems.

Network Interface Cards and Drivers

The data is transferred along the network through the network cabling. Different types of cabling are supported by different types of NICs. Figure 1.1 shows how the NICs are attached to the main circuit board (motherboard) inside the computer.

For a company's LAN to work with a manufacturer's network interface card (NIC) in the workstation, there must be a network interface card driver. The driver is a file, written by the NIC manufacturer to activate the actual hardware component (NIC) and serve as an interface between the NIC and the network operating system, NOS (in this case, NetWare). Many network operating systems can work with a variety of NICs because they are compatible with a variety of drivers. NIC manufacturers keep in close contact with NOS vendors to assure compatibility and maximize their product's marketability.

Network Interface Card (NIC)
Also called Network Adapter Board. Expansion component (adapter board) which interconnects workstation(s) and server(s) using the network cabling system.

The **network interface card** is usually referred to as the NIC, but can also be called a LAN card, network adapter card, network adapter board, or network interface adapter. The NIC is an add-in, expansion board that is installed in a PC's expansion slot, allowing it to communicate as part of the LAN. The server receives requests through its NIC. Refer to Figure 1.1.

NICs can be classified into four categories: ARCnet, Ethernet, Token Ring, or proprietary. Broadly, networks are divided into patterns of information sent in unmatched types of frames based upon by the different type of category. Theoretically, NICs of the same classification are

FIGURE 1.1

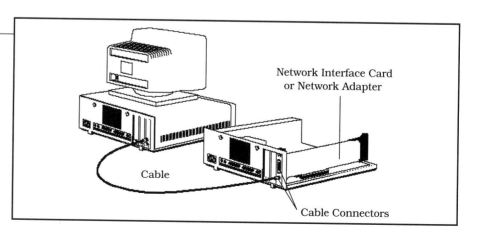

Network Interface Card
or Network Adapter

Cable

Cable Connectors

Baseband
Network transmission used by most LANs which transmits signals as direct current pulses. A single digital signal describes the channel (bandwidth).

Broadband
Network transmission which includes voice, video, and data over the same medium. This transmission divides the channel into several distinct channels that can be used concurrently.

Twisted-Pair Cabling (TP)
Cable comprised of two or more pairs of insulated wires, twisted together, at six twists per inch. The cable may be shielded or unshielded. In twisted-pair cabling, one wire carries the signal and the other is for grounding.

interchangeable. In reality, you must ask the network software manufacturer, and/or NIC manufacturer, if a specific brand has been tested with a particular NOS manufacturer's software to support a classification such as ARCnet, Ethernet, Token Ring, or proprietary. Novell tests manufacturer's NICs and certifies these products by allowing the manufacturer to market the product using the Novell logo as an authenticating "stamp of approval."

THE PHYSICAL AND ELECTRICAL NATURE OF CABLING

The issues that define what kind of cable is suited for varying physical and electrical environments differ by network type. **Baseband** is a network type where an electrical signal is transmitted on a physical medium (cable). **Broadband** is the other network type that simultaneously transmits multiple electrical signals at different frequencies. Baseband is cheaper than broadband, and is classified as a bounded medium—a way to classify devices physically attached by cabling.

Cabling is often defined by its rate of speed, type of cabling, and maximum length in hundreds of meters. For example, 10BASE2 cabling is 10 megabits per second (Mbps), baseband, and 200 meters before a connector or repeater is needed.

LAN Cabling Types

Twisted-Pair Cabling

The most popular type of cabling is **twisted-pair cabling**. Figure 1.2 provides an example of twisted-pair cabling, a flexible, inexpensive, and easy to install cable. Twisted-pair (TP) cable uses two wires that are separately insulated and twisted together. Twisting the wires increases the conductivity and reduces external electromagnetic interference. One or more wire pairs may exist inside an insulating sheath. Most TP cables, such as standard telephone cabling, is unshielded. In some situations,

FIGURE 1.2

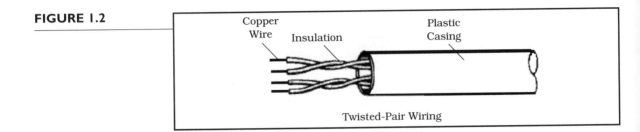

Twisted-Pair Wiring

the existing telephone cabling is used since it eliminates the need to install more cabling and is twisted-pair.

Twisted-pair comes in different sizes and may be shielded by different materials. Most twisted-pair is shielded by PVC (Poly Vinyl Chloride), but this material emits toxic fumes, so TP insulated near air ducts must be shielded in another substance, often Teflon (or plenum). TP cables have different electrical properties caused by differences in wire size, insulation, and pair twisting. Compared to other bound media, TP is more common, less expensive, more readily available, and more susceptible EMI and tapping.

Coaxial Cabling

Coaxial Cabling (COAX)
A high-capacity cable that contains a solid, inner copper wire acting as a conductor and surrounded by plastic insulation and an outer braided copper or foil shield.

Other types of cabling include coax and cable TV (CATV) type cables. These cable types are also fairly inexpensive, but are a bit more difficult to work with. Figure 1.3 illustrates **coaxial cabling**.

Coax is derived from the fact that two conductors (an inner conductor and an outer conductor) share the same axis. The center of the cable is a relatively stiff wire encased in insulating plastic foam. This foam is surrounded by the second conductor, a wire mesh tube (some include conductive foil wrap) that also serves as shielding. A thick, insulating plastic tube forms the cable's external cover. Coaxial cable comes in a variety of types and thickness. Thicker coax carries signals longer distances than thinner cable, but thicker cable is also more expensive and less flexible. Compared to TP, coax is faster (supports higher data rates), less susceptible to EMI and tapping, less common, more expensive, and has a more complex insulation process. Cable TV and Ethernet both use coaxial cable.

Fiber Optic Cabling
Cabling that sends pulses of light along optical fibers. Immune to electrical interference and often used as a high-speed transmission medium.

Fiber Optic Cabling

Fiber optic cabling is another type of cabling that is a very expensive option. Fiber is increasing in popularity because it meets such needs as increasing network performance between buildings. Refer to Figure 1.4.

FIGURE 1.3

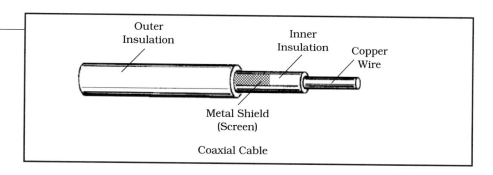

Outer Insulation

Inner Insulation

Copper Wire

Metal Shield (Screen)

Coaxial Cable

FIGURE 1.4

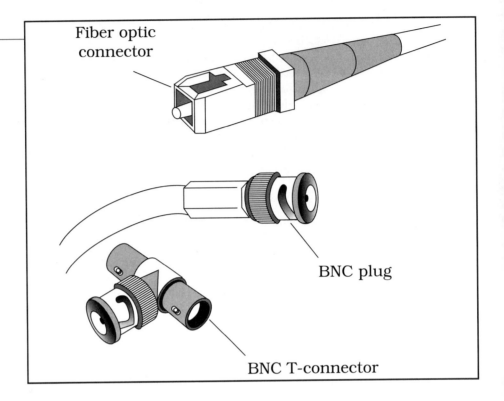

Fiber optic connector

BNC plug

BNC T-connector

Fiber optic cable is made of light-conducting glass or plastic fibers, centered in a thick tube of protective cladding surrounded by a tough outer sheath. One or more fibers can be bundled in the center of the cable, which can be entirely nonmetallic. Pulses of light are transmitted by either lasers or LEDs over the length of the fibers and received by photodetectors at the far end. Optical fibers are much smaller and lighter than both TP and coax. Large, multiple-connection trunk lines, using fiber optic cables, can carry more conductors than similar-sized wire cables. Fiber optic cables support much higher data rates than TP or coax. Light signals do not attenuate (lose strength) over distance to the same degree as electrical signals. Fiber transmission, therefore, requires fewer intermediate signal regeneration devices.

Fiber is not susceptible to EMI and is very difficult to tap. The principle disadvantage with fiber optic cabling is its relatively high cost, although this is changing as it becomes more popular. Fiber offers the highest bandwidth and is emerging as one of the more exciting network technologies.

CONNECTORS: THE CONNECTING PIECES

There are several ways to connect or network computers. There is also a wide variety of connectors, or connecting pieces, attached to the medium between NICs. The purpose of connectors is to join wiring and to boost signal strength to account for such problems as attenuation or EMI.

SOME COMMON CONNECTORS

T connectors	Require you to cut the cable and fix a bayonet connector to the end.
BNC (or bayonet) connectors	Lock the T-connector so you get a three-way connection to provide a straight line for the network cabling to pass through and a tap for the PC network interface card to attach.
DB connectors	Located on cables with a male (the end with the pins) and a female end piece, both in the shape of a D. There are three common forms of DB connectors: DB-9, with 9 pins, DB-15, with 15 pins, and DB-25 with 25 pins. DB connectors are commonly used to connect serial devices, such as printers.
Repeaters	Differ from other connectors because they serve as a means of overcoming limitations in length or constraints surrounding loss of signal strength. A repeater's functions is to recondition and regenerate signals from one piece of cable to another.
RJ connectors	Are a family of connectors, such as RJ-45, that support two or four wires. The RJ-11 family member is used for telephone installations and thought to be somewhat undesirable in a network due to confusion and complications arising from plugging a PC into a telephone wall socket. The RJ-45 connector is larger than the RJ-11 and preferred because it supports eight wires. Both RJ-45 and RJ-11 are connections for twisted-pair cabling, also called 10BASET cable.

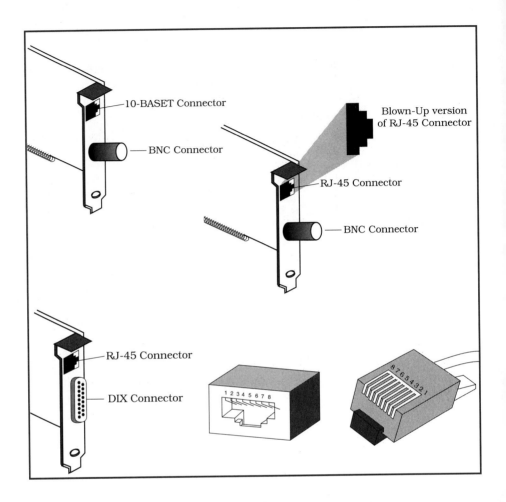

SOME COMMON CONNECTORS (CONT.)

Terminating connectors   Involve putting a resistor (the terminator) across the pair of conductors (wires) at opposite ends of the cable length. This resistance absorbs the energy of the signal at the cable ends and prevents reflection which distorts the upcoming signals. Each network requires different termination resistances (e.g., thin Ethernet cabling uses 50-ohm terminations).

Unique connectors   There are other connectors, such as the hermaphroditic connector used with Token Ring cabling, or the optical connectors used with fiber optic cabling.

LAN TOPOLOGIES

Network Topology
The map of the network. The physical arrangement describes the physical topology. The logical path the message takes to get from one computer to another is the logical topology.

Most networks serve as the electronic communications pathway or the "backbone" for the company's computing needs. The physical arrangement of network nodes (workstations and servers) is called the **network topology**.

Different networks require different types of topologies. There are three major types of topologies: *bus*, *star*, and *ring*. With the bus topology, shown in Figure 1.5, all the nodes are connected to a single trunk cable in a linear fashion, resembling clothes hanging on a line. The star topology, Figure 1.6, consists of a central connecting device (called a hub) with branches going off to each workstation. With the ring topology, Figure 1.7, all nodes connect to a single cable to form a ring.

LAN PROTOCOLS

Protocol
A set of specifications defining the procedures to follow for format, timing, sequence, and error checking when a message is transmitted and received.

With a LAN, each workstation attaches to the network via the cabling, which is attached to the Network Interface Card (NIC) inside the computer. There are many varieties and types of NICs, and almost all of them have different characteristics. The most important characteristics are protocol, access method/scheme, and speed.

A **protocol** describes how the network interface cards make contact with and recognize each other. Further, protocols are the building

FIGURE 1.5

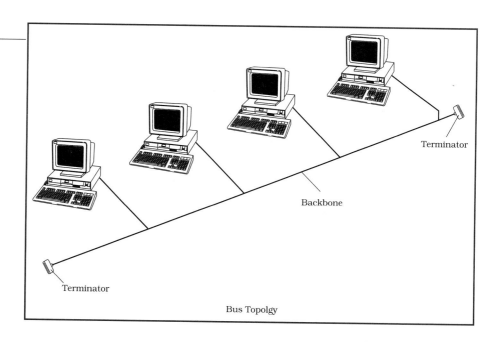

Terminator

Backbone

Terminator

Bus Topolgy

FIGURE 1.6

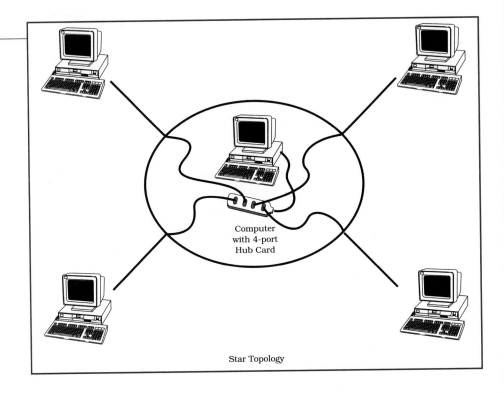

Star Topology

FIGURE 1.7

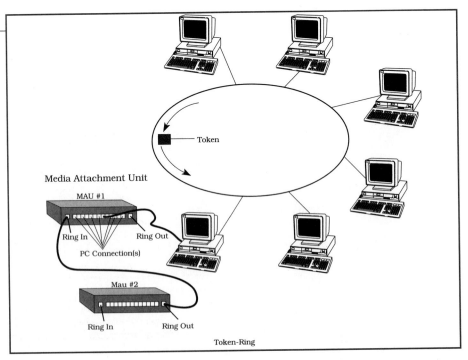

Token-Ring

blocks that turn cables and attached computers into smooth functioning communications systems.

Protocol specifications are formal documents that describe how the protocol will operate and specify the rules for communication. *Protocol implementations* is only one vendor's implementation of a protocol specification which is why no two network installations are exactly alike.

LAN STANDARDS

Standards
Establishing connectivity using multiple vendors within an open architecture. Standards, such as the OSI model, are formed by committees, such as the International Standards Organization.

Protocols become **standards** as a result of superior features or simply because they are supported by large, influential vendors. Take the scenario of a customer purchasing a household light bulb. The size and threading of the bulb is a standard. Although there are different types of light bulbs, virtually all manufacturers build lamps that take standard-size bulbs. Hence, the result is that customers purchase light bulbs from various retail outlets and rest assured that the light bulbs will fit the lamps in their homes.

Compare the purchase of light bulbs to the purchase of automobile tires. Tires come in standard sizes. Customers purchase tires specific to certain automobile types. Thus, the conclusion is that light bulbs are more standard than tires.

As the network industry has matured, some organizations have attempted to legislate protocol standards. These efforts have met with varying degrees of success. The more "standard" the protocol, the more implementations there are available from which to choose.

Every protocol offers certain features. Developed by the International Standards Organization, the OSI reference model represents protocols created at all layers. The OSI reference model, pictured in Figure 1.8, is comprised of seven layers.

FIGURE 1.8

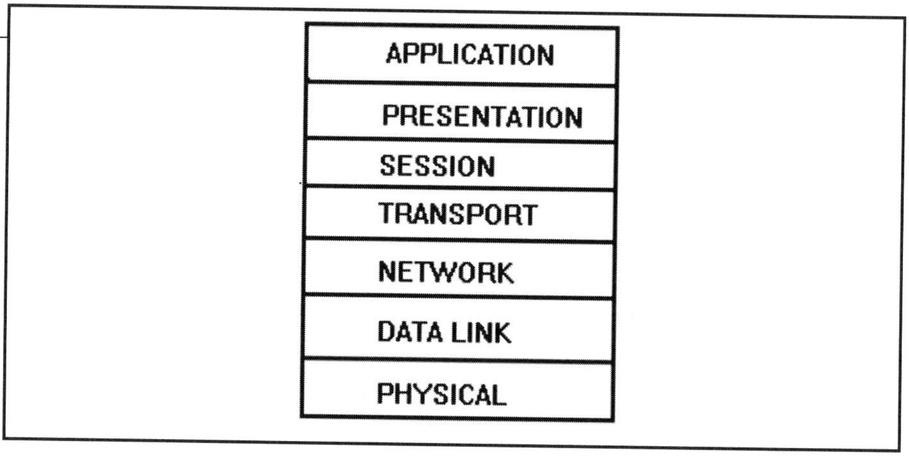

Network architectures are layered for better comprehension, increased modularity and more consistent problem solving. The OSI Reference Model divides communication tasks into layers and solves each individually. Thus, the "Divide-and-Conquer" model for networking calls for tiered-step solution. The layers of the OSI interact, but in minimal, well-defined ways. The top (Application) layer, is closest to the user. The bottom (Physical) layer, is closest to the actual network medium (cabling). Communication through these tiered-steps of the architecture are necessary for optimal communication. The same is true of communication between two computers on a network.

Networks send data across the cabling in what is called packets. These packets are composed in such a way that they can be recognized and read by other NICs that use the same protocol. The idea is similar to language. In order to communicate with someone, you both need to be speaking the same language. Similarly, network interface cards need to use the same protocol in order to communicate. NetWare's protocol is IPX/SPX (Internetwork Packet Exchange/Sequenced Packet Exchange).

CABLING ACCESS METHODS

Access Method
A set of rules determining which workstation has access to the medium at any moment.

Carrier Sense Multiple Access
(CSMA). Popular baseband protocol where each node listens. CSMA/CD networks transmit only when the line is free, avoiding collisions and detecting when a collision occurs by waiting a random length of time before retrying the transmission.

An important characteristic of NICs is their **access method** or access scheme. The access method or access scheme describes the way network interface cards gain access to the cable to send their packets. An access method is needed if two or more computers on the network transmit data simultaneously, otherwise the data will collide and disable either computer's transmission. NICs need some way to determine when the line (cable) is free so they can send their data packets. This is accomplished through the access method or access scheme. The type of access method used will affect the network's performance.

In most networks, multiple devices are connected to a single channel. Usually this model provides efficient use of bandwidth and related cost benefits. If two devices on the network transmit information simultaneously, problems arise—such as signals mixing with one another and becoming unintelligible. The task to ensure simultaneous transmission either does not occur or is improperly handled. Access methods provide this assurance.

A network's access method describes the manner and order in which devices access the physical medium. Three basic channel access methods are contention, token passing and polling.

Contention Access Method

The **carrier sense multiple access** (CSMA) method is a very popular contention access method. In CSMA-type networks, all network cards "listen" to the line (cable) and send data packets whenever they detect that the line is free. It is possible for two nodes to be listening, detect a free line, and then both send data simultaneously. CSMA-type networks are further categorized as either Collision Avoidance (CSMA/CA) or Collision Detection (CSMA/CD). CSMA/CA could be thought of as carrier avoidance and CSMA/CD as carrier detection.

CSMA/CA networks use a mechanism to avoid collisions that might be thought of, in simple terms, as needing a permission slip for the NIC to enter data onto the line. The NIC waits until the line is free before actually sending the data. Each computer in a CSMA/CA network senses the line for an existing signal and if a signal exists, the station waits. If no signal exists, the station transmits. CSMA/CA gives the best performance in small networks.

CSMA/CD use a newer contention system for detecting collisions. The NICs detect when there has been a data collision and instruct the NIC to resend the data.

The Institute of Electrical and Electronics Engineers (**IEEE**) develops standards for LANs, known as the 802 series standards. CSMA/CD LANs use IEEE 802.3 standard, token ring LANs use IEEE 802.5, which utilize the token-passing access method.

Token Passing Access Method

With the **token-passing access method,** a token is generated and passed around the network. The token is the authorizing entity for node data transmission. Since only one node can have the token at a time, only one node can transmit data at a time. This eliminates data collisions but places an artificial time constraint on sending data. Each node must wait until it has the token before it can transmit, even though the line may be free.

The token moves unidirectionally in the logical ring, regardless of network topology or physical structure. It designates different primary devices, in turn, by passing a token from one to another. (A token is a special authorizing entity that temporarily gives control of the channel to the device holding it.) The rest of the devices on the network remain as secondaries. Each device knows from which device it received the token and to which device it must pass the token. Token-passing design rules limit the duration each device can control the token.

Polling Access Method

With the **polling access method,** one device is designated or called a primary controller (master device). The master device query (poll) each of the other devices, called secondary devices in a predetermined order

IEEE
A coordinating body founded in 1963 to develop computing and communications standards. Particularly noted for the IEEE 802-series standards.

Token Passing Access Method
Network access method which uses an electrical signal, called a token. The token passes from node to node, providing access to the medium for the node controlling the token.

Polling Access Method
Network access method where a host device controls communications in a predetermined order between secondary devices.

to see whether they have information to transmit. Polling may incur substantial channel access overhead. The polling mechanism takes time and restricts transmission opportunities of each secondary device. When secondary devices have no data to transmit, network bandwidth is still used for polling messages and responses. On the positive side, polling completely eliminates collisions. When secondary devices regularly have information to transmit, this method can make the best use of network bandwidth. On the negative side, overhead and delay, caused by polling many transmitters, may be excessive.

Both polling and token-passing eliminate collisions and utilize network bandwidth optimally when devices frequently have information to send. Both methods also incur some overhead in determining who can access the network.

The major benefit of token passing over polling is distributed (token) vs. centralized (polling) control. Damage to any signal device in a token-passing network does not necessarily disable the network, whereas damage to the primary in any polling environment often disables that portion of the network. On the other hand, token-passing requires intelligence in every device, since every device is the primary on a regular basis.

NETWORK CABLING TRANSPORT SUBSYSTEMS

There are many schemes for managing the physical aspects of cabling. The components of the transport lie in the subsystem of the cables and in the way you detect and correct errors in the sending and receiving of data. An analogy would be for you to dial the number for a telephone call. In reality, the telephone company is managing all the wires and switches that are hidden from you. Similarly, network transport subsystems are what is hidden when you send a message from a networked workstation to the server.

ARCnet Network Cabling Transport Subsystem

Attached Resource Computer Network (ARCnet)
A network cabling transport system that uses a token-passing access method to connect as many as 255 workstations, using coaxial, twisted-pair, or fiber optic cabling.

Attached Resource Computer Network (ARCnet) was created by Datapoint Corporation in the late 1970s and is one of the oldest network transport subsystems. Today, ARCnet is manufactured by Thomas Conrad Corporation. When Datapoint was manufacturing ARCnet, the speed was 20 Mbps. The Thomas Conrad version of ARCnet runs at 100 Mbps and is used for fiber optic, twisted-pair or coax signals, and is thought to be as easy to install as other ARCnet versions.

ARCnet uses the token passing access method on a bus topology, thus called a *token bus*. For a station to transmit a message on an ARCnet network, it must be in possession of the token. As defined earlier, the token is the authorizing agent that allows messages to be passed from one station to another. If you think of this exchange as a baton being passed to your hand in a relay race you know you are not being able to run unless you have the token (baton) in your hand. The sequence for passing the token is important for it is passed in numerical order, sequencing to the next highest number. Because the station number may not exist, each station determines which is the next in line to receive the token by sending out an inquiry message. If stations enter or leave the network, the network reconfigures. If the network has just started, or the token is lost due to station failure, the station with the highest numbered address initiates a new token.

When ARCnet stations enter or exit the network, the autoreconfiguration process is performed where all stations participate in recognizing the new or deleted address (number). Since, the addressing (or numbering) is dynamically assigned, it governs the transmission not only the order of the token-passing, but also for the speed of the network. It is estimated that because of the inquiry messaging, token-passing, and reconfiguration inherent to the nature of ARCnet, the total overhead in some ARCnet systems can reduce the data throughput to as much as 50 to 60 percent of the theoretical maximum level of possible transfer rates.

To cable an ARCnet network, you need to use a wiring hub. The wiring hub serves as a concentrator (a device that provides the connection between the rest of the network and a PC). The hubs can be thought of as "wiring boxes." Two types of hubs can be used, either an active or a passive hub. With the passive hub, four connectors are wired together using resistors. This conditions the signals and ensures that reflections and other electrical problems do not occur. Active hubs are 8-port devices that condition and amplify signals. All unused connections on a hub, either active or passive, should be terminated.

If the network only consists of two PCs, no hubs are required as long as the maximum cable length of 2,000 feet is not exceeded. Neither the maximum cable length between two hubs, nor the longest cable run between an active hub and a PC can exceed 2,000 feet. The longest cable run between a passive hub and a PC is 100 feet. The total overall cable length for an ARCnet network cannot exceed 20,000 feet and should end at routers if they are used.

Ethernet and IEEE 802.3 Network Cabling Transport Subsystem

Ethernet is a network transport subsystem created in the late 1970s, known today as the IEEE 802.3 standard. Ethernet's roots lie in its development by Xerox Corporation, for whom Ethernet is a trademark.

Ethernet
Network cabling transport system using CSMA/CD to prevent failures or collisions when two nodes try to access the cabling system at the same time. Ethernet uses coaxial, fiber optic or twisted-pair cabling connected with a bus topology.

The first Ethernet system Xerox produced connected more than 100 computers, communicating at a signaling rate of 2.94 megabits per second (Mbps). Shortly following this success in the late 1970s, companies such as Digital and Intel collaborated on the more familiar 10 Mbps standard. Because of the collaboration between the three companies, the DIX connector (named after Digital, Intel, and Xerox) was developed as the connecting device for the cable to be attached.

There are actually two standards, Ethernet and IEEE 802.3 to consider. Originally, Ethernet existed alone and then the IEEE (the Institute for Electronic and Electrical Engineers) developed IEEE 802.3 standard. The two standards are not compatible. If a computer tries to send an Ethernet message to a IEEE 802.3 computer, the IEEE 802.3 will not be able to interpret the Ethernet message. However, you can mix the two types on the same network if the LAN drivers for the NIC permit this. Hence, mixing the two standards on a LAN is simply a matter of implementing the software driver to handle the two types of messages.

Both Ethernet and IEEE 802.3 use a contention method for allowing the workstation to access the network cabling. This method requires that prior to transmitting the workstation listen for traffic and check for voltage on the cable. If there is no traffic, transmission begins. The workstation must then immediately check if there has been a collision due to another workstation sending data at the same time. If this is the case, the workstation stops, waits a given amount of time, and retries the transmission. All of this is handled by the NIC, and has no impact upon the workstation's performance.

Ethernet supports coxial cable. There are three media types for coaxial cable and two for twisted-pair for the IEEE 802.3 standard. IEEE 802.3 supports 1BASE5, and 10BASET for the twisted-pair cable types and 10BASE5, 10BASE2, and 10BROAD36 for the coaxial implementation to the IEEE 802.3 standard. To define the media types, 10BASE2 can be divided into three parts: speed, cable type, and segment length. So, 10BASE2 would be 10Mbps, baseband cabling, at a maximum segment length of 200 meters. Refer to Figure 1.9.

Ethernet permits a bus topology where IEEE 802.3 permits various topologies. The data transfer rate for Ethernet is 10Mbps and IEEE 802.3 can range from 1Mbps to 10Mbps.

Token Ring and IEEE 802.5 Network Cabling Transport Subsystem

IEEE originally proposed the Token Ring network technology in 1969; however, IBM publicly demonstrated interest in 1982 and announced related products in 1985. The first version of Token Ring ran at 4Mbps and supported 260 workstations.

FIGURE 1.9

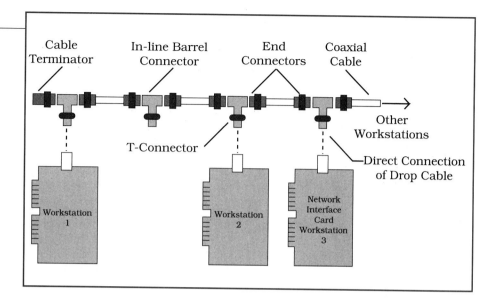

Token Ring
Cabling transport
subsystem which
uses a ring structure
to pass a token to
regulate traffic on
the network.

Token Ring conforms to the IEEE 802.5 standard. The token-passing access method used by token ring networks is called deterministic. It is deterministic because the maximum time required for information to flow from one node to another may be calculated. Each node on the ring may hold the token for a given amount of time, and since the number of nodes on the ring is known, the maximum token transit time can be calculated. These deterministic networks are always implemented where delays are of no particular value, such as automobile assembly lines.

The IEEE 802.5 network uses a rather complex priority system. If a node with a higher priority wants to monopolize the token, it may do so by increasing the priority of the token, thus preventing it from being seized by the nodes with lower priority.

The NICs use a DB-9 connector for Token Ring cards and primarily use only shielded or unshielded twisted-pair cable; although it can be run over coaxial cable (but not as reliably unless very short cable lengths are involved). The cable attaches to a *Media Attachment Unit* (*MAU*) that is similar to the hub described in the ARCnet section. MAUs usually have 8 ports, although some vendors offer 24-port versions. MAUs contain relays that contact and connect a PC to the ring as it is powered up. The interconnection of MAUs is due to RI (ring in) and RO (ring out) ports. Where IEEE 802.5 media is unspecified, IBM Token Ring uses IBM-specific, shielded, twisted-pair wiring. Refer to Figure 1.10.

Token Ring is a logical ring with a physical layout of a star. This means there is a path (a set of wires) running from one PC to the next

A TABLE RECAP OF NETWORK
CABLING TRANSPORT SUBSYSTEMS

The advantages and disadvantages of ARCnet, Ethernet, and Token Ring transport subsystems are as follows.

	Advantages	**Disadvantages**
ARCnet	Easiest to install. Least costly.	Automatically reconfigures itself, as workstations enter and exit the network.
	Relatively stable, understood and supported by a wide variety of vendors. Can be implemented in a bus or star topology. Can use shielded or unshielded twisted-pair wiring.	Dynamically assigns a numbered address per workstation, up to 255 addresses on any single network.
Ethernet	Standard Ethernet runs at 10Mbps. Fast Ethernet runs at 100Mbps. Contention access method.	Only Bus Topology permitted. Coaxial cable is only media type supported.
IEEE 802.3	Various topologies permitted. Supports three types of coaxial and two types of twisted pair cabling. Supports data rates from 1Mbps to 10MBbps.	Some wiring types supported susceptible to EMI. Cable segment lengths must be closely watched to guard against signal loss.
Token Ring	Permits 4 or 16Mpbs data rates.	Specifies IBM cabling type, shielded twisted-pair only.
IEEE 802.5	Permits various topologies. Uses amplifiers to boost the signal as the token is passed around the ring.	Deterministic with a complex, monopolistic tendency for nodes with higher priorities always seize and control the token, keeping it away from lower priority nodes. Permits 1Mbps to 4Mbps.

FIGURE 1.10

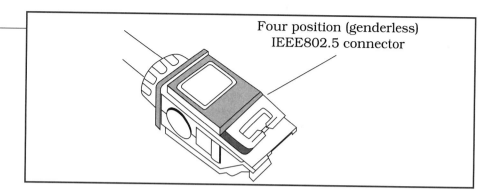

Four position (genderless)
IEEE802.5 connector

with only two PCs on each path. The physical layout of Token Ring consists of a star based on each MAU, or the arrangement of MAUs on the ring. Thus, the topology permitted for IEEE 802.5 varies where IBM Token Ring permits star/ring topology of 260 stations per ring. The data rate for IEEE 802.5 is 1Mpbs to 4Mbps while IBM Token Ring permits 4Mbps to 16Mbps.

Bandwidth Compared to Transmission Speed

Bandwidth
The transmission capacity of a network medium, typically stated in megabits per second (Mbps).

Bandwidth designates the amount of cabling media the NIC can actually use. Many networks have a maximum rated bandwidth. In other words, under optimal theoretical conditions, each network is supposed to be able to transfer a given number of megabits per second (Mbps). A network's rated bandwidth is based upon physical rather than practical limits.

Network speed should be a relatively simple equation. NICs are designed to transmit data at a specific maximum transmission rate. This rate is usually expressed in megabits per second (Mbps). Typical NIC transmission rates for data transfer can be either 4Mbps or 10Mbps. A natural assumption is that a 10Mbps NIC will give a better performance than a 4Mbps NIC, but such is not always true. Actual network performance is also affected by (1) the efficiency of the access scheme, (2) the actual bandwidth usage of the NICs, (3) the efficiency of the network driver the NIC uses, and (4) the network operating system itself.

Relatively few NICs actually deliver data at the maximum transmission rating because they are restricted by bandwidth usage. A simple analogy might be to compare highway lanes—a two-lane highway versus a four-lane highway. Each highway has a posted speed limit of 55 mph but more cars can travel the four-lane highway, even though the speed limit is the same for both. This is similar to bandwidth usage on a network since the higher the bandwidth usage, the more data can be delivered in a given amount of time. Bandwidth usage is a function of the efficiency of the NIC design and the chips that are used on the card;

efficiencies vary from one manufacturer's NIC to another. Contrary to popular belief, networks rarely, if ever, reach their theoretical limit.

In addition to transmission speed, bandwidth usage, and access scheme, the software driver for the NIC, the network operating system, and what the network user community is doing on the network at a given time all affect performance. Determining performance is never simple, so some companies invest in special network monitoring hardware and are able to watch the performance of the network and closely monitor bottlenecks.

SUMMARY

Today, the trend in networks for a company is moving away from the mainframe and minicomputer environments to a network of interconnected PCs, called a LAN. The network is a tool for facilitating employee communications and conducting business in a timely fashion through the access and sharing of programs and data files.

The network server is where the network operating system is installed. Though the server looks no different than the client workstation from the outside, the server is configured with a very fast microprocessor, contains as much as four times the amount of RAM as the clients, and typically equipped with a large amount of disk storage capacity. Once installed on a server, Novell's version 3.1x network operating system can address up to 32TB of disk storage and can address up to 4 GB of RAM.

Some kind of electrical communication system is necessary to coordinate the electrical signals that travel along the cabling systems, between the network interface cards. Rules or standards specify the signal's transmission, limiting how fast and how far you can send electrical signals. This coordination of the signals between the interface cards is the essence of data transmission.

Network Interface Cards are classified into four categories: ARCnet, Ethernet, Token Ring, and proprietary. LAN cabling types include twisted-pair, coaxial, and fiber optic. LAN topologies are the physical arrangement of network nodes and include bus, star, and ring arrangements.

LAN protocols are characterized by access method and speed in which each workstation can attach to the network cabling system. The protocols establish rules for communication, but can vary slightly between each vendor's implementation of a protocol's specification, making no two network installations alike.

A LAN is characterized as being located within a close geographic location, such as a building. Compared to LANs, a metropolitan area network (MAN) is usually spread across a city, where a wide area network (WAN) is spread across states.

END OF CHAPTER REVIEW

Important Terms

Access Method
Attached Resource
  Computer Network
Bandwidth
Baseband
Broadband
Carrier Sense
  Multiple Access
Centralized
  Network
Client
Client-Server
  Network
Coaxial Cabling
  (COAX)
Distributed
  Network
DOS
Downsizing
Ethernet

Fiber Optic Cabling
Groupware
IEEE
Local Area
  Network (LAN)
Medium
Metropolitan Area
  Network
NetWare
Network
Network Interface
  Card (NIC)
Network Operat-
  ing System
Network Server
Network Topology
Node
PC
Peers
Peer-to-Peer

Polling Access
  Method
Protocol
Pure Network
  Applications
Stand-Alone
  Applications
Standards
Terminal
Terminal Emulation
Token Passing
  Access Method
Token Ring
Twisted-Pair
  Cabling (TP)
Upsizing
Wide Area
  Network
Workstation

True/False Questions

1. The server is where the network operating system is installed.

2. NetWare file servers are designed to handle system security.

3. All network installations are exactly alike.

4. The physical attachment of all the computers to the centralized cabling establishes a WAN.

5. Most LANs are privately owned and maintained.

6. Bandwidth usage refers to how much of the cabling media the NIC can actually use.

7. When network nodes perform the same function, they are called clients.

8. NetWare is a network operating system (NOS) that works with only DOS workstations.

9. The term client refers to computers connected to the server.

10. An example of unbounded media is twisted-pair wiring.

IN YOUR OWN WORDS

1. Investigate the network at your site. List the specific problem(s) the network solves. Discuss the purpose of networking as being beneficial to workgroup computing for your site. Speak with an individual with network administration responsibility. From your discussion, explain if there were/are possible tradeoffs or alternatives to networking. Also from your discussion, list any changes that could be made, list what the changes would be and why.

2. Research the components of your network.

   Server   List the brand, model, processor, memory (RAM), number of hard disks, and disk storage capacity.

   NetWare   What version(s) of NetWare is installed in your organization? What is the node capacity for the server(s)?

   Cabling   List the type(s) of cabling installed at your site. List the most pervasive type of cable if there is more than one type.

   NICs   List the type and brand of NICs installed at your site.

   Other   How secure is the network?
              Does the server remain operational 24/7 (24 hours per day, 7 days per week)?
              Are log in restrictions enforced? If so, what restrictions?
              List the brand of UPS or power conditioning equipment utilized at your site.
              List any specific equipment used to backup the server.
              List how often the server is backed up.

3. The network is down. The panic has set in. For whatever reason, the LAN is not functioning properly and you cannot log in. The server might be having a problem, or perhaps your workstation is having a problem. Some possible causes are:

   — The Network Administrator forgot to upgrade your workstation to match the server's upgrade performed last night.
   — Your network card is having a problem with the attachment to the cabling.

— The NIC in the server is not working properly.
— The server's hard disk has failed (crashed).
— The Supervisor (accidentally) deleted your account.

Pick one or a combination of the above possible causes and explain who you would contact. Discuss these causes with your LAN administrative personnel and list the steps necessary to solve the problem. Discuss if your solution would mean bringing the server down.

4. Compare a terminal to stand-alone computer and network workstation.

5. Define a server.

6. Differentiate between a client and a server.

7. Compare mainframe and minicomputer networks to peer-to-peer and client-server networks.

8. Describe the difference between distributed networks to distributed processing.

9. Specify the difference between the local operating system and the network operating system.

10. Distinguish the difference between bounded and unbounded media.

11. List the three types of LAN cabling systems.

12. Define the terms topology, standard, and protocol.

13. Explain the concept and list three types of access methods.

14. Distinguish between ARCnet, Ethernet, and Token Ring transport subsystems.

15. Clarify the meaning of a network backbone.

16. Define bandwidth.

17. Compare pure network applications to stand-alone applications adapted to run on the network.

18. Distinguish between a LAN, MAN, and WAN.

19. List the four components of a data communication system.

ON YOUR OWN

I. A Case of Collaborative Learning
You are a student enrolled in a course where the instructor wants you to work in groups, dividing the work evenly among the members, and authenticating your own work. How could the network help you:

   A. Communicate with your classmates?
   B. Complete your project?
   C. Communicate with your instructor?
   D. Authenticate your own work?

II. Clarkdale College Bookstore
Joyce Seymore and Jack Milano are employees at the Clarkdale College Bookstore. The bookstore is privately owned by LaFolet, Inc. Joyce and Jack use the network to post daily sales, keep track of inventory, and prepare reports to send to LaFolet's regional office in Denver. They have a modem to use Internet and access LaFolet's corporate network.

Cite the advantages and disadvantages of using the local area network at Clarkdale's College Bookstore. Explain how you think this network might be managed.

Making the Physical and Logical Connections

OBJECTIVES

- Log in and log out of NetWare.

- Use NetWare's SLIST, WHOAMI, and USERLIST command-line utilities.

- Separate the purpose of Users and Groups and NetWare's use of special accounts for system administration.

- Overview shortcut keys used in a NetWare's menu utilities.

- Use NetWare's SYSCON menu utility to view user account restriction information.

- Use NetWare's FILER menu utility to navigate NetWare's directory structure.

- Compare using the DOS Shell with NetWare's utilities to navigate the local and network directory structure.

CHAPTER INTRODUCTION

In the beginning..... you owned a stand-alone, *personal computer* (PC). Next you added a fancy printer. Before long, all wanted to borrow your computer for printing their work. Soon, all were playing the game of "sneakernet;" with their sneakers on, they carried disks to your computer (or another) for processing or printing.

Alas, today... all enter the Local Area Network (LAN).

In the **booting** process, **Disk Operating System (DOS)** is the local operating system which coordinates between all programs running on the local workstation and the workstation's hardware components. DOS acts more like a resource manager—or a director of services—for loading and executing the stand-alone, local workstation operations.

Booting
Starting or restarting the workstation.

Disk Operating System (DOS)
The most common local operating system for NetWare client workstations. Macintosh, OS/2 and Unix are other operating systems that NetWare will service as clients.

DOS is the master control program for the stand-alone computer. You may not have thought of it quite this way, but the main function of DOS on the local workstation is to oversee all disk activities and to act as a resource controller and director of services. The network server, which houses the Network Operating System (NOS), also performs this but for multiple client workstations.

When the computer first boots, DOS watches the time and date, memory, and networking considerations. DOS facilitates the local workstation booting to the network. DOS is a foundation for the stand-alone workstation, upon which the network services build.

You can tell when DOS is active by the *DOS prompt* (for example, C:\>). You can tell when the network is active by the *network prompt* (for example, F:\>). The DOS prompt is typically displayed as drive letters A through E, where the network prompt usually ranges from drive letters F through Z.

Physical Connection
Activates the Network Interface Card (NIC) inside the workstation to receive information from the network cabling and file server.

Upon *boot-up* (turning on the power) to their workstation, the network user isn't aware of the connectivity taking place as the workstation attaches to the network server. Little or no thought is given as the stand-alone computer extends itself to make the **physical connection** to the cabling system, attach to the **server**, and then enter network as a client workstation.

Server
A powerful PC configured to load the network operating system and direct resources to network clients.

First, the workstation boots locally by activating the local operating system, usually DOS. Next, the workstation loads the file (driver) to activate the network interface card and then runs the program file(s) to seamlessly connect to the network as a client. DOS service requests are directed to DOS on the local workstation while requests for NetWare services are sent through the cabling system to the server.

The purpose of this chapter is to provide a hands-on perspective to the concept that drive letters are used to identify and inform the computer of where to retrieve and store information. Separating the drive letter assignments to indicate local from network resources is the job of

SLIST
Command-line utility is used to view information about your physical connection and other available file server(s) on a NetWare LAN. The Status column will display DEFAULT for your active physical connection and ATTACHED for other logical connections you establish with other servers.

LOGIN
NetWare's Command to activate and open a session (log in) to the Network Operating System (NOS) for a user. The full syntax for the LOGIN command is LOGIN *servername/ username*. The *severname* option is only used to specify a particular server, and usually not needed to log in. The LOGIN *username* option is typically given at the command-line to log in to your workstation's default server. Refer to Exercise 2.1 to see your default server.

both the local and Network Operating Systems working together. Understanding the layering of the stand-alone computer first booting DOS and then attaching to the network will help you comprehend the transformation of the stand-alone computer into a client workstation that can be both physically and logically recognized by the network server and other clients.

This chapter is designed to give you this understanding through hands-on, step-by-step instruction. You will use both **SLIST** and **LOGIN** commands in this chapter. You will discover that your workstation has activated a network connection and been recognized by the NetWare network operating system located on the server when you see either the LOGIN directory prompt or the first network drive prompt (typically, F:\>) displayed on your screen. These exercises assume your network is set up accordingly.

The network workstation is sometimes referred to as a *node* on the network. Where the network server is the "front end," responsible for supplying network services, the network workstation is the "back end," receiving the services requested from the server. A network server is usually responsible for handling workstation requests and controlling access to the network services. The network operating system (installed on the server) connects the front and back ends together, making the underlying physical and logical network connections and connectivity devices obscure to the network workstation's (client's) boot-up process.

The network server is presented in this chapter as a means of recognizing NetWare's client-server network operating system. The client is synonyamous with the name network workstation. The concept of the network server as presented in this chapter as a computer (PC) that is configured as the device where the network operating system is installed, configured to share or direct the sharing of network resources among the clients. As explained in Chapter One, the network server is typically a microcomputer (or PC), with a very fast microprocessor and a vast capacity of disk storage space.

The network server has traditionally had many names. For the purposes of this chapter and remainder of this book, the server (network server) is referenced as either the server or the file server. The function of a file server is to store and share its disk resources (such as application programs and data files) with network client workstations that are attached to the network cabling system and recognized by the server. The term *disk server* is an older term often found in other books and used to mean a file server functioning to share files as if the hard disk resources were inside the local computer. The older, disk server terminology is the same as the newer term, file server. The newer term of file server is actually a better description of what service that the server is providing.

The network server is flexible in its function. The file server could also be providing print services, and thus configured as a file and print server, controlling the printer(s) directly attached to it. With newer and advancing technologies, most file servers are being alleviated of the print server function/task. Newer printing devices are entering the marketplace which have the print server capability built-in. Further information about network printing can be found in Chapter Six.

This chapter and remainder of the book will rely upon you grasping the concept that the network server orchestrates or performs many functional tasks for the client workstations. For the purpose of definition, you should think of the server as a specially configured PC that is installed to contain the network operating system and functions to coordinate the requests it receives from the network clients/workstations.

In this chapter, you will examine the LOGIN directory and work with the SLIST and LOGIN commands. First, you will use the LOGIN command to log in to a NetWare server and then use the SLIST command to view information about your server and other servers on your LAN.

Logical Connection
Logging on to the network. Also called network session or user connection.

The primary purpose of this chapter is to give you a hands-on perspective of the stand-alone workstation becoming a network workstation. You use the LOGIN command to establish the **logical connection** between your workstation and the NetWare server. With a valid username and password, you log in to any NetWare server on your LAN.

Your LAN may have only one server, or it could have many. The first hands-on exercise using NetWare's SLIST command will show you the number of servers on your LAN and from which one you are active (logged in).

LOGOUT
NetWare's command to terminate a logical connection.

LOGOUT is the Netware command you will use in this chapter; it terminates your logical connection with the network. Although you log out and end your network session (or logical connection), the physical connection between the network interface card located inside your workstation being active with the network cabling system, is ongoing. Using SLIST after you log out assures you that the workstation is still physically active and connected to the network.

You will examine logging in and using the LAN to discover the security structure of NetWare. NetWare's security structure is revealed in this chapter. It is very flexible for widening user accounts to establish greater levels of security for individual users who need to help manage a specific task or group on the network.

Network administration is often a team effort in companies where on-site support of a particular aspect of the network is determined necessary to keep workflow and workgroup computing operational. The network administrator may delegate system responsibilities to other staff members (user accounts). In this chapter, you are given insight into your own user account restrictions as well as information on

DOS Shell
Menu-driven, user interface utilized for processing DOS commands.

FILER
NetWare's menu-drive interface for changing directory and file security, and controlling volume, directory and file information.

Command-Line Utility
NetWare commands issued from the network drive prompt (or command-line prompt). SLIST is an example of one of NetWare's command-line utilities.

special rights granted to other accounts who are designated to share administrative duties with the network administrator.

As you progress through the hands-on exercises, you are shown the groups to which you belong on the LAN. Rather than deal with individual user accounts, NetWare administration uses the creation of groups to deal with users collectively.

At the end of this chapter, you are shown the **DOS Shell** and NetWare's **FILER** menu utility, two ways to navigate the network's directory structure. This will prepare you for managing the directory structure in Chapter Three.

2.1 SLIST

SLIST is the only NetWare **command-line utility** that you use without logging in. In this exercise, SLIST is used to demonstrate the physical connectivity your workstation can establish. Your workstation must first be configured to activate the physical connection to the LAN. Then, you will invoke a logical connection, by logging in with your valid username and password. SLIST is used in this exercise to confirm your workstation made the physical connection and is actively communicating with other devices on the network.

NOTE: **Your LAN may show a letter other than F for the first network drive, depending upon your workstation's configuration. You will know your workstation has successfully booted and made a physical connection to the network, ready for you to log in, when you see the first network drive letter or the \LOGIN> directory prompt on your screen.**

This exercise assumes you have booted your workstation to your LAN, the *F* drive letter as the first network drive, with your cursor at the F:\LOGIN> directory prompt. You can use CD\LOGIN if you need to change to the LOGIN directory prompt.

Hands-On Exercise

At the \LOGIN> prompt,

   1. **Type** *SLIST*

      Press `Enter`

NOTE: **NetWare Commands can be typed using uppercase or lowercase letters as they are not case sensitive. In this book, commands are uppercase.**

Your screen displays a list of server names on your LAN. If you are working on a LAN with many servers, and when the screen fills, it will pause for you to advance through the listing.

***NOTE:* You can press the letter C to *continuously* scroll through the listing of servers.**

Search the listing for the server's name showing Default in the Status column on your screen. The word *Default* in the Status column displays your active server. Make note of the server name.

At the prompt,

2. **Type** *SLIST* servername (type SLIST followed by a space and then type the name of your server)
   (Your servername is listed in the Status column as Default)

   Press Enter

You should see a listing of just the one active server your workstation has attached to. If you found only one server on your LAN from using SLIST in the previous step, this command looks no different from your previous listing, from Step 1. Refer to Figure 2.1.

3. **Type** *SLIST /C*

   Press Enter

Use the /C option when you're working on a LAN with many NetWare file servers and you want to list the file servers continuously on screen, scrolling through the screens without stopping. If you found only one server on your LAN, using the SLIST/C, this command looks no different from your previous listing(s). Refer to Figure 2.1.

KEY RELATED POINTS

SLIST is one of many NetWare command-line utilities. You can issue the SLIST command whether you've logged in or not. SLIST is used to list the available servers on the LAN. Its purpose is to provide the valid name of the specific NetWare server you wish to specify logging in to, or are presently logged in to, on the LAN.

NetWare commands are not case sensitive. As you enter the command from the command-line, uppercase or lowercase letters are accepted.

NetWare uses a forward slash (/) after a command to identify command options. You may or may not use a space between the forward slash (/) and the command option (i.e., SLIST/C or SLIST /C).

FIGURE 2.1

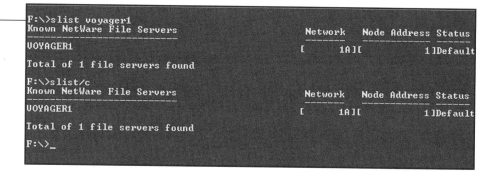

```
F:\>slist voyager1
Known NetWare File Servers                    Network   Node Address Status
                                              ----------- ------------ --------
VOYAGER1                                       [      1A][             1 ]Default

Total of 1 file servers found
F:\>slist/c
Known NetWare File Servers                    Network   Node Address Status
                                              ----------- ------------ --------
VOYAGER1                                       [      1A][             1 ]Default

Total of 1 file servers found

F:\>_
```

NetWare offers either command-line or menu utilities. Command-line utilities are commands executed from the network drive prompt in NetWare. LOGIN and SLIST are examples of command-line utilities. **Menu utilities** provide a menu to allow you to choose options from menus. SYSCON and FILER are examples of menu utilities you will work with in this chapter. NetWare's utilities are designed to be expanded in security access to provide greater security options for those needing to administer the network.

With SLIST, the word DEFAULT in the Status column displays your active server. All other servers you have logged in to and established logical connections with will be depicted by the word ATTACHED in the Status column of SLIST.

Menu Utility
Type of interface used to provide menu options, rather than entering commands to perform network task, SYSCON and FILER are examples of NetWare's menu utilities.

OPTIONS AVAILABLE WITH SLIST

Command	Description
SLIST	List of available file servers on the LAN.
SLIST servername	List one server.
SLIST B*	List all of the server names beginning with the letter B.
SLIST /C	Continuously scroll through the listing of server names on screen without pausing as the screen fills.

2.2 LOGIN, WHOAMI, USERLIST

USERLIST
Lists users currently logged in and their connection information.

LOGIN is the command you use to log in to a NetWare server and establish a logical connection, if you possess a valid username (user account) and password. Your username and password must be valid on whatever server you choose to log in to. **USERLIST** and **WHOAMI** are command-line utilities used in this exercise to display information about your logical connection and your access rights on the network.

This exercise assumes that F is your first network drive letter and that you are at the F:\LOGIN> directory prompt on your NetWare LAN. You can use CD\LOGIN to change to the F:\LOGIN> directory prompt.

Hands-On Exercise

LOGIN
See page 35.

WHOAMI
Lists information about your connection and privileges on the network. (See page 39.)

LOGIN Directory
Created upon installation of a NetWare file server. Used for logging in to the network. Contains the LOGIN.EXE file.

Public Directory
Created upon installation of a NetWare file server. Contains NetWare's utility command files.

To log in,

    1. **Type** *LOGIN*

        Press ⌷Enter⌷

You should see the prompt, Enter your login name:

***NOTE:* If you see the message Bad command or file name on your screen, booting to the LAN was not successful as this is a DOS error message. You may need to reboot the workstation to the network and retype LOGIN from the first network drive letter prompt or \LOGIN> directory prompt.**

At the Enter your login name: prompt,

    2. **Type** Your Username (or Guest)

        Press ⌷Enter⌷

At the Enter your password: prompt,

    3. **Type** the password you were given

        Press ⌷Enter⌷

When you logged in, you may have seen some connection information displayed on your screen similar to Figure 2.2, except your server name will replace the server name Voyager1 and your drive G may not appear as shown in Figure 2.2.

NOTE: As a security feature, your password is not visible as you type it on screen. If you see a warning message to change your password you are advised to seek assistance before continuing.

Move to the **PUBLIC directory**.

    4. **Type** *CD\PUBLIC*

        Press ⌷Enter⌷

***NOTE:* If you see a different drive letter than F, your LAN has been configured with another first network drive letter. If you don't see the \PUBLIC> directory path, you may need to log in again and retype CD\PUBLIC.**

FIGURE 2.2

```
F:\>login
Enter your login name: guest
Enter your password:

Drive   A:    maps to a local disk.
Drive   B:    maps to a local disk.
Drive   C:    maps to a local disk.
Drive   D:    maps to a local disk.
Drive   E:    maps to a local disk.
Drive   F:  = VOYAGER1\SYS:  \LOGIN
Drive   G:  = VOYAGER1\VOL1:  \

SEARCH1:  = Z:.  [VOYAGER1\SYS:  \PUBLIC]
SEARCH2:  = Y:.  [VOYAGER1\SYS:  \PUBLIC\IBM_PC\MSDOS\V5.00]

F:\LOGIN>_
```

FIGURE 2.3

```
F:\PUBLIC>dir userlist.*

 Volume in drive F is SYS
 Directory of F:\PUBLIC

USERLIST EXE     23175 05-06-93  10:59a
        1 file(s)        23175 bytes
                       5398528 bytes free

F:\PUBLIC>userlist

User Information for Server VOYAGER1
Connection  User Name         Login Time
-----------------------------------------
    1     * GUEST             11-19-1994  3:15 pm
F:\PUBLIC>_
```

At the \PUBLIC> prompt,

5. **Type** *DIR USERLIST .**

   Press [Enter]

You should see the listing of the USERLIST.EXE file on your screen. The Public directory is the directory where NetWare's utility command files are kept. The utilities in the Public directory are available to most users.

To activate the USERLIST command, with your cursor at the F:\PUBLIC> Directory prompt,

6. **Type** *USERLIST*

   Press [Enter]

You should see a listing of usernames logged in and working from the same server you are. Your screen may look similar to Figure 2.3. You can find your connection quickly as it is noted by an asterisk (*) after the first column (connection) displayed on your screen.

NetWare's WHOAMI command-line utility lists information about your network connection. To use WHOAMI,

7. **Type** *WHOAMI*

   Press [Enter]

You should see your username, the name of the file server name you are attached to, and other connection information listed on your screen. WHOAMI can be used to display various information about your access rights (or privileges) and other information about your network connection.

At the prompt,

WHOAMI/G
Adds a listing of the Groups of which you are a member to the WHOAMI command.

8. **Type** *WHOAMI /G*

   Press Enter

At the end of the WHOAMI listing, you should see the groups of which you are a member. Your screen should look similar to Figure 2.4. (NetWare allows network administration to be simplified by creating Groups and dealing with users collectively.) Both Groups and Users are created in NetWare's System Configuration (SYSCON) menu utility. NetWare automatically assigns new users to the system-created group, Everyone.

To log out, at the prompt,

9. **Type** *LOGOUT*

   Press Enter

You should be at the first network drive prompt, depending upon how your workstation is configured. Logout displays your connection information and lists the time you logged in and the time you logged out. LOGOUT returns you to where the LOGIN.EXE file is located.

At the prompt,

10. **Type** *DIR*

    Press Enter

Your screen displays a listing of files, which include the LOGIN.EXE and SLIST.EXE files. From the previous exercise, recall you can log in to the network and list available servers from using these commands.

FIGURE 2.4

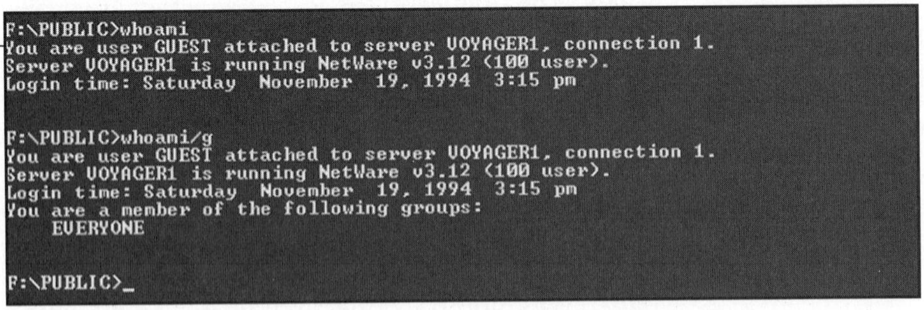

```
F:\PUBLIC>whoami
You are user GUEST attached to server VOYAGER1, connection 1.
Server VOYAGER1 is running NetWare v3.12 (100 user).
Login time: Saturday  November  19, 1994  3:15 pm

F:\PUBLIC>whoami/g
You are user GUEST attached to server VOYAGER1, connection 1.
Server VOYAGER1 is running NetWare v3.12 (100 user).
Login time: Saturday  November  19, 1994  3:15 pm
You are a member of the following groups:
    EVERYONE

F:\PUBLIC>_
```

NETWARE'S BASIC ACCOUNT SECURITY

Supervisor	This account is automatically created upon installation of a NetWare server. The username for the network supervisor or system administrator. The Supervisor account has all rights throughout the NetWare server.
Supervisor Equivalent	The account(s) are designated with security equivalence equal to the Supervisor account.
Workgroup Manager	The user account(s) are identified to have supervisory rights to manage assigned user accounts and groups. They can be given rights to modify files and directories, volume restrictions, and disk space restrictions of the User and/or Groups they are assigned.
User Account Manager	A user or Group account(s) identified to have routine maintenance rights to manage assigned User accounts and Groups.
Group	A group is identified as a way to collectively deal with users. Only one Group, Everyone, is system-created. All other Groups are created by the Supervisor or Supervisor equivalent(s) to simplify network administration. All newly created Users automatically belong to Everyone.
Everyone	This group is created upon installation of a NetWare server. All newly created Users are included in this Group. The system-created accounts of Guest and Supervisor belong to this Group.
Guest Account	This is the account used typically for anyone needing temporary, restricted access to the server. The Guest account is automatically created upon installation of a NetWare server.

KEY RELATED POINTS

- Part of NetWare's login security involves restrictions placed upon user accounts as they log in. For example, restrictions can be imposed upon the time of day you log in, to limit and control initial access. You may not be able to log in because of these restrictions, even if you have a valid username and password. Unless otherwise specified, NetWare will automatically choose the logically closest server to your workstation for you to log in.

- The **ATTACH** Command can be used after you LOGIN to establish a connection with other server(s). As with LOGIN, to use ATTACH you must have a valid username and password on the other server(s). You must know the name of the server when using ATTACH.

- To use the LOGIN command a second time implies a logout, where the ATTACH command is used to open a connection needed with another server and remain logged in to your current server.

- The SLIST command is used to list the server names on your LAN.

- The Guest account, along with the Supervisor account are created upon installation of NetWare. The Guest account can be deleted because it is usually utilized for those needing temporary access for a limited period of time. However, the Supervisor account should not be deleted for this account has full access rights throughout the server.

- When you first set up the NetWare file server, the SYSCON menu utility is used for creating and defining users, groups, and other system configuration activities. You work with SYSCON in Exercise 2.3.

- Upon creation, all users have access to the Public directory, where NetWare's command-line and menu utility command files are located. The other directories created upon installation are LOGIN, Mail, and SYSTEM.

- When a Netware server is first installed, the option for passwords is not activated. System Supervisors control the implementation and parameters for passwords. Thus, by default, passwords are not required to log in to NetWare. Passwords are implemented as a measure of establishing system security.

- Passwords are first configured by the System Supervisors. System-wide Account Restrictions are set in the Supervisor Options section of NetWare's SYSCON menu utility. This is where supervisor or equivalents can require passwords.

Password security includes such items as:

1. The length of days a password is valid.
2. How many characters the password must be.
3. How often you must change your password.
4. Whether you can change your own password.
5. How many times you can type your password incorrectly before the system is alerted of a possible intruder.
6. How many times you can put off changing your password before the system locks you out.
7. Which workstation you must log in from.
8. What time periods you can log in to the network.
9. How many workstations you can log in from with the same user account.
10. Whether your account is currently active for use.

ATTACH
NetWare command used to open another logical connection with another server. Type ATTACH servername/LOGIN name at the command line. This command depends upon you having access (a valid username and password) for another server. (See page 44.)

DEFAULT ACCOUNT RESTRICTIONS SYSTEM-WIDE

Account Expiration Date	None
Limit Concurrent Connections	No
Create a Home Directory as Users are Created	Yes
Require a Password	No
Login Times	Not restricted
Intruder Detection/Lockout	None

2.3 SYSCON—VIEWING YOUR LOG IN RESTRICTIONS

NetWare's log in restrictions can be placed on any user account and can be applied to specify which (1) workstation(s) you can log in from, (2) limitations on the number of workstations you can concurrently log in from, (3) set restrictions on the time of day for logging in, (4) set how often passwords need to be changed, or (5) establish whether the user can change their own password. With this exercise, you will use NetWare's **SYSCON** (system configuration) menu utility to view your account's configuration and restrictions.

SYSCON
NetWare menu utility used to configure and restrict accounts.

This exercise assumes that F is your first network drive letter and that you are logged in your NetWare LAN. You may refer to steps 1–3 of Exercise 2.2 to LOGIN.

Hands-On Exercise

At the F:\> prompt,

     1. **Type** *SYSCON*

       Press [Enter]

The main menu of Syscon, Available Topics, should be showing on your screen. Syscon is one of NetWare's menu utilities. System configuration information is available for each user to view configuration information about their own account in Syscon. Unless User account management is delegated and rights to manage users granted to others, the Supervisor account retains all rights to create, delete, or modify all User accounts.

To view the account restrictions of your username,

2. **Type** *U* to select User Information

   Press ⌗Enter⌗

You should be at the User Names submenu, showing a list of your server's usernames.

***NOTE:* Entering the first letter of a selection item (option) listed in NetWare's menu utilities is a quick way to move the highlight bar to select that item.**

3. **Press** ⌗↓⌗ until you move the highlight bar through the list to highlight your username,

   Press ⌗Enter⌗ highlighted on your username

You should be at the User Information submenu.

***NOTE:* Either the down arrow key or the first letter of a menu option will move the highlight bar to that location.**

4. **Press** ⌗↓⌗ once to move the highlight bar to the Account Restrictions menu option

   Press ⌗Enter⌗

Your screen should display the account restrictions for your username. Use Figure 2.5 as a reference point, and realize your screen display may vary slightly.

FIGURE 2.5

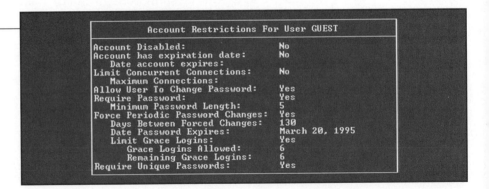

FIGURE 2.6

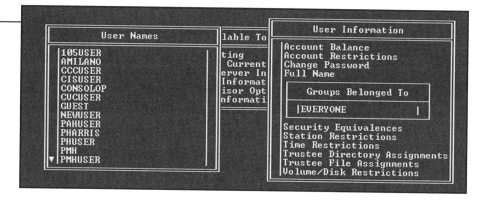

NOTE: **Account restrictions may control the time of day to log in, the minimum character length for a password, and more.**

5. **Press** Esc once

   Type *G* to highlight Groups Belonged To

   Press Enter

You should now see the Groups to which you belong listed on your screen. NetWare automatically assigns new users to the Group Everyone. Any other groups you belong to have been added as part of system management for your account. Refer to Figure 2.6, and realize your screen display may vary.

6. **Press** Esc once

   Type *O* to highlight Other Information

   Press Enter

Your screen shows your last log in. If you have file server console operator privileges, it shows your disk space in use, and your User ID number.

7. **Press** Esc once

   Type *T* to highlight Time Restrictions

   Press Enter

Your screen will display a table of allowed log in times. Asterisks (*) indicate times you can log in during the week. The absence of an asterisk tells you you cannot log in during the week.

8. **Press** Esc once

   Press ↓ once to highlight Trustee Directory Assignments

   Press Enter

Your screen displays the Trustee Directory Assignments pop-up window, showing you the directories you have been given rights to work with on the network. The exact directory rights are displayed in the column on the right of this window, where the letters representing the various rights are enclosed in the square brackets ([ ]).

9. **Press** F1

You should see an on-line Help screen that is available as you work through NetWare's menu utilities. The Help screen, in this case, displays a brief description of directory assignments.

10. **Press** F1 again

You should see a listed description of each function key assignment. Pressing F1 twice provides the function key assignments for any NetWare menu utility.

11. **Press** Alt F10 simultaneously

Press Enter highlighted on Yes to Exit Syscon

SHORTCUTS AND KEYS USED IN A MENU UTILITY

Up or Down Arrow icons	Used to move the highlighted selection bar in the menu.
First Letter	Type the first letter of the menu item to move the highlighted selection bar there quickly.
Ins key	Used to display a list of options or to insert a new item.
Enter key	Generally used to take you to the submenu or accept your entry. With the highlighted selection bar over a particular menu option, use this key to select the option.
F1 key	NetWare's Help key, used to access a brief, on-line description.
F1 F1 keys	Used within a menu utility to obtain a list of function key assignments available.
F3 key	Used to edit or modify an item in a list box/window.
F5 key	Used as a toggle to mark (highlight or select) or unmark one or more items in a list box/window. You can then edit, modify or delete the item(s), once marked.
Alt F10	Used to quickly exit a menu utility from anywhere in the submenu structure.

You should have exited SYSCON. The [Alt] [F10] key combination work to quickly exit you from anywhere in a menu utility.

12. **Type** *LOGOUT*

    Press [Enter]

You should be either at the first network drive prompt, likely shown as the F:\> directory prompt.

KEY RELATED POINTS

Menu utilities provide you a menu from which you choose options. SYSCON is an example of a menu utility. Chapter Five holds further information about NetWare's system configuration utility, SYSCON.

Randomly, NetWare automatically assigns a user identification number when the user is created. Step 6 of Exercise 2.3 displayed your user ID number. NetWare references this ID number when the user logs in to organize and secure the user's operating environment based upon a data-base definition for this entity. The database files for defining users and other entities is contained in what is known as NetWare's Bindery files.

A trustee directory assignment (as shown in step 8 of Exercise 2.3) is granted to a user account (or group) and is the permission to access this location in NetWare's directory structure. Trustee assignments is discussed further in Chapter Four and Five.

NetWare references database definition files (Bindery files) when the user logs in. The Bindery files use the User ID (identification number) to organize and configure the operating environment based upon the definition they contain for each user's ID. You saw the User ID number in Step 6 of Exercise 2.3 when you selected Other Information from Syscon's User Information submenu.

NetWare's Mail directory holds numbered subdirectories which correspond to the User ID number. The numbered subdirectories in Mail are created when the user is created. Your numbered Mail directory was shown in Step 8 of Exercise 2.3. The log in process references this numbered subdirectory as this subdirectory is where the user login script resides. More information on login scripts can be found in Chapter Eight.

NetWare 3.12 uses Windows to launch the hypertext help system, ElectroText, from a CD-ROM. NetWare 3.11 uses the Folios program installed on the server for expanding topics using an on-line help facility.

COMMON NETWARE MENU UTILITY WINDOWS

Confirmation	Yes or No selections appear as a confirmation pop-up window to confirm your changes.
Entry	Used to enter (type) requested information, such as a directory location.
Form(s)	Used to select from available choices (options). Typically, you use the tab or arrow key to move to a field, select your displayed option and then type or select the necessary information from the choices available.
Insert or View	These windows are typically given to show information rather than to be able to change information about a selection. These boxes could change, depending upon if you are logged in as Supervisor, a Manager account, or an Operator account. Typically, an Insert or View window will be surrounded by a single (versus a double) bar border.
List	Used to display a listing, usually so you can select, add, or delete one or more items from the list.

2.4 NAVIGATING THE NETWORK FROM THE DOS SHELL

DOS Shell
See page 37.

In this exercise, you gain a perspective of working with the NetWork from the DOS Shell menu. The DOS Shell is used in this exercise to demonstrate the vast directory and file management, as well as, interactive capabilities this menu-driven interface holds after you've logged in to the network. This exercise assumes that DOS is located on your C drive, your hard disk, in a subdirectory called \DOS. For this exercise, you will first need to log in to NetWare, and then move to the C:\DOS> directory prompt on your workstation.

Hands-On Exercise

After logging in, at the C:\DOS> prompt,

    I. **Type** *DOSSHELL*

       Press [Enter]

You should be at the MS-DOS Shell main menu.

To acquaint yourself with the DOS Shell,

2. **Press** Alt H simultaneously or with a mouse, click left mouse button once on Help

Type P to select procedures

Your screen displays the MS-DOS Shell Help Procedures and acquaints you with how to navigate using either a keyboard or a mouse. For the remainder of this exercise, the keyboard, command version will be given.

To get out of Help,

3. **Press** Esc

Your screen places you back at the MS-DOS Shell.

To adjust your viewing window,

4. **Press** Alt V simultaneously

You should have pulled down the View menu and be highlighted on Single File List. While highlighted on Single File List,

Press Enter (on Single File List)

NOTE: If you press Enter in the View menu and nothing happens, the DOS Shell is already in the Single File List mode and you need to press Esc instead of Enter to continue.

To make sure your screen is adjusted properly for working with this exercise,

5. **Press** Alt O simultaneously

You should have pulled down the Options menu and be highlighted on Confirmation.

Type F to select File Display Options...

You should be at the File Display Options window, highlighted opposite Name:.

Type *.*

Press Tab 3 times to move to Sort by:

Press ↓ to move the radio button to highlight Name

Press Enter

To switch to viewing the network drives,

6. **Press** → to highlight F

When the drive letter F is highlighted,

Press Enter

You should see the directory tree for F:\ on the left side of the split window, and F:*.* on the right side of the window.

7. **Press** Tab until you highlight Directory Tree

When Directory Tree is highlighted,

Press ↓ until you highlight LOGIN directory.

Logged in as Guest. your screen should look similar to Figure 2.7.

You should notice that your display adjusts in the right split window to reference F:\LOGIN*.*, which means you are viewing all the files in the LOGIN directory. Notice that there is a plus (+) on the LOGIN directory folder, shown in the left split window, titled Directory Tree. The plus (+) indicates that a directory is an expandable directory branch.

To move to the Mail directory,

8. **Press** Down Arrow until you highlight Mail

When your highlight bar is on Mail,

Press Alt T simultaneously to pull down the Tree menu

Type x to expand the tree one level

Your screen should look similar to Figure 2.8, except you should see the numbered directory under Mail for your User account. This is your User ID number, and your location within the Mail directory that is

FIGURE 2.7

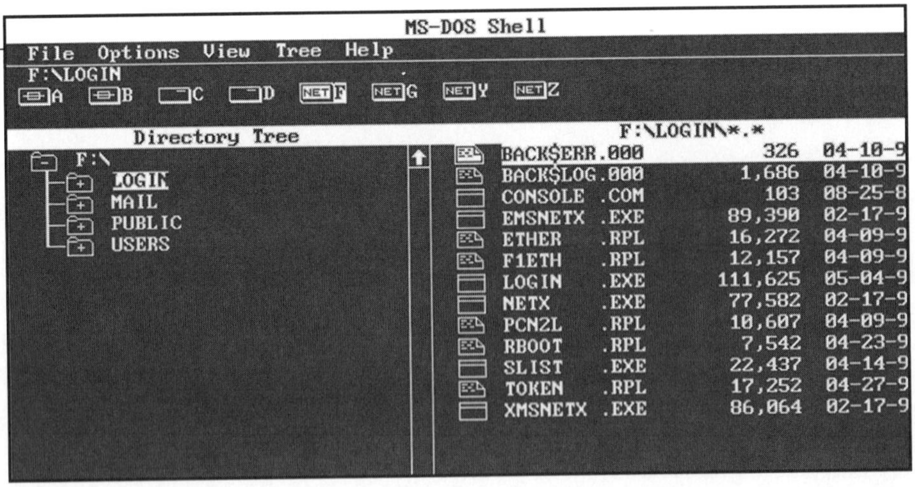

FIGURE 2.8

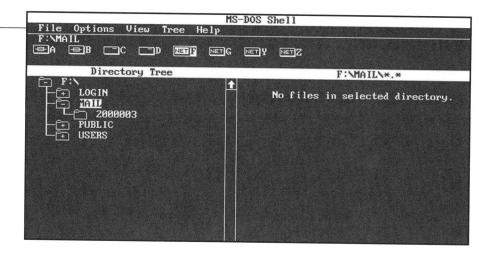

checked every time you log in. Notice your Mail folder shows a minus (–) symbol. A collapsable directory branch (where there are no further levels) is indicated by the minus (–) symbol.

To move to the PUBLIC directory,

> 9. **Press** ↓ until you are highlighted on PUBLIC

When your highlight bar is on PUBLIC,

> **Press** Alt F simultaneously
>
> **Type** *H* to select Search
>
> **Type** *.EXE
>
> **Press** Tab to move to [X] Search entire disk
>
> **Press** Spacebar until [ ] is blank for Search entire disk
>
> **Press** Enter

Your screen shows the results of your search of all the files that have an *.EXE extension in the Public directory. Using DOS Shell is a handy way of working from a menu to help you work with files and directories on the network.

To exit DOS Shell,

> 10. **Press** Alt F simultaneously
>
> **Press** *X* to select exit

You should be returned to the F:\PUBLIC> directory prompt.

From the F:\PUBLIC> prompt,

   11. **Type** *LOGOUT*

      Press Enter

You are logged out of the network. You don't have to be logged in to the network to work with the DOS Shell. However, when you are logged in, you can use the DOS Shell to work with files and directories on your local workstation or those available to you on the network.

KEY RELATED POINTS

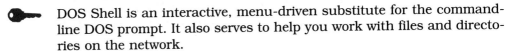 DOS Shell is an interactive, menu-driven substitute for the command-line DOS prompt. It also serves to help you work with files and directories on the network.

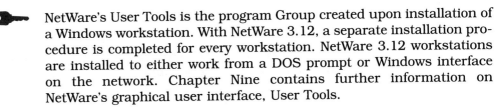 NetWare's User Tools is the program Group created upon installation of a Windows workstation. With NetWare 3.12, a separate installation procedure is completed for every workstation. NetWare 3.12 workstations are installed to either work from a DOS prompt or Windows interface on the network. Chapter Nine contains further information on NetWare's graphical user interface, User Tools.

2.5 NAVIGATING THE NETWORK FROM NETWARE'S FILER

FILER
See page 37.

FILER is NetWare's menu utility to control volume, directory, and file information. You will use FILER in this exercise to learn how to navigate the directory structure.

This exercise assumes that you are logged in and at either the first network drive F:\> prompt or the F:\LOGIN> directory prompt on your NetWare LAN. You can use CD\LOGIN to get to the LOGIN directory prompt.

Hands-On Exercise

From the F:\LOGIN> prompt,

   1. **Type** *FILER*

      Press Enter

Your screen displays the Available Topics main menu, within FILER.

With your highlight bar on Current Directory Information,

2. **Press** (Enter)

Your screen displays Directory Information for the LOGIN directory. The listing displays the owner, creation date and time, as well as other security information about the LOGIN directory.

To return to Available Topics,

3. **Press** (Esc)

You should be at FILER'S main menu, Available Topics.
From Available Topics, select Directory Contents,

4. **Press** (↓) once

Press (Enter) highlighted on Directory Contents

You should be at the Directory Contents screen for the LOGIN directory. The LOGIN.EXE and SLIST.EXE files are displayed in your viewing window.

5. **Press** (↓) to move the highlight bar to LOGIN.EXE

Press (F5)

The LOGIN.EXE file should be blinking. (F5) is used to mark files.
With LOGIN.EXE still blinking,

6. **Press** (↓) to move the bar to SLIST.EXE

Press (F5)

The SLIST.EXE file should now be blinking, with the LOGIN.EXE file highlighted. You have now marked both files.
With the SLIST.EXE file blinking,

7. **Press** (Enter)

Your screen displays a pop-up window, Multiple File Operations, with Copy Marked Files as an option selection for this window. It is a common practice to use FILER for copying files on the network.

To end this process,

8. **Press** (Esc) once

You should be back at Directory Contents. Since you aborted or escaped the copying process, the marking was automatically removed on SLIST and LOGIN files.

To go to the parent directory,

9. Move the highlight bar to the top of the window where

.. parent is shown and

Press (Enter)

Your screen should look similar to Figure 2.9.

The pop-up window asks if you want to make this your current directory, with your highlight bar on Yes,

> **Press** Enter

Your screen should resemble Figure 2.10.

> **Press** Esc

10. Move the highlight bar to LOGIN (subdirectory) selection, and then

> **Press** Enter

Your screen displays a Subdirectory Options pop-up window. You could (1) copy or move the entire subdirectory structure, including any subsequent contents, (2) make this your current directory, or (3) view directory information.

From this window, to make this directory your current directory,

11. **Type** M

> **Press** Enter

This was the same screen, Directory Contents, you were working with before, similar to the one pictured in Figure 2.9.

With Directory Contents showing, to make a quick exit from FILER,

12. **Press** Alt F10 simultaneously

> **Press** Enter highlighted on Yes to Exit FILER

You should be at the LOGIN directory prompt, your last navigated directory location within FILER.

At the \LOGIN> prompt, end your network session.

13. Log out of the network using NetWare's LOGOUT command-line utility.

FIGURE 2.9

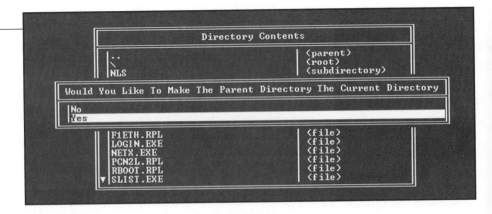

FIGURE 2.10

KEY RELATED POINTS

NetWare's directory structure begins with the file server. The next level is the volume, which is equivalent to the root level in DOS. Followed by the volume, is the directory and subsequent subdirectory level(s).

NetWare's directory structure is written:

Servername \ Volume: Directory \ Subdirectory

Example: ACADEMIC4C   \   SYS: LOGIN

servername   volume   directory

The F5 key is used to mark entries in NetWare's menu utilities.

Access Rights is the level of security, past LOGIN security, where network administrators must grant access privileges to users to work with directories and files. System Supervisors can set up security for each directory, controlling the access rights for each user of a directory. File access is controlled through attributes. Attributes are designed to be placed on files, but some can be placed on the directory. Directory and file access rights are covered in Chapter Three and Four.

FILER is NetWare's menu utility that will allow you to easily copy or move all or a portion of a directory structure. FILER can be used as an alternative to DOS or NetWare's command-line utilities for managing directories and files. FILER is explored further in Chapter Four.

END OF CHAPTER REVIEW

Important Terms

Booting	LAN	Physical Connection
Client	Logical Connection	PUBLIC Directory
Command-Line	LOGIN	Server
Utility	LOGIN Directory	SLIST
DOS	LOGOUT	USERLIST
DOS Shell	Menu Utility	WHOAMI
FILER	Network Connection	WHOAMI/G

True/False Questions

1. DOS is the local operating system which coordinates between all programs running on the local workstation and the workstation's hardware components.

2. Booting the local workstation means first loading the network operating system.

3. Pressing the [F1] [F1] key combination inside a menu utility provides a listing of NetWare's key (keyboard) assignments.

4. SLIST is used to view information about other users on the system.

5. To use the LOGIN command a second time, after already logging in, implies a logout.

6. The [F5] key is used to mark entries in NetWare's menu utilities.

7. Your USER ID numbered assignment, and your numbered directory location within the Mail directory is checked every time you log in.

8. The DOS Shell serves to help you work with files and directories on only the local workstation.

9. Entering the first letter of a selection item listed in a NetWare menu utility is a quick way to select that item.

10. Each user can view account configuration information about their own username in SYSCON.

11. The Supervisor and Guest account are automatically created upon installation of a NetWare server.

12. Every new user account belongs to the group, Everyone, when they are first created.

13. All users automatically have access to the Public directory when first created.

14. After log in, the next level of establishing security restrictions and access for NetWare is the directory rights assignments.

15. The USERLIST command lists the username, server you're attached to, the version of NetWare you are using, and the log in time and date.

ON YOUR OWN

1. What is your User ID number? What utility did you use to find it?

2. Find your connection number. What utility did you use to find your connection number?

3. What causes your prompt to show Enter your username: ? How could you combine this command at the command-line prompt to bypass the Enter your username: prompt, going directly to Enter your password: ?

4. Why do passwords not show on your screen as they are typed?

5. What information does USERLIST provide?

6. What information does WHOAMI provide?

7. Give at least 3 examples of reasons to use SYSCON.

8. What is the purpose of the Public directory?

9. What information does SLIST provide?

10. What is the purpose of creating Groups?

IN YOUR OWN WORDS

1. Investigate the network at your site. How are the workstations booting to the LAN? Are they configured as DOS-based or Windows-based interface for the network?

2. Describe the boot process of a NetWare workstation. Differentiate between physical and logical connections.

3. Define a User Account.

4. Define Group membership.

5. Distinguish between a User account and Group membership.

6. Explain NetWare's use of special accounts for system administration.

7. Explain the concept of user account restrictions.

8. Define and compare NetWare's SYSCON and FILER menu utilities.

9. Distinguish between NetWare's LOGIN, PUBLIC, and Mail system-created directories.

10. Differentiate between the listing obtained with SLIST compared to USERLIST.

11. Compare the LOGIN to the ATTACH command.

12. Name and define the accounts created upon installation of a NetWare 3.1x server.

CHAPTER 3

Exploring NetWare's Directory Structure

OBJECTIVES

- Compare NetWare's directory structure to DOS directory structure.

- Use command-line and menu utilities to navigate the directory structure.

- Compare local drives, network drives and search drives.

- View information about the server's volume(s) with VOLINFO and CHKVOL.

- Use CHKDIR and DSPACE to view directory space restrictions.

- View the directory structure using LISTDIR.

- Create and manipulate network and search drives with the MAP command.

- Map a fake root drive.

- Use MAP INSERT to add and reposition existing search drives.

- Add and change network drives using NetWare's SESSION menu utility.

CHAPTER INTRODUCTION

This chapter addresses both DOS and NetWare directory structures. It compares DOS to NetWare and introduces you to working with directory structures in NetWare. Both DOS and NetWare use the DOS MD (make directory) command to create directories. The DOS CD (change directory) command is also a valid way to navigate the directory structure(s) of both DOS and NetWare. With DOS, the CD command is valuable in navigating the directory structure. With NetWare, this chapter illustrates how the CD command can be a hindrance in navigating NetWare's directory structure.

In this chapter, you will find that a network drive letter can be established (usually drive letters F through Z) to move quickly to any logical location in NetWare's directory structure. In comparision, with DOS, once you used the drive letter to navigate to the physical disk on the network workstation, you then had to enter the path every time you wanted to move from the root.

The punctuation that always follows a NetWare volume name is a colon (e.g., SYS:). To illustrate, suppose you had the directory name "One" with a subdirectory name "Two" located off the volume SYS on file server FS1. You would list this as FS1\SYS:ONE\TWO.

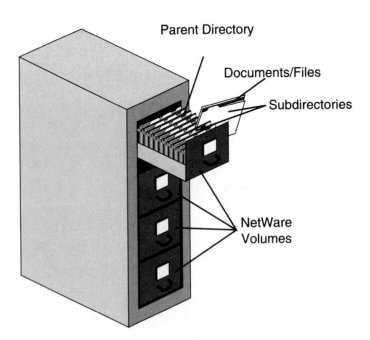

A NetWare File Server's Hard Disk

The NetWare directory structure can be visualized if you correlate this to filing cabinets in an office. All file cabinets, together, would be the network server. Each individual file cabinet would be the server's hard disk. Each file drawer could be thought of as being equal to a NetWare volume, but since a volume can span physical disks, you could also correlate a volume to all the parent drawers in a series of filing cabinets. The directories, underneath each volume, could be thought of as the hanging folders in each file drawer. The subdirectories would then be the manila file folders inside the hanging folders. The files are then the documents inside each manila folder. (See figure on page 62.)

Rights on a Network

In this chapter, you will also begin to work with NetWare's security. *Network security* means granting rights to users and collectively dealing with them as much as possible by placing them in groups and granting them rights. Granting access rights means granting access to volumes, directories, subdirectories and files. Granting access rights is generally done in combination with the needs of a particular user through the automatic assignment of security rights granted when a user logs in to NetWare. In this chapter, you will use the WHOAMI command (introduced in the previous chapter) with a new option, WHOAMI /R, to find out your security access rights.

Upon logging in to the NetWare server, your access rights are checked. You are granted access to NetWare because you have been defined and hold a valid account on a particular NetWare server.

The log in level is often thought of as the first level of security in NetWare. You may log in (or attach) to more than one server on a network where you possess a valid username and password.

System Created Directories

Upon installation of a NetWare v3.x server, volume SYS is created and certain files are copied to system-created directories named:

LOGIN, PUBLIC, MAIL, SYSTEM

The LOGIN directory, mentioned in the previous chapter, contains the LOGIN.EXE program for logging in to the network. Prior to logging in to the network, it is important to note that the first network drive or the Login directory are the only options available to a user (depending upon your workstation's network boot process configuration), aside from the DOS drives and directories on the workstation's local hard disk.

The Public directory holds the NetWare command-line and menu utilities for network users. The WHOAMI and USERLIST command files used in the previous chapter's exercises are located in this directory. Losing your search drive to this directory could automatically log you out of the network. It is important that this directory is mapped as your first search drive directory and that you NOT lose your search drive to the public directory for you risk being automatically logged out.

The Mail directory, also mentioned in the previous chapter, contains a hexadecimal-numbered subdirectory for each user, known as their User ID. This hexadecimal number is assigned automatically when the user is created. The Mail directory is where your personal, User LOGIN Script is located (if you create one). You will work with LOGIN Scripts in Chapter Eight to personalize and define your working session after you log in.

The SYSTEM directory contains supervisory and system administrative command files. This directory also holds files specific to the NetWare server.

Drive Pointers

This chapter introduces you to drive letter assignments. You can establish a drive letter to point to a specific subdirectory location within NetWare's directory structure. The assignment of drive letters is called *establishing drive pointers.*

A DOS drive letter (drive pointer) could be established to a directory path location on the local workstation's hard disk with the SUBST command. Though rarely used because you can run into problems, this is one way of establishing a drive letter to designate a location within the DOS directory structure.

With a networked workstation, drive letters A to E point to physical drives on the local workstation. NetWare recognizes and automatically reserves drive letters A through E for the local workstation. However, with NetWare 3.12, using DOS LASTDRIVE in the CONFIG.SYS file and FIRST NETWORK DRIVE in NetWare's NET.CFG file you can alter what is reserved for the local workstation and what is available, or left over, for **network drive pointers**.

NetWare assigns drive pointers to logical locations on the physical disk(s) located on the network server. Network drives begin with the drive letter F and range through Z. A drive pointer is configured to be either a Network or **search drive pointer**. Creating drive pointers for a network workstation is termed *mapping a drive.* The MAP command is used to establish network drives in NetWare.

Network Drive Pointer
Defined using the MAP command. Used to assign a single drive letter as an identifier or shorthand notation for a directory path location for a specific server volume.

Search Drive Pointer
Like a Network Drive Pointer, defined using the MAP command, and assigns a drive letter as an identifier. Unlike Network Drives, Search Drives only work to point to executable Files, much as the DOS path command does as it searches in order of the path in memory. The first search drive is drive Z and are lettered in reverse order through the alphabet.

3.1 VOLUMES OF INFORMATION

As mentioned in Chapter 2, the naming conventions are the same with NetWare as with DOS. What differs is the path identified. To review, with NetWare, the directory path is identified as:

SERVER \ VOLUME: DIRECTORY \ SUBDIRECTORY

As you can see, the NetWare directory structure is hierarchical. NetWare's directory structure really begins at the file server level and then branches to the volume(s), tiers to the directory level, and continues on with any subsequent subdirectories, ending at the file level.

VOLINFO
Menu utility to show volume information.

NetWare's volume level can be thought of as equivalent to the root level in DOS. NetWare's **VOLINFO** menu utility is used to view information about each volume on your server. CHKVOL is another command-line utility which utilizes volume information. Both commands are explored in this exercise.

This exercise assumes you're already logged in to NetWare.

Hands-On Exercise

Once you've logged in, at the prompt,

1. **Type** *VOLINFO*

   Press Enter

Your highlight bar should be on Change Servers in the Available Options screen of NetWare's VOLINFO menu utility. Using VOLINFO is the simplest way to view free space on the volume(s). The table above the Available Options menu displays the total volume and free volume space per volume as well as total and free directory entries per volume. One directory entry is used for each DOS file, subdirectory, and other items which characterize the NetWare volume. The F2 function key toggles the VOLINFO display between kilobyte and megabyte.

***NOTE:* If you do not have a search path to Public, you cannot run the VOLINFO utility. Common practice is to map the first search drive (usually letter Z:) to the Public directory. NetWare command-line and menu utilities must be in the search path.**

Figure 3.0 displays the VOLINFO in the kilobyte format. To view the megabyte format,

2. **Press** F2

To exit VOLINFO,

3. **Press** Esc once

You should be highlighted on Yes in the Exit VOLINFO pop-up window. Press Enter highlighted on Yes.

From the command-line prompt, to work with **CHKVOL**,

CHKVOL
Command-line utility
to show volume
information.

4. **Type** *CHKVOL*

   Press Enter

You should see a listing on your screen displaying information about the volume on which you are working. Figure 3.1 displays the CHKVOL command for the VOYAGER1 server. The CHKVOL command displays total space on the volume in use and space available on the volume as does VOLINFO. CHKVOL breaks down the space in use by deleted files and also shows the space available to you as a user, both of which VOLINFO did not display.

To use CHKVOL, if you had more than one volume on the server, at the prompt you would issue the following:

Terabyte(TB)
One TeraByte is equal
to approximately
1,000 GigaBytes.

5. **Type** *CHKVOL* *

   Press Enter

GigaByte(GB)
One GigaByte is equal
to approximately
1,000 MegaBytes.

VOLUME CAPACITY IN NETWARE

MegaByte(MB)
One MegaByte is equal
to approximately
1-million bytes
of information.

Feature	Maximum Amounts
Volumes on each file server	64
Hard disks on each volume	32
Maximum hard disks per server	2,048
Maximum volume size	32 (**T**era**B**yte)
Maximum addressable disk storage	32 (**T**era**B**yte)
Maximum file size	4 (**G**iga**B**yte)

FIGURE 3.0

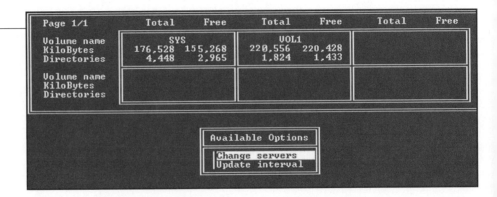

FIGURE 3.1

```
F:\LOGIN>chkvol

Statistics for fixed volume VOYAGER1/SYS:

Total volume space:                          136,528   K Bytes
Space used by files:                          31,260   K Bytes
Space in use by deleted files:                   224   K Bytes
Space available from deleted files:              224   K Bytes
Space remaining on volume:                   135,268   K Bytes
Space available to GUEST:                    135,268   K Bytes

F:\LOGIN>_
```

FIGURE 3.2

```
F:\LOGIN>chkvol *

Statistics for fixed volume VOYAGER2/SYS:

Total volume space:                          136,528   K Bytes
Space used by files:                           1,260   K Bytes
Space in use by deleted files:                   224   K Bytes
Space available from deleted files:              224   K Bytes
Space remaining on volume:                   135,268   K Bytes
Space available to GUEST:                    135,268   K Bytes

Statistics for fixed volume VOYAGER2/VOL1:

Total volume space:                           40,556   K Bytes
Space used by files:                          39,128   K Bytes
Space in use by deleted files:                    32   K Bytes
Space available from deleted files:               32   K Bytes
Space remaining on volume:                     1,428   K Bytes
Space available to GUEST:                      1,428   K Bytes

F:\LOGIN>_
```

The CHKVOL * command provides statistics for all volumes on the server which VOLINFO is designed to show. Figure 3.2 displays a two-volume listing for the VOYAGER2 server.

KEY RELATED POINTS

- The length of a server's volume name can be assigned between 2 and 15 characters.

- The punctuation that always follows a volume name is a colon (e.g., SYS:).

- The top level of a server is the volume, which is equivalent to the root in the DOS directory structure. Below the volume level is the directory level and subsequent subdirectory level(s). A DOS volume is noted by a backslash (\) character where a NetWare volume is noted by a colon (:). With both DOS and NetWare, the volume is the highest level in the directory structure.

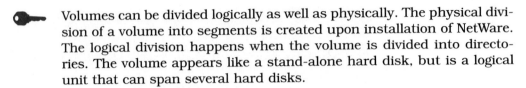 Volumes can be divided logically as well as physically. The physical division of a volume into segments is created upon installation of NetWare. The logical division happens when the volume is divided into directories. The volume appears like a stand-alone hard disk, but is a logical unit that can span several hard disks.

SYS is the first volume of every server. SYS volume is created with the installation of NetWare. The minimum volume size for the first volume, SYS, is 2.5MB.

A server cannot have the same name for any two volumes.

A NetWare 3.1x server can contain up to 64 volumes per server.

3.2 DIRECTORIES AND ACCESS RIGHTS

LISTDIR
Command used to view directory structure and rights information.

In this exercise, the **LISTDIR** command is used to list information about directories and subsequent subdirectories within NetWare's hierarchical directory structure on a server. DOS refers to a directory as a Directory Tree structure and uses the TREE command to view the directory, represented as a tree structure. In this exercise, you will use the DOS TREE command equivalent, NetWare's LISTDIR.

In this exercise, it is assumed that you are logged in to a NetWare server and that your first network drive is F.

Hands-On Exercise

To assure you are at the root of drive F,

    1. **Type** CD\

       Press [Enter]

This should take you to the root level of the volume, SYS. Your prompt should be the highest level in the directory structure for the first network drive, assumed to be F, and your prompt showing F:\>.

At the F:\> prompt,

    2. **Type** LISTDIR

       Press [Enter]

You should now see a listing on your screen of the network's directories you have rights to view, located directly off the SYS volume. There may be many more directories originating from the volume, but you may not be given rights to view or access them.

To view the directory structure, at the prompt,

FIGURE 3.3

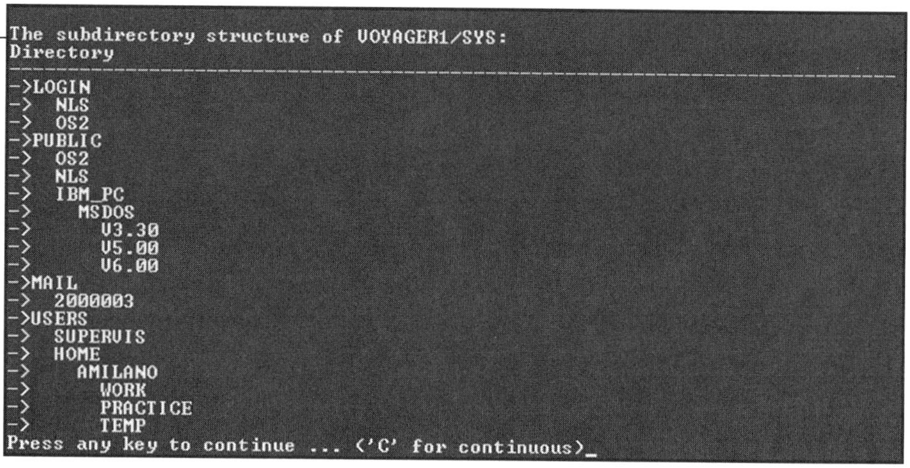

```
The subdirectory structure of VOYAGER1/SYS:
Directory
────────────────────────────────────────────────────────────────────────
->LOGIN
->   NLS
->   OS2
->PUBLIC
->   OS2
->   NLS
->   IBM_PC
->      MSDOS
->         V3.30
->         V5.00
->         V6.00
->MAIL
->   2000003
->USERS
->   SUPERVIS
->   HOME
->      AMILANO
->         WORK
->         PRACTICE
->         TEMP
Press any key to continue ... ('C' for continuous)_
```

3. **Type** *LISTDIR /S*

   Press Enter

You should see a complete listing on your screen of the directory structure originating from volume SYS which you have been given rights to work with and your screen will likely resemble Figure 3.3. Though you can see the directories, establishing security through the granting of NetWare's suite of rights enables you to perform tasks such as saving or overwriting files.

To see a listing of your rights, at the prompt,

4. **Type** *LISTDIR /R*

   Press Enter

You should see a listing of the rights for the directories you can work with displayed on your screen. NetWare's rights assigned to the directory flow down the directory structure. Once rights are granted for a directory, at a specific directory level in the directory structure, they flow underneath to subsequent subdirectories until they are redefined at a subsequent subdirectory level. To see a listing of your rights throughout the network directory structure,

5. **Type** *LISTDIR/SUB/R*

   Press Enter

You should see a combined list of the access rights for all the directories and subsequent subdirectories displayed on your screen where you have been given access rights. When working with NetWare commands, you can combine the command options or use the options separately.

To see a complete LISTDIR listing,

6. **Type** *LISTDIR /A*

   Press Enter

You should see a listing displayed on your screen which gives all the data LISTDIR offers, including the time that the directories and subsequent subdirectories were created.

To look at your rights on the network in another way,

7. **Type** *WHOAMI /R*

   Press Enter

You should then see your connection information as well as your effective directory rights listed for each level in the directory structure.

8. **Type** *CD\PUBLIC* to move to the Public directory

   Press Enter

From the F:\PUBLIC> directory prompt,

9. **Type** *LISTDIR /S/E*

   Press Enter

This gives you a list of your effective rights, not only in the Public directory but in any subsequent subdirectories below Public as well.

KEY RELATED POINTS

- The output from the LISTDIR command depends upon where it is issued in the directory structure. You can provide a directory path with NetWare's commands (e.g., LISTDIR SYS:PUBLIC) or move to make the desired directory your current directory prompt and then issue the LISTDIR command (e.g., F:\PUBLIC> LISTDIR).

- Directory rights apply to all files in the directory. With file attributes, discussed in the next chapter, you are able to apply certain attributes to a specific file within a directory. You can apply some attributes to all files in the directory.

- Inherited rights are those that flow down the directory structure from the Parent directory.

- Effective rights are the actual access rights you can exercise within a given directory.

WHOAMI/R shows your effective access rights throughout that portion of the network directory structure you can access.

 The listing obtained from LISTDIR depends upon where you are located in the directory structure when the command is issued. WHOAMI, with the /R option shows what directories and rights you have, and is the same listing regardless of where it is issued in the directory structure.

A FEW OF NETWARE'S RIGHTS
ASSIGNMENTS FOR DIRECTORIES

S	Supervisory rights hold all rights to the directory and files.
R	Read or open a file.
W	Write or update a file.
C	Create subdirectories and files.
E	Erase or delete directory and files.
M	Modify or rename directory and files.
F	File Scan or see names of files and directories.
A	(Access Control or change access) Grants any right but S to any user.

3.3 CHECKING THE STORAGE SPACE ON THE VOLUME AND DIRECTORY

CHKDIR
Command-line utility for viewing directory and volume disk storage space available and in use.

NetWare's **CHKDIR** provides a listing of space in use and what is available for you to use on the file server by server volume and directory location. The DOS CHKDSK command is similar to NetWare's CHKDIR. DOS CHKDSK is used on local workstation drives and cannot be used on network drives.

NetWare's **DSPACE** command is the menu-utility that lists disk space available for a user on a volume. DSPACE or SYSCON are two of NetWare's menu utilities that can be used by the system administrator to limit user disk storage space on a volume.

This exercise assumes that you are logged in to a NetWare server, and located at the F:\LOGIN> directory prompt.

Hands-On Exercise

At the F:\LOGIN> prompt,

    1. **Type** *CHKDIR*

       Press [Enter]

DSPACE
Menu utility for
viewing directory and
volume disk storage
space available and
in use. The System
Administrator may
use this utility to
change disk storage
space on a volume or
directory. (See page
71.)

You should see a listing of your space limitation for the LOGIN directory as well as the SYS: volume.

To launch the DSPACE menu utility,

2. **Type** *DSPACE*

   Press Enter

You should see the Available Options menu within Netware's DSPACE menu utility.

3. **Press** ↓ once to highlight User Restrictions

   Press Enter

You should be highlighted on your username in the Users on Server submenu within DSPACE.

4. **Press** Enter highlighted on your username

You should be highlighted on the volume name of SYS in the Volumes on Server submenu.

5. **Press** Enter highlighted on SYS

Viewing the listing of your available disk space and space limitation for the SYS volume, Figure 3.4 should look somewhat similar to what your screen displays.

6. **Press** Alt F10 simultaneously

By holding Alt continuously while pressing F10 you should bring up the Exit DSPACE pop-up window and your highlight bar should be on Yes.

7. **Press** Enter on Yes to Exit

You should be back at the command-line prompt.

To view your disk space in SYSCON, at the prompt,

FIGURE 3.4

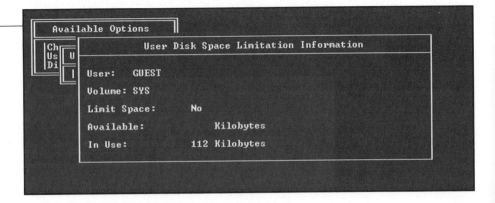

FIGURE 3.5

```
         User Volume/Disk Restrictions

Limit Volume Space?                    No
Volume Space Limit:                    KBytes
Volume Space In Use:           112 KBytes
```

8. **Type** *SYSCON*

   Press [Enter]

   Type *U*

   Press [Enter]

Under the User Information submenu screen,

9. **Press** [↓] until you move the highlight bar to your username

   Press [Enter] highlighted on your username

Select Volume/Disk Restrictions submenu option for the volume SYS:. Your screen may resemble Figure 3.5. When you're finished viewing your storage space restrictions, you can use [Alt] [F10] to exit SYSCON.

KEY RELATED POINTS

 From SYSCON, User Information submenu for your username, the Volume/Disk Restrictions menu option will show your volume and disk storage restrictions. Figure 3.5 displays an example of the restrictions for the Guest account on this particular NetWare server.

The system administrator can limit disk storage space by volume or directory using either the SYSCON or DSPACE menu utility.

3.4 GETTING OUT THE MAP FOR THE DIRECTORY STRUCTURE

MAP
Used to create, change, or view network drive mappings.

NetWare's **MAP** command is used to list, create, or change network drive letter assignments. A drive designation is represented by a letter, assigned to specific, frequently accessed locations within NetWare's directory structure. NetWare recognizes three types of drives: local, or those reserved for the workstation; network, those which point to the file server's hard disk; and search drives, or those NetWare keeps in memory to search a path, like DOS uses PATH, if a file is not located at the current directory prompt. In this exercise, you will be introduced to all three drive types and NetWare's MAP command.

This exercise assumes that you are logged in to a NetWare server, and located at the F:\LOGIN> directory prompt. Use the CD\LOGIN command to move to the F:\LOGIN> directory prompt.

Hands-On Exercise

At the F:\LOGIN> prompt,

    1. **Type** *MAP*

       Press Enter

You should see a listing of the drive mappings configured for your workstation. As part of the log in process, your drive assignments are established. To create a drive mapping, render the following:

MAP drive letter:=volume:directory path

To map drive G to the LOGIN directory,

    2. **Type** *MAP G:=SYS:LOGIN*

       Press Enter

You see NetWare's confirmation to your drive mapping on your screen, *Drive G: = servername\SYS: \LOGIN*. Your screen may resemble Figure 3.6. Supplying the servername is optional. NetWare assumes your current server.

***NOTE:* If you did not receive NetWare's confirmation for your drive mapping, check to see that you've used the colon equals (:=) after the drive letter. A colon (:) must be placed after SYS, the volume name. The colon is easy to overlook.**

To see a complete listing of your current mappings, at the prompt,

    3. **Type** *MAP*

       Press Enter

MAP DEL
Used to delete drive mappings. Referred to as NetWare's Map Delete command. Works the same as MAP REM.

You see drive G has been added to your drive assignments.
To delete the map for drive G, at the prompt,

    4. **Type** *MAP DEL G:*

       Press Enter

Your screen shows, *"The mapping for drive G: has been deleted."*

***NOTE:* With DOS and NetWare you must make sure you add the colon (:) after the letter to designate a drive assignment (e.g., G:).**

FIGURE 3.6

```
F:\LOGIN>MAP G:=SYS:LOGIN
Drive  G: = VOYAGER1\SYS:  \LOGIN
F:\LOGIN>_
```

To map a drive to a directory path,

> 5. **Type** *MAP G:=SYS:PUBLIC\IBM_PC*
>
> **Press** (Enter)

Drive G is now mapped to the subdirectory location, IBM_PC in the PUBLIC directory.

To move to that location quickly,

> 6. **Type** *G:*
>
> **Press** (Enter)

You should be at the G:\PUBLIC\IBM_PC> subdirectory location.

***NOTE:* If you were not successful, you may not have access to this directory (e.g., SYS:PUBLIC\IBM_PC) or you may need to use another subdirectory under Public for this step.**

To view your new mappings, at the prompt,

> 7. **Type** *MAP*
>
> **Press** (Enter)

Now NetWare recognizes that drive G is mapped to the PUBLIC\ IBM_PC directory location (or another if you had to choose another).

At the G:\PUBLIC\IBM_PC> prompt, move back to drive F.

> 8. **Type** *F:*
>
> **Press** (Enter)

Remove the drive mapping for drive G.

MAP REM
Same as MAP DEL.
Referred to as
NetWare's MAP
REMove command.

> 9. **Type** *MAP REM G:*
>
> **Press** (Enter)

Your screen shows, "*The mapping for drive G: has been deleted.*" NetWare's MAP REM (remove) works just like the MAP DEL (delete) command.

***NOTE:* You do not need to move away from the drive letter to be deleted to remove the drive mapping to that location, but you will receive an error message that your current drive is no longer valid and could risk being automatically logged out of the network.**

KEY RELATED POINTS

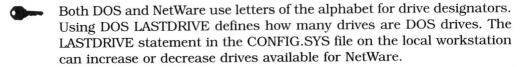

Both DOS and NetWare use letters of the alphabet for drive designators. Using DOS LASTDRIVE defines how many drives are DOS drives. The LASTDRIVE statement in the CONFIG.SYS file on the local workstation can increase or decrease drives available for NetWare.

DOS assigns letters to designate physical disk drives and can assign a letter to a directory path using the DOS SUBST command or by creating a RAM drive. With the DOS SUBST command, the drive letter assignment works like a NetWare network drive. A RAM drive works like a NetWare search drive. Exercise 3.9 is the hands-on exercise for creating search drives.

The letters A through E are usually reserved for local drives, pointing to physical disk drives on the local workstation. A NetWare workstation is typically configured to recognize drive letters A to E for local drives and reserves letters F to Z for pointing to logical locations within the network's directory structure.

Local drives are listed on your screen with the MAP command as "*maps to a local disk*". After the local disk drives, the network drives are listed, which point to logical locations on the file server's hard disk. Search drives direct NetWare to search memory for files not at the current directory prompt. With the MAP command, search drives are listed at the end of the listing. Search drives correlate to the DOS PATH command.

Drive mappings are temporary unless you save them in your login script, to execute mappings automatically each time you log in. Login scripts are covered in Chapter Eight.

You can use either the backslash (\) or forward slash (/) with the MAP command.

3.5 NAVIGATING IN THE DIRECTORY STRUCTURE

In this exercise, you will learn how to navigate through NetWare's directory structure and use the MAP command to view your changes.

This exercise assumes that you are logged in to a NetWare server, and located at the F:\LOGIN> directory prompt.

Hands-On Exercise

At the F:\LOGIN> prompt,

1. **Type** *MAP G:=SYS:PUBLIC\IBM_PC*

   Press [Enter]

You should have received the confirmation for mapping drive G.
To create a drive mapping for drive H,

2. **Type** *MAP H:=SYS:PUBLIC*

   Press [Enter]

You should now see NetWare's confirmation of your mapping to drive
H displayed on your screen.

To move around the network directory structure quickly, at the
prompt,

3. **Type** *G:*

   Press [Enter]

   Type *H:*

   Press [Enter]

   Type *F:*

   Press [Enter]

CD
DOS Command to be
avoided in NetWare,
unless you want the
drive remapped. CD\
is used to change
your directory to the
Root of a DOS
Directory structure.
CD\ is to be avoided
with NetWare for
CD\ remaps your
network drive letter.

CD..
DOS command to be
avoided in NetWare.
Used to move
backwards one
directory level in the
DOS directory tree
structure. To be
avoided with NetWare
unless you want the
drive remapped as
you go.

You should always avoid using the **cd** or **cd..** to navigate NetWare's
directory structure. Although this was essential for navigating DOS
directory structures, in NetWare it should be avoided.

To illustrate this point, at the prompt,

4. **Type** *G:*

   Press [Enter]

You should be at the G:\PUBLIC\IBM_PC> directory prompt.
To view and check your mapped drives,

5. **Type** *CD*

   Press [Enter]

You can see that your directory path has disappeared from your
prompt.

To view the effect of this on your drive mapping, at the prompt,

6. **Type** *MAP*

   Press [Enter]

Drive G has been remapped and the new mapping gives a prompt
that shows G:\> as a result of using CD\ in the previous step. Refer to
Figure 3.7 and compare the listing on your screen for steps 5 and 6.

At the G:\> prompt,

7. **Type** *CD\LOGIN*

   Press Enter

   Type *MAP*

   Press Enter

You see that NetWare remaps your drive assignment to yet another location as you use CD.. or CD\. Your screen may resemble Figure 3.8. To remove the map to drive letter H,

8. **Type** *MAP REM H:*

   Press Enter

The confirmation message, "*The mapping for drive H: has been deleted*", should appear on your screen.

At the prompt,

9. **Type** *LOGOUT*

   Press Enter

You should be at NetWare's F:\LOGIN> directory prompt. NetWare leaves you at your last active network drive prompt or the LOGIN directory each time you log out.

KEY RELATED POINTS

 Logical locations within NetWare's directory structure on the file server are remapped in NetWare when you use CD\ or CD.. to navigate.

 You should navigate the directory structure using the mapped drive letter assignments rather than DOS CD\ or CD.. to change directories.

FIGURE 3.7

```
G:\PUBLIC\IBM_PC>CD\

G:\>MAP

Drive  A:    maps to a local disk.
Drive  B:    maps to a local disk.
Drive  C:    maps to a local disk.
Drive  D:    maps to a local disk.
Drive  E:    maps to a local disk.
Drive  F: = VOYAGER1\SYS:   \LOGIN
Drive  G: = VOYAGER1\SYS:   \
Drive  H: = VOYAGER1\SYS:   \PUBLIC

SEARCH1:   = Z:. [VOYAGER1\SYS:   \PUBLIC]
SEARCH2:   = Y:. [VOYAGER1\SYS:   \PUBLIC\IBM_PC\MSDOS\U5.00]

G:\>_
```

FIGURE 3.8

```
G:\LOGIN>MAP

Drive   A:    maps to a local disk.
Drive   B:    maps to a local disk.
Drive   C:    maps to a local disk.
Drive   D:    maps to a local disk.
Drive   E:    maps to a local disk.
Drive   F: = VOYAGER1\SYS:   \LOGIN
Drive   G: = VOYAGER1\SYS:   \LOGIN
Drive   H: = VOYAGER1\SYS:   \PUBLIC

SEARCH1:   = Z:. [VOYAGER1\SYS:   \PUBLIC]
SEARCH2:   = Y:. [VOYAGER1\SYS:   \PUBLIC\IBM_PC\MSDOS\V5.00]

G:\LOGIN>_
```

3.6 THE PURPOSE OF MAP ROOT

MAP ROOT
Used to create a fake
root directory. Can
be assigned to any
location in the
directory structure.

The **MAP ROOT** command is used to make a fake root directory. The fake root is a location that appears as if this were the first level of the directory structure.

In this exercise, it is assumed that you are logged in to NetWare and the prompt on your screen displays F:\LOGIN>.

Hands-On Exercise

To create a fake root,

  1. **Type** *MAP ROOT G:=SYS:USERS*

     Press [Enter]

You should have received confirmation of your mapping from NetWare.
     To view your new drive assignment for G,

  2. **Type** *MAP G:*

     Press [Enter]

You now should see the path which drive G is mapped to, and after the directory path you should see a backslash (\) symbol. This backslash (\) is used to indicate a root drive mapping. Take a look at this drive mapping compared to the other drive mappings.
     At the prompt,

  3. **Type** *MAP*

     Press [Enter]

You should have noticed that drive G, in relation to other drive mappings, has the backslash (\) at the end of the directory path and can easily be spotted in the listing, similar to Figure 3.9.

To move to drive G,

   4. **Type** *G:*

      Press Enter

You should have received the G:\> prompt. The directory path does not display. When you use the MAP ROOT command to designate a fake root drive mapping, the path does not show at the drive letter prompt. Putting this to the test, see if you can move back toward the root (volume level) in the directory structure.

   5. **Type** *CD*

      Press Enter

      Type *LISTDIR*

      Press Enter

You can see that your directory path is not displayed and your location has not changed. Using either CD\ or CD.. with a fake root mapping will not alter your inability to move backward in the directory structure. You can, however, move farther down the directory structure.
   To move down the directory structure,

   6. **Type** *CD HOME*

      Press Enter

You should see that your directory prompt changed from G:\> to G:\USERS>, now showing the path.

NOTE: If you were not successful in moving to the HOME directory under the USERS directory, it may need to be created on your directory structure.

To see if the root is now remapped,

   7. **Type** *MAP*

      Press Enter

You should see that drive G now ends the path with \HOME, which verifies that you have moved the drive pointer.
   To see if you have changed the root mapping too,

   8. **Type** *CD*

      Press Enter

      Type *MAP*

      Press Enter

FIGURE 3.9

```
F:\LOGIN>MAP ROOT G:=SYS:USERS\

Drive  G: = VOYAGER1\SYS:USERS  \

F:\LOGIN>MAP G:

Drive  G: = VOYAGER1\SYS:USERS  \

F:\LOGIN>MAP

Drive  A:    maps to a local disk.
Drive  B:    maps to a local disk.
Drive  C:    maps to a local disk.
Drive  D:    maps to a local disk.
Drive  E:    maps to a local disk.
Drive  F: = VOYAGER1\SYS:  \LOGIN
Drive  G: = VOYAGER1\SYS:USERS  \

SEARCH1:  = Z:. [VOYAGER1\SYS:  \PUBLIC]
SEARCH2:  = Y:. [VOYAGER1\SYS:    \PUBLIC\IBM_PC\MSDOS\V5.00]

F:\LOGIN>_
```

Your screen displays that you did not remove the root drive mapping assignment for drive G. To actually delete the fake root map, you can either remap the drive to another location or delete the drive mapping.

To remove the root mapping,

9. **Type** *MAP DEL G:*

   Press Enter

You should have received, "*The mapping for drive G: has been deleted*" on your screen.

NOTE: **You received the message, "Current drive is no longer valid>" because you removed your active drive pointer.**

10. **Type** *F:*

    Press Enter

Your active drive is now F.

KEY RELATED POINTS

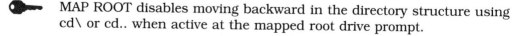 MAP ROOT disables moving backward in the directory structure using cd\ or cd.. when active at the mapped root drive prompt.

MAP ROOT changes the path, and remaps the drive pointer as you move down the directory structure but does not allow moving toward the root of the directory structure using CD.. or CD\.

3.7 SHORTCUTS WITH MAP

There are shortcuts to remapping your drives. In this exercise, it is assumed that you are logged in and your prompt shows F:\LOGIN>.

Hands-On Exercise

To begin, at the F:\LOGIN> prompt,

    1. **Type** *MAP G:=SYS:USERS/HOME/SHORTCUT*

        Press [Enter]

NOTE: **If you were not successful in moving to the Shortcut directory, it may need to be created on your directory structure.**

You should be at the G:\USERS\HOME\SHORTCUT> prompt. NetWare recognizes the forward slash (/) as well as the backslash (\) to separate subdirectories when a directory path is given.

To quickly remap drive G,

MAP ..
Remap one level back in the directory structure

    2. **Type** *G:*

        Press [Enter]

        Type *MAP ..* (type 2 dots after MAP)

        Press [Enter]

Your screen displayed the confirmation of your remapping, changed the path shown at the prompt for drive G to one level back in the directory structure, and positioned you at the G:\USERS\HOME> prompt. Refer to Figure 3.10.

NOTE: **You needed to move the active drive before you were able to take the first shortcut given to simplify drive mapping. Your active drive prompt is important for taking shortcuts.**

MAP ...
Remap two levels back in the directory structure.

At the G:\USERS\HOME> prompt,

    3. **Type** *CD SHORTCUT*

        Press [Enter]

        Type *MAP ...* (type 3 dots after MAP)

        Press [Enter]

Your screen displayed the confirmation of your remapping, changed the path for drive G two levels back in the directory structure, and positioned you at the G:\USERS> prompt. Refer to Figure 3.10. Type MAP at the prompt to check your drive mappings.

FIGURE 3.10

```
G:\USERS\HOME\SHORTCUT>MAP ..
Drive  G:  = VOYAGER1\SYS:   \USERS\HOME
G:\USERS\HOME>CD SHORTCUT
G:\USERS\HOME\SHORTCUT>MAP ...
Drive  G:  = VOYAGER1\SYS:   \USERS
G:\USERS>_
```

To work with shortcuts and remap a fake root, at the G:\USERS> prompt,

    4. **Type** *MAP ROOT /USERS/HOME/SHORTCUT*

       Press Enter

You should be at the G:\> prompt.

To check your directory path for drive G, at the G:\> prompt,

    5. **Type** *MAP*

       Press Enter

**MAP **
Remap to the root directory, NetWare's volume level.

You should see that NetWare recognizes drive G as a fake root drive mapping as there is a backslash (\) after the directory path showing for G drive on your screen.

To take a shortcut in remapping a fake root,

    6. **Type** *MAP *

       Press Enter

You received the confirmation message of the remapping from NetWare on screen, and your prompt shows G:\USERS\HOME\SHORTCUT>. You have removed the fake root. Type MAP at the prompt to check and then map drive G to the volume level (root) of NetWare's directory structure.

At the G:\USERS\HOME\SHORTCUT> prompt,

    7. **Type** *MAP *

       Press Enter

The backslash (\) showing in this step indicates the root of NetWare's directory structure, or the volume level. Type MAP at the prompt to verify your mapping.

To take still another shortcut in mapping, at the G:\> prompt,

    8. **Type** *MAP /USERS/HOME*

       Press Enter

While at a drive letter prompt, you can use MAP followed by the directory path from the root (or volume level) to extend your drive letter mapping. Type MAP to verify your remapping, and then delete your mapping.

At the prompt,

9. **Type** *F:*

   Press Enter

   Type *MAP REM G:*

   Press Enter

NetWare provides a message confirming your deletion of the map for drive G.

KEY RELATED POINTS

NetWare places a backslash (\) at the end of the directory path listed with the MAP command to indicate a fake root drive mapping.

You can use either the forward slash (/) or backslash (\) when entering a directory path for drive mapping.

To extend or remap a drive mapping within the same drive letter designation, move to the location using DOS CD to change to that subdirectory, or use MAP followed by just the directory path, such as: MAP USERS/HOME/SHORTCUT.

3.8 MAPPING NETWORK DRIVES USING NUMBERS

MAP NEXT
Used to map the next available network drive letter to a directory path specified.

Instead of creating a drive mapping by using a letter, you can use the numerical equivalent to the letter to create a mapped drive. If the first network drive is F, this corresponds to the number 1 drive. Drive G would be number 2, and so on. In this exercise you will work with the MAP command using the numerical equivalent instead of using letters to map drives. You work with the **MAP NEXT** command to map the next available drive letter to a specific directory path.

This exercise assumes that you are logged in and your prompt shows F:\LOGIN>.

Hands-On Exercise

To begin,

1. **Type** *Z:*

   Press Enter

MAP *(*number*):=
Used to assign the
second network drive
letter to a directory
path. (e.g., MAP
*2:=/USERS).

You should be at the Z:\PUBLIC> prompt.
To quickly map drive G to the PUBLIC directory,

2. **Type** *MAP *2:=*

   Press Enter

You see the confirmation on your screen, "*Drive G: = server
name\SYS: \PUBLIC*" for mapping drive G. The asterisk (*)
followed by the numerical equivalent to the drive letter is another way
to perform drive mapping.

**NOTE: The := (colon equals) after the *2 assumes the active loca-
tion within the directory structure.**

At the Z:\PUBLIC> prompt,

3. **Type** *G:*

   Press Enter

   Type *MAP NEXT SYS:LOGIN*

   Press Enter

Your screen should show a message confirming drive H was mapped
to the LOGIN directory. MAP NEXT is a command used to quickly assign
the next available drive letter to the directory location within the volume
specified. MAP NEXT even works with the last drive, Z, and will rotate to
assign the next available network drive letter in position of the alphabet.
   To see how this works, at the G:\PUBLIC> prompt,

4. **Type** *Z:*

   Press Enter

   Type *MAP NEXT SYS:LOGIN*

   Press Enter

You should have returned to the Z:\PUBLIC> prompt and received the
message that drive I is mapped to the LOGIN directory. Drive letters F
through H were taken, so the next available drive letter for NetWare to
assign was the letter I. Refer to Figure 3.11. Type MAP at the prompt to
verify your mappings.
   Then,

5. **Type** *MAP *6:=/PUBLIC*

   Press Enter

You should have received the message that drive K (or the 6th network drive letter) was mapped to the Public directory. Move to drive I.
   At the prompt,

6. **Type** *I:*

   Press Enter

Type *MAP NEXT /LOGIN*

Press Enter

You should have seen drive J is assigned as a mapped drive to the LOGIN directory. Type MAP at the prompt to verify your current mappings, and then move to drive J.

At the prompt,

7. **Type** J:

   Press Enter

   Type *MAP NEXT /USERS*

   Press Enter

You should have received the message that drive L is mapped to the USERS directory. Drive K was taken, so NetWare skipped to the next available drive letter, drive L.

To gain a perspective of how temporary your mappings are, log in again.

8. **Type** *LOGIN*

   Press Enter

Then, provide your username and password. You will recall from the previous chapter that using LOGIN a second time, after you are already logged in, implies a log out.

Use the MAP command to verify your default mappings assigned upon logging in. Once you're logged in again, at the prompt,

9. **Type** *MAP*

   Press Enter

FIGURE 3.11

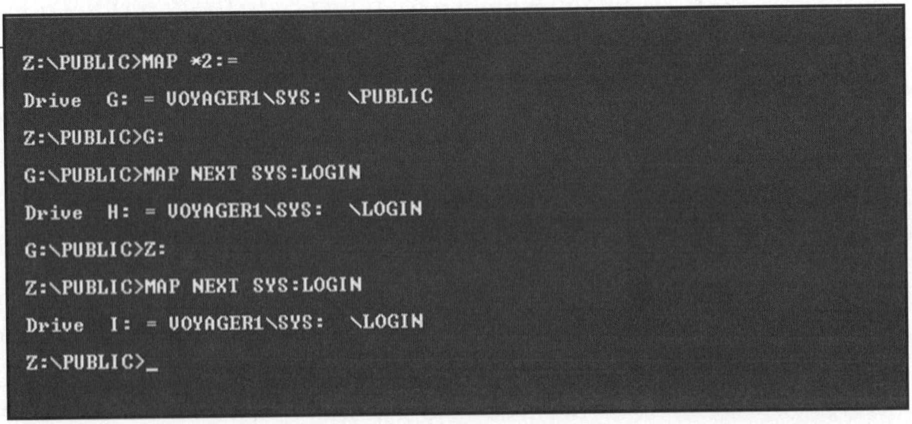

```
Z:\PUBLIC>MAP *2:=
Drive   G: = VOYAGER1\SYS:   \PUBLIC
Z:\PUBLIC>G:
G:\PUBLIC>MAP NEXT SYS:LOGIN
Drive   H: = VOYAGER1\SYS:   \LOGIN
G:\PUBLIC>Z:
Z:\PUBLIC>MAP NEXT SYS:LOGIN
Drive   I: = VOYAGER1\SYS:   \LOGIN
Z:\PUBLIC>_
```

The mappings which appear on your screen are your default drive mappings or the ones saved to a LOGIN Script. In order to save drive mappings, you write them to a LOGIN Script file. LOGIN Scripts are covered in Chapter Eight.

KEY RELATED POINTS

 Drive mappings are temporary unless saved to a LOGIN Script file (a text file which executes automatically when you log in to initialize and customize your network session). LOGIN Scripts are similar to DOS configurable batch files, but are executed as part of the LOGIN procedure.

NETWARE DRIVE LETTERS AND CORRESPONDING DRIVE NUMBERS

NetWare Drive Letter	NetWare Drive Number
F*	1
G	2
H	3
I	4
J	5
K	6
L	7
M	8
N	9
O	10
P	11
Q	12
R	13
S	14
T	15
U	16
V	17
W	18
X	19
Y	20
Z	21

* F is usually the first drive letter for NetWare, however, the first network drive letter could be drive D for NetWare 3.12. The ending drive letter is established in the CONFIG.SYS file using DOS LASTDRIVE. FIRST NETWORK DRIVE (in the workstation's network configuration file, NET.CFG) establishes the assignment for the first network drive letter.

With NetWare, your drive mappings can be saved to your personal LOGIN Script file. Your personal LOGIN Script can be created, viewed or edited in SYSCON, by selecting LOGIN Script from the User Information submenu for your username.

The asterisk (*) followed by the numerical equivalent to the drive letter matching the number given is another way to perform drive mapping.

3.9 CREATING SEARCH DRIVES

In this exercise, you will become acquainted with NetWare's search drive mapping. You will use COPY CON to make a test file, and to search through the directory structure as you work with search drives. NetWare's search drives check for executable files, typically those that end with .EXE, .COM, or .BAT extensions.

NetWare uses MAP S1 to designate the first search drive. Search drives are in descending alphabetical order. Thus, the first search drive (S1) corresponds with the letter Z, and the second search drive (S2) corresponds to Drive Y, and so on.

This exercise assumes that you have just logged in and your prompt shows F:\LOGIN>.

Hands-On Exercise

At the F:\LOGIN> directory prompt,

1. **Type** *MAP G:=SYS:USERS\HOME*

   Press [Enter]

   Type *G:*

   Press [Enter]

You should be at the G:\USERS\HOME> directory prompt. You need to make a subdirectory under USERS that begins with your first initial, followed by as many letters in your last name that you can fit in the remaining seven (7) letters. For example, Joe Davis would type: MD JDAVIS

At the G:\USERS\HOME> prompt,

2. **Type** MD (your directory name)

   Press [Enter]

   Type CD (your home directory name)

   Press [Enter]

You should be at the directory prompt for your home directory, under the USERS\HOME directory, *G:\USERS\HOME\your home directory* *name>*. Next, create a test file to use with this and the coming exercises dealing with NetWare's search drives.

At the G:\USERS\HOME\your home directory name> prompt,

3. **Type** *COPY CON TESTIT.BAT*

   Press Enter

The cursor should appear at the far left of your screen, under the G of the drive prompt.

To begin your first line of text for this file,

4. **Type** *@ECHO OFF*

   Press Enter

The cursor should be blinking under the @ symbol. The @echo off will not display commands or messages during execution of this file.

To type the next line of this file,

5. **Type** *ECHO* A file for <your name here> to use with the MAP command.

   Press Enter at the end of the line of text. The cursor should be blinking under the letter E of the word *echo*. The *echo* command is used so that the message following it will display on your screen.

To type the last line of this file,

6. **Type** *@ECHO OFF*

   Press Enter

The cursor should be blinking under the @ symbol.

To begin to save what you've typed on screen to the *TESTIT.BAT* file,

7. **Press** Ctrl z simultaneously to initiate saving the file

To finish the saving process and write the file to your home directory on the server's disk,

8. **Press** Enter to complete saving this file

You should have received the "*1 file copied*" message and returned to your home directory prompt for drive G. To check that your file is in your home directory, use the DOS DIR command.

To run or execute this batch file,

9. **Type** *TESTIT*

   Press Enter

You should have received the 1-line message, "*A file for <your name here> to use with the MAP command,*" similar to what is shown in Figure 3.12.

To establish a search drive pointing to your home directory, at the prompt,

10. **Type** *MAP S3:=*

    Press (Enter)

You should have received a message on your screen to echo your SEARCH3 location, confirming your search drive mapping to the location of your active prompt, your home directory. You can type MAP at the prompt to check your mappings. To test your batch file and search drive mapping, move to another directory location.

At your home directory prompt for drive G,

11. **Type** *F:*

    Press (Enter)

At the prompt for drive F,

    Type *TESTIT*

    Press (Enter)

Your cursor should be returned to drive F prompt. You should see the 1-line message from the TESTIT.BAT file above your blinking cursor.

This proves that NetWare first surveys the active drive prompt and then looks to the search path established. To view your search path, at the prompt for drive F,

12. **Type** *PATH*

    Press (Enter)

You should see a listing of the search path for your workstation. This is the search path your workstation follows, beyond your active drive prompt.

NOTE: **Search drives will map around network drives, which means that if the first network drive is mapped to Z, then the first search drive, listed as S1, will begin at the letter Y. The maximum search drives is 16, but not necessarily ending at the letter K. The next exercise dealing with S16 will display the variable nature of search drives.**

KEY RELATED POINTS

- COPY CON is the command used to copy what is typed at the console prompt to create a text file. Using .BAT file extension creates a batch file which can be called to run from any drive prompt in the directory structure, provided a search drive mapping (search path) has been established.

- The drive designations (drive pointers) NetWare recognizes are either local workstation drives, network drives, or search drives.

FIGURE 3.12

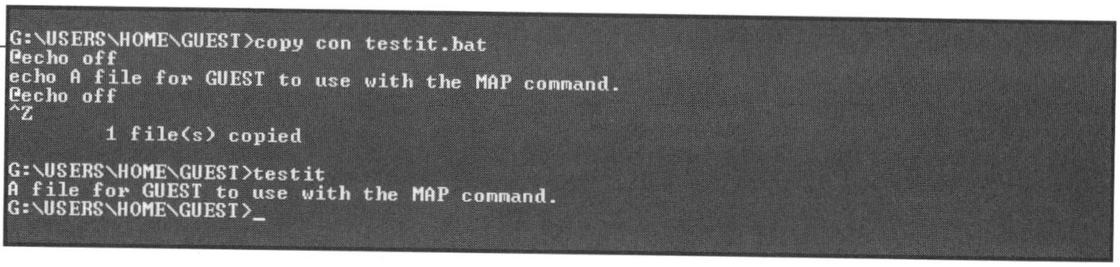

```
G:\USERS\HOME\GUEST>copy con testit.bat
@echo off
echo A file for GUEST to use with the MAP command.
@echo off
^Z
        1 file(s) copied

G:\USERS\HOME\GUEST>testit
A file for GUEST to use with the MAP command.
G:\USERS\HOME\GUEST>_
```

If the first network drive letter is drive F, you have up to 5 drives designated for the local workstation (drive letters A through E), and have 21 drives (F through Z) which can be used for either network or search drive mappings.

Search drives are established by using the letter S followed by a number (e.g., MAP S2:=SYS:USERS).

Search drives correlate to the DOS PATH command. With DOS, the PATH was established to point to directory locations where DOS could search to find executable files.

Search drives begin with drive Z (or S1). Search drives are in descending alphabetical order, thus the first search drive, SEARCH1:, corresponds with the letter Z.

With NetWare, you can have a maximum of 16 search drives.

NETWARE'S SEARCH DRIVE NUMBERS AND CORRESPONDING DRIVE LETTERS

NetWare Search Drive	NetWare Drive Letter	Count
S1	Z	1
S2	Y	2
S3	X	3
S4	W	4
S5	V	5
S6	U	6
S7	T	7
S8	S	8
S9	R	9
S10	Q	10
S11	P	11
S12	O	12
S13	N	13
S14	M	14
S15	L	15
S16	K	16

3.10 DELETING SEARCH DRIVES; USING S16 TO CREATE SEARCH DRIVES

In this exercise, you will create a search drive using S16. You will delete search drives first using the search drive letter and then the search drive number. You will see how NetWare remaps search drives when you try to overwrite them. This exercise is designed to reveal NetWare's variability in the assignment and reassignment of search drives.

This exercise assumes that you have just logged in, that your first search drive shows SEARCH1:=Z:[servername\SYS:\PUBLIC], mapping and your cursor is blinking at the prompt shown as F:\LOGIN>.

Hands-On Exercise

At the F:\LOGIN> directory prompt,

    1. **Type** *CD\USERS*

       Press [Enter]

You should be located at the F:\USERS> prompt.

To map drive X to this location,

    2. **Type** *MAP X:=*

       Press [Enter]

You should have received confirmation on your screen that drive X was mapped to the USERS directory. Type MAP at the prompt to check it. Refer to Figure 3.13.

MAP S16
NetWare assigns the next available search drive when using S16 as a way to prevent overwriting existing search drive mappings. Sixteen search drives are possible with NetWare. Defining drive mappings using S16 will map the next available search drive number. (Refer to table on pg. 91.)

NOTE: The := after X assumes the active directory prompt. If you receive the message that drive X is already in use as a search drive, answer X for yes to overwrite this drive letter assignment.

With your prompt showing F:\LOGIN>, to use S16 to create a search drive,

    3. **Type** *MAP S16:=*

       Press [Enter]

You should see confirmation of your search drive mapping displayed on your screen. Creating search drives with S16 assures that the next available search position is chosen, rather than designating the position, such as S2 for example. Type MAP at the prompt to check it.

See what happens when you try to overwrite a search mapping, at the F:\USERS> prompt,

FIGURE 3.13

```
F:\LOGIN>cd\users

F:\USERS>map x:=

Drive   X: = VOYAGER1\SYS:  \USERS

F:\USERS>map

Drive   A:    maps to a local disk.
Drive   B:    maps to a local disk.
Drive   C:    maps to a local disk.
Drive   D:    maps to a local disk.
Drive   E:    maps to a local disk.
Drive   F: = VOYAGER1\SYS:  \USERS
Drive   G: = VOYAGER1\VOL1:  \

SEARCH1:   = Z:. [VOYAGER1\SYS:   \PUBLIC]
SEARCH2:   = Y:. [VOYAGER1\SYS:   \PUBLIC\IBM_PC\MSDOS\V5.00]
SEARCH3:   = X:. [VOYAGER1\SYS:   \USERS]

F:\USERS>_
```

   4. **Type** *MAP S2:=*

      Press [Enter]

Now you should see the confirmation of your drive mapping displayed on your screen. NetWare assigned the next available search drive letter, but retained the location SEARCH2.

   To examine this further,

   5. **Type** *MAP*

      Press [Enter]

Your screen displays that NetWare took your previous drive letter assignment for S2 and reassigned it to a network drive mapping. You should also see that your S2 mapping from step 4 was given the next available drive letter assignment, and took the SEARCH2: position. Write down the SEARCH2 drive letter assignment now showing on your screen.

MAP DEL S(*number*):
Used to delete search drive mappings.

   To view what happens when you try to delete a search drive,

   6. **Type** *MAP DEL* <drive letter from step 4>:

      Press [Enter]

You receive the message from NetWare on your screen, telling you your search drive assignment for that drive letter is used for SEARCH2 drive mapping. The question asks if you want to change it, and you're given a Y prompt.

   With your cursor on Y,

   7. **Type** *N*

      Press [Enter]

MAP DEL drive letter:
Commonly used to delete network drive mappings. When used to delete a search mapping, NetWare notifies you of deleting your search map and asks for confirmation.

NetWare responds that there was NOT a deletion performed for that drive letter. Use the MAP command to view and verify you retained SEARCH2. Rather than use the drive letter, try using the S2 designation to delete the search drive and compare the difference between the two methods of deleting search drives.

At the prompt,

> 8. **Type** *MAP DEL S2:*
>
>   **Press** Enter

NetWare did not ask you to respond (Y/N) to continue. By providing the S2 versus the drive letter assignment, NetWare assumes you are sure of your request and executes the deletion without question. Use the MAP command to view and verify you removed the SEARCH2 from step 4.

KEY RELATED POINTS

- Rather than use the drive letter, use the S(number) designation to delete a search drive.

- Using S16 assures you will not overwrite existing search mappings, but rather create a search mapping for the next available search drive position.

- Overwriting existing search drive mappings using MAP S(*number*) causes NetWare to throw the mapping to the next available network drive letter.

3.11 MAP INSERT

In this exercise, you will use **MAP INS** to work with inserting search drive mapping. You will be able to compare this to overwriting and remapping an existing search drive from the previous exercise.

This exercise assumes that you've just logged in and your prompt shows F:\LOGIN>.

Hands-On Exercise

At the F:\LOGIN> directory prompt,

> 1. **Type** *CD\USERS*
>
>   **Press** Enter

Your F drive prompt should have changed to F:\USERS.

FIGURE 3.14

```
F:\USERS>map s3:=
SEARCH3:   = X:.  [VOYAGER1\SYS:   \USERS]
F:\USERS>map ins s3:=
SEARCH3:   = W:.  [VOYAGER1\SYS:   \USERS]
F:\USERS>_
```

MAPS INS
Used to create a search drive mapping by inserting a mapping at a specified search numbered location. MAPS INS automatically renumbers and rotates the existing search mapping(s), moving them farther down the search path to make room for the inserted search drive mapping. (See page 94).

At the F:\USERS> prompt,

2. **Type** MAP S3:=

   Press Enter

NOTE: If you receive the message that drive X is in use as a search drive, type Y to answer yes to the question to overwrite it.

You should have received confirmation that S3 was mapped to the USERS directory.

To see how MAP INS works,

3. **Type** MAP INS S3:=

   Press Enter

You should have received confirmation that S3 was mapped to the *next available*, descending ordered letter of the alphabet for the USERS directory. Refer to Figure 3.14.

To view what happened to the previous S3 mapping and the status of your current mappings,

4. **Type** MAP

   Press Enter

You should see that your drive letter assignments are out of alphabetic order because SEARCH3 drive letter took the *next available letter.* Hence, MAP INS actually inserted the search drive map at the search location requested, SEARCH3, yet took the next available descending letter of the alphabet. The previous SEARCH3 was moved down one position in the search drive order, to SEARCH4.

To see what benefit using S16 holds,

5. **Type** MAP S16:=

   Press Enter

Your screen shows that the next available search drive number along with the next available search drive letter were assigned to the S16 mapping. Type MAP to view your drive mappings. Refer to Figure 3.15.

Moving your drive pointer can remap your search drive. From the F:\USERS> prompt,

6. **Type** *CD\LOGIN*

   Press [Enter]

   Type *MAP X:=*

   Press [Enter]

NetWare asks you again if you want to reassign this search drive. Refer to Figure 3.16.

At the Y prompt, to accept remapping,

7. **Press** [Enter]

NetWare responds that drive letter X was remapped. Refer to Figure 3.16. To see if it was retained as a search drive,

8. **Type** *MAP*

   Press [Enter]

You see that not only was drive X retained as a search drive, it also retained its search number position. Moving the drive pointer and issuing a new mapping using the drive letter is handled differently by NetWare than remapping a search drive using the search drive number.

To review this difference, while still at the F:\LOGIN> prompt,

9. **Type** *MAP S3:=*

   Press [Enter]

   Type *MAP*

   Press [Enter]

FIGURE 3.15

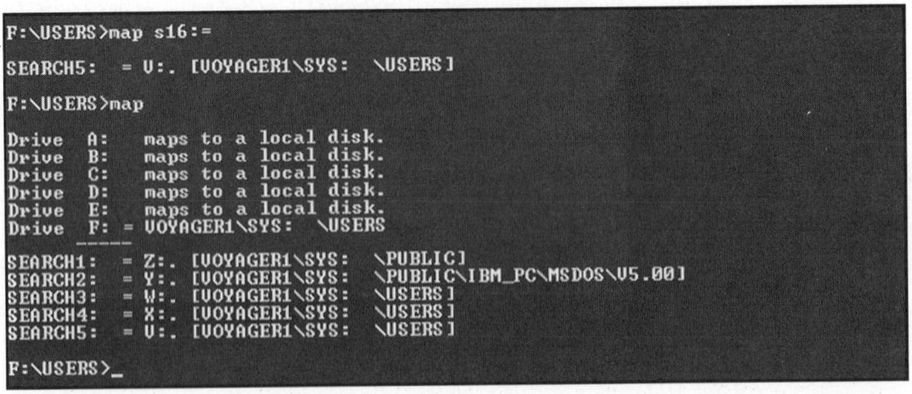

```
F:\USERS>map s16:=

SEARCH5:  = U:. [VOYAGER1\SYS:   \USERS]

F:\USERS>map

Drive  A:     maps to a local disk.
Drive  B:     maps to a local disk.
Drive  C:     maps to a local disk.
Drive  D:     maps to a local disk.
Drive  E:     maps to a local disk.
Drive  F: = VOYAGER1\SYS:   \USERS

SEARCH1:  = Z:. [VOYAGER1\SYS:    \PUBLIC]
SEARCH2:  = Y:. [VOYAGER1\SYS:    \PUBLIC\IBM_PC\MSDOS\V5.00]
SEARCH3:  = W:. [VOYAGER1\SYS:    \USERS]
SEARCH4:  = X:. [VOYAGER1\SYS:    \USERS]
SEARCH5:  = U:. [VOYAGER1\SYS:    \USERS]

F:\USERS>_
```

FIGURE 3.16

```
F:\USERS>cd\login

F:\LOGIN>map x:=

Drive X is in use as a search drive.
Do you want to reassign this search drive? (Y/N) Y
Drive  X: = VOYAGER1\SYS:  \LOGIN

F:\LOGIN>map

Drive  A:    maps to a local disk.
Drive  B:    maps to a local disk.
Drive  C:    maps to a local disk.
Drive  D:    maps to a local disk.
Drive  E:    maps to a local disk.
Drive  F: = VOYAGER1\SYS:  \LOGIN

SEARCH1:  = Z:.  [VOYAGER1\SYS:   \PUBLIC]
SEARCH2:  = Y:.  [VOYAGER1\SYS:   \PUBLIC\IBM_PC\MSDOS\V5.00]
SEARCH3:  = W:.  [VOYAGER1\SYS:   \USERS]
SEARCH4:  = X:.  [VOYAGER1\SYS:   \LOGIN]
SEARCH5:  = V:.  [VOYAGER1\SYS:   \USERS]

F:\LOGIN>_
```

You see that SEARCH3 took the next available drive letter assignment. The previous SEARCH3 was automatically reassigned to the next available network drive letter. This confirms the difference between remapping a search drive using the drive number vs. using the drive letter.

KEY RELATED POINTS

 MAP INS works only with Netware's search drive mappings.

3.12 GETTING A LITTLE HELP—ADDING DRIVE MAPPINGS WITH SESSION

SESSION
Netware's menu utility to enable users to set up and change their own working environment.

The **SESSION** menu utility enables you to set up your own working environment without having to know the corresponding NetWare command-line utility. SESSION allows you to change to another server, map drives, and send messages. In this exercise you will use SESSION to view and add a network drive mapping.

This exercise assumes that you've just logged in and your prompt shows F:\LOGIN>.

Hands-On Exercise

At the F:\LOGIN> directory prompt,

    1. **Type** *SESSION*

       Press Enter

You should be looking at the Available Topics main menu of NetWare's SESSION menu utility.

To view your network drive mappings,

2. **Type** D

   Press Enter

You should be at the Current Drive Mappings submenu. Your current drive mappings are listed on your screen. Add a drive mapping for drive G, mapped to the Public directory.

From the Current Drive Mappings screen,

3. **Press** Ins

You should see a suggested drive letter in the Drive pop-up window.

To select L as the drive letter assignment,

4. Type L

   Press Enter

You should be at the Select Directory pop-up window.

To walk down the directory structure,

5. **Press** Ins

You should at the File Servers pop-up window, highlighted on the name of your active server.

To select your server,

6. **Press** Enter

You should be at the Volumes pop-up window.

To select volume SYS,

7. **Type** S to move the highlight bar to highlight SYS

   Press Enter

You should be at the NetWork Directories pop-up window.

To select PUBLIC,

8. **Type** P to move the highlight bar to highlight PUBLIC

   Press Enter

You should be highlighted on .. in the NetWork Directories pop-up window.

To quit selecting and move out of the subdirectory selection window,

9. **Press** Esc

You should be at the Select Directory pop-up window and viewing a directory path that begins with the name of your active server, followed

FIGURE 3.17

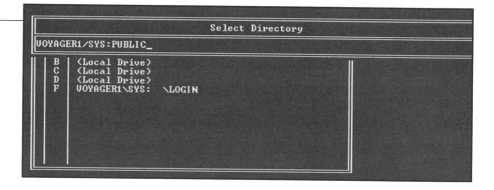

by /SYS:PUBLIC. You can edit this entry now. You can type the path or walk down the directory structure. Refer to Figure 3.17.

To select the /SYS:PUBLIC directory path for your server,

    10. **Press** ⌈Enter⌉

You should be viewing a pop-up window asking if you want to map root this drive.

To answer No,

    11. **Press** ⌈Enter⌉ highlighted on No

You should see drive L, mapped to PUBLIC, added to your Current Drive Mappings screen.

To exit to the SESSION's main menu,

    12. **Press** ⌈Esc⌉

You should be back at the Available Topics menu, ready to complete the next exercise, 3.13.

KEY RELATED POINTS

When you are not sure of the directory path, you can walk down the directory structure by pressing ⌈Ins⌉ at each level, selecting what you need from each subdirectory.

You press ⌈Esc⌉ in NetWare's menu utilities to indicate your entry is complete and also to stop the selection process. Using ⌈Esc⌉ in NetWare's menu utilities also exits to the previous level, or provides an exit to the menu utility.

To add a search drive map in the SESSION menu utility, select Search Mapping from the Available Topics menu and follow the same steps as used to create a network drive map.

3.13 CHANGING DRIVE MAPPINGS USING NETWARE'S SESSION MENU UTILITY

In this exercise you will use SESSION to change your default drive pointer and delete a network drive mapping. This exercise assumes that you've completed the previous exercise to add a MAP for drive G and you are currently at the Available Topics main menu of NetWare's SESSION menu utility.

Hands-On Exercise

From SESSION's Available Topics menu,

1. **Type** *SEL*

You moved the highlight bar to Select Default Drive menu item.

    Press Enter

You should be at the Select Default Drive screen.
To change your active drive,

2. **Type** *Z*

    Press Enter

You should be back at the Available Topics menu.
To verify your change was effective,

3. **Press** Esc

    Press Enter highlighted on Yes to Exit SESSION

You should see your active drive prompt is Z:\PUBLIC>.
To return to SESSION,

4. **Type** *SESSION*

    Press Enter

You should be back at the Available Topics menu.
To institute deleting your drive mapping for drive L,

5. **Type** *D* to move the highlight bar to Drive Mappings

    Press Enter

You should be at the Current Drive Mappings screen.
To delete your drive mapping for drive L,

6. **Type** *L*

    Press Del

    Press Enter highlighted on Yes to Delete drive mapping

You should have seen drive L removed from the Current Drive Mapping submenu listing.

7. **Press** Esc

You should have returned to the Available Topics menu.
To return to the command-line and check your mappings,

8. **Press** Esc

Press Enter highlighted on Yes to exit SESSION

You should have returned to the Z:\PUBLIC> directory prompt.
Next, to check your drive mappings,

9. **Type** *MAP*

Press Enter

You should see that drive L was, in fact, removed.

KEY RELATED POINTS

🔑 The MAP command-line utility corresponds to creating network and search drive mappings in NetWare's SESSION menu utility.

🔑 MAP DEL or MAP REM are the command-line utilities that correlate to deleting drive mappings in SESSION.

🔑 You cannot delete your active drive location within SESSION, but can delete your active drive from the command-line using MAP DEL or MAP REM.

END OF CHAPTER REVIEW

Important Terms

CHKDIR	MAP DEL drive letter	MAP..
CHKVOL	MAP DEL S(*number*):	MAP...
CD..	MAP INS	MAP\
CD\	MAP NEXT	Network Drive Pointer
DSPACE	MAP REM	Search Drive Pointer
LISTDIR	MAP ROOT	SESSION
MAP	MAP S16	VOLINFO
MAP DEL	MAP *(number)*:=	

True/False Questions

1. CHKVOL displays the name of the volume, total number of directories, and number of free directories.

2. The CHKDIR command lists the space available on the file server, volume, and directory.

3. MAP is a command that allows the user to define frequently accessed directories and subdirectories.

4. A network drive mapping points to a specific directory location.

5. In order to map a network drive, only a letter is assigned to indicate a specific directory path.

6. The alphabet letters A–E are generally available for mapping to a search drive.

7. Logical drives are given letter A–E assignments.

8. Search drives look first to the path and then to the active directory prompt.

9. A valid map command is MAP j=server1/sys:users/home.

10. You may have up to 17 search drive mappings.

11. You can move backward, toward the volume, in a fake root mapping.

12. The drive designation for S1 is usually drive letter F.

13. When you log out of a NetWare server, you are automatically taken to the LOGIN directory prompt.

14. When you log out of a server, you lose your drive mappings created during your working session.

15. VOLINFO displays information for all volumes on your server.

16. DSPACE is used for limiting space on the volume only.

17. NetWare recognizes three drive types: network, search, and mapped drives.

18. Search drive mappings are similar to the DOS PATH command.

19. Mapping a drive to S2 will always provide the drive letter Y assignment.

20. The SESSION menu utility is only used to map drives.

ON YOUR OWN—HANDS-ON

Mapping and Displaying Information on the NetWork.

Directions: For this exercise, you will need to have a formatted diskette located in drive A on your local workstation. You will use the DOS redirector (>) and the DOS append (>>) symbols to store files containing listings of information about your network. You will be given instruction for making printouts of these files.

1. Use LOGIN to log in to NetWare. At the F:\LOGIN> prompt,
   TYPE: MAP > A:MAPPING
   You should have returned to your F:\LOGIN> drive prompt. Nothing appears on your screen, so use the DOS DIR to check that the MAPPING file was created on the disk you have in drive A. If the MAPPING file did not save, check to see that the diskette is formatted.

2. Use the DOS TYPE command to check the contents of the MAPPING file. At the F:\LOGIN> prompt,
   TYPE: TYPE A:MAPPING
   You should see the contents of the MAPPING file displayed on your screen.

3. To add to the MAPPING file,
   TYPE: USERLIST >>A:MAPPING
   This will add the USERLIST command information, output to the previous file, MAPPING. Use DOS TYPE command to check your output.

4. To make a printout of this file, at the F:\LOGIN> prompt,
   TYPE: TYPE A:MAPPING>LPT1
   This output will work, assuming you have been given instructions on how to capture a network printer or have captured a network printer upon logging in. You could also use this on any computer, networked or not, that has a locally attached printer.

5. To begin displaying information, the following assumes you have your formatted diskette in drive A and have either gone through or read through the instructions for steps 1–4, above, as this assignment refers back to them.

5a. ON YOUR OWN: MAP drive G to your home directory in the /USERS/HOME directory structure. Use MAP >>A:MAPPING once you have completed this task. Then,
TYPE: ECHO LISTING 5A >>A:MAPPING and
PRESS [Enter]. This will add the label "LISTING 5A" to your MAPPING file.

5b. ON YOUR OWN: MAP the next available search drive, using S16, to the LOGIN directory. Use MAP >>A:MAPPING once you have completed this task. Then,
TYPE: ECHO LISTING 5B >>A:MAPPING and
PRESS [Enter]. This will add the label "LISTING 5B" to your MAPPING file.

5c. ON YOUR OWN: MAP drive H to the /USERS directory. From the H:\USERS> prompt, use MAP >>A:MAPPING once you have completed this task. Then,
TYPE: ECHO LISTING 5C >>A:MAPPING and
PRESS [Enter]. This will add the label "LISTING 5C" to your MAPPING file.

5d. ON YOUR OWN: Use LISTDIR /S to view the subdirectory structure from the H:\USERS> prompt. Use LISTDIR/S >>A:MAPPING once you have completed this task to save the output to the MAPPING file. Then,
TYPE: ECHO LISTING 5D >>A:MAPPING and
PRESS [Enter]. This will add the label "LISTING 5D" to your MAPPING file.

5e. ON YOUR OWN: Use LISTDIR/S, adding the option which would also provide your security rights. Use THE LISTDIR [WITH THE APPROPRIATE OPTION(S)] followed by >>A:MAPPING to save the output to the MAPPING file. Then,
TYPE: ECHO LISTING 5E >>A:MAPPING and
PRESS [Enter]. This will add the label "LISTING 5E" to your MAPPING file.

5f. ON YOUR OWN: Use CHKDIR from drive H prompt to view the information about the network's directory structure. Use CHKDIR >>A:MAPPING once you have completed this task to save it to the MAPPING file. Then,
TYPE: ECHO LISTING 5F >>A:MAPPING and
PRESS [Enter]. This will add the label "LISTING 5F" to your MAPPING file.

5g. ON YOUR OWN: Use the WHOAMI command from the drive H prompt that would show all of the rights and options WHOAMI recognizes. Use THE WHOAMI COMMAND WITH THE APPROPRIATE

OPTION(S) followed by >>A:MAPPING to save the output to the MAPPING file. Then,
TYPE: ECHO LISTING 5G >>A:MAPPING and
PRESS (Enter). This will add the label "LISTING 5G" to your MAPPING file.

5h.   ON YOUR OWN: Move to drive G.
TYPE: CD\ at the H:/ USERS/HOME/your home directory name> prompt. From the H:\> prompt, use the command that would show your current drive mappings. Use THE COMMAND followed by >>A:MAPPING to save the output to the MAPPING file. Then,
TYPE: ECHO LISTING 5H >>A:MAPPING and
PRESS (Enter). This will add the label "LISTING 5H" to your MAPPING file.

5i.   ON YOUR OWN: From the H:\> prompt, use the LISTDIR command that would show all the directory and subsequent subdirectories. Use THE LISTDIR [WITH THE APPROPRIATE OPTION(S)] followed by >>A:MAPPING to save the output to the MAPPING file. Then,
TYPE: ECHO LISTING 5I >>A:MAPPING and
PRESS (Enter). This will add the label "LISTING 5I" to your MAPPING file.

5j.   ON YOUR OWN: From the H:\> prompt, use the MAP INS command to place a mapping at S2 for the /USERS/HOME/your home directory. From the H:\> prompt, use the command that would show your current drive mappings, followed by >>A:MAPPING to save the output to the MAPPING file. Then,
TYPE: ECHO LISTING 5J >>A:MAPPING and
PRESS (Enter). This will add the label "LISTING 5J" to your MAPPING file.

6.   Make a printout of the MAPPING file. Refer to step 4 as needed.
TYPE: TYPE A:MAPPING>LPT1

IN YOUR OWN WORDS

1.   Describe the types of basic drive mappings you would recommend for all users working on wordprocessing in the MicroView company. Draw a map of the directory structure that would fit your mapping(s).

2.   Draw a directory structure for a multiple-server environment of a college. Account for administrative and instructional uses. For each server, list all the volumes, directories, subdirectories, and

directory rights you might assign to various college employees. Make sure you have included a home directory location for each user as well as a shared data directory(s) and common application directory(s) where appropriate. List the hardware capacity and configuration of the servers the college uses, including CPU size, disk storage space, and amount of RAM.

3. Compare NetWare's directory structure to DOS directory structure.

4. Distinguish between local drives, network drives and search drives.

5. Explain the statement, "Granting access rights means granting access to volumes, directories, subdirectories and files."

6. What is contained in the SYSTEM directory?

7. How can you establish a drive pointer in NetWare?

8. Explain the concept of volumes being divided logically as well as physically.

9. What would be the advantage of having Read and File Scan rights applied to a directory?

10. When would you need to have the Modify or Write access rights?

11. List the advantages and disadvantages of mapping a fake root directory.

12. Discuss the benefit of MAP S16? Discuss any unfavorable uses to using MAP S16.

Working with Files and NetWare's Security Rights

OBJECTIVES

- View and list files with NDIR.

- Rename directories using RENDIR.

- Distinguish rights assigned to the directory from those applied to a file.

- Modify directory rights and control file attributes with FILER.

- Control individual and groups of files with FILER.

- Compare working with files in NetWare to DOS.

- Show and change file attributes using FLAG.

- Extend trustee rights using GRANT.

- Examine trustee assignments using TLIST.

- View effective rights with RIGHTS.

- Recover deleted files with SALVAGE.

CHAPTER INTRODUCTION

This chapter addresses both DOS and NetWare directory structures, comparing DOS to NetWare by working with files within directory structures.

NetWare's Directory Rights

The following describes NetWare's Directory Rights, stating how these rights apply to directories and files.

Supervisory (S) applied to directories, grants all rights to the directory, its files and subdirectories and overrides any restrictions from the inherited rights mask. When applied to files, it grants all rights to the file. A user with supervisory rights can grant that right to other users for that file or directory.

Read (R) grants the right to open files in a directory and read their contents (which also means you can run the file if it is a program). For a file, (R) allows it to be opened and read.

Write (W) in a directory grants the right to open and modify files. For a file, (W) allows the opening and modification of the file.

Create (C) allows files and subdirectories to be created in a directory. If this is the only right in a directory, it is a drop box. For files, this right allows the user to recover (using SALVAGE) a file after it is deleted.

Erase (E) for directories allows the deletion of a directory, it's file's subdirectories, and the subdirectory's files. For files, (E) allows them to be deleted.

Modify (M) permits the changing of directory and file attributes and their renaming when applied to directories, and the changing of attributes and renaming of files only when applied to files. Having this right doesn't allow you to change the contents of files.

File Scan (F) for directories, grants the right to see the file in the directory, and for files, allows the filename to be seen and grants the right to see the directory structure above the subdirectory the file is in.

Access Control (A) in a directory allows the modification of directory and file trustee assignments and inherited rights mask, and the granting of any right except supervisory to any other user, including granting rights the user does not have. For a file, the same applies to that file only.

NetWare's File Attributes

The status of a file ultimately determines which functions you can perform. Directory rights apply to all files in a directory. File attributes are secured by placing conditions (attributes) on the file. The attributes control the file and with many combinations of attributes, files and directories are controlled on the network.

The file attributes of DOS are Archive, Hidden, Read-only, and System. DOS attributes are assigned using the ATTRIB command file. To assign an attribute, use the (+) before the letter and, to delete the attribute, use the (–) before the letter. An example of the assignment of file attributes in DOS using the ATTRIB command would be: ATTRIB FILE1.TXT +R. This would make the FILE1.TXT file Read-only. If you replaced the plus (+) with a minus (–) you would remove the attribute.

FLAG is a command used in this chapter to verify or change a file's attributes. A "flagged" file is one that has been marked with one or more of NetWare's attributes. These attributes regulate whether files or directories may be changed or shared. Ways in which the FLAG command are used include:

1. Prevention of accidental changes to or deletions of individual files.

2. Protection of public information files.

3. Alteration of the attributes of many files at one time.

A good understanding of how file attributes could limit the use of files and directories will help you to understand network security. When changing file attributes, the FLAG command requires you have MODIFY as an effective directory right, assigned to that specific directory.

FLAG is a command-line utility located in the SYS:PUBLIC directory. An example of a FLAG command is: FLAG SERVER1/SYS:USERS\ HOME\BILL\WP.EXE RO S.

Since the path is provided above, the FLAG command could be issued from any NetWare directory prompt to flag WP.EXE with the Read-only (Ro) and Shareable (S) attributes. If a file is flagged with the Ro and S attributes, it can be used by more than one person at a time. This is very valuable to keep in mind when trying to launch or open multiple copies of a file.

Netware assigns file attributes using the FLAG or FLAGDIR commands. Some attributes apply to DOS users and some to Macintosh users.

Some attributes apply to directories (all files in the directory) and some to a file.

NetWare's File Attributes for Directories

Delete Inhibit (D) applies to directories and files, preventing erasure even when the user has the Erase right.

Purge (P) immediately purges a file, when it is deleted. For directories, NetWare immediately purges any file that is deleted in the directory.

Rename Inhibit (R) prevents users from renaming files or directories even if they have the Modify right.

Hidden (H) prevents the directory from being seen with a DOS DIR command, but allows it to be seen by NDIR scans, and the directory cannot be deleted. If a user has the File Scan right, files hidden with this attribute appear when using NDIR.

System (Sy) is applied for directories only and prevents the directory from not only being seen with a DOS DIR command, but also from being copied or deleted. If a user has the File Scan right, files hidden with this attribute appear when using NDIR.

NetWare's File Attributes for DOS Workstations

Execute Only (X) applies to executable files ending in COM or EXE only and prevents them from being copied or backed up. This attribute cannot be removed once assigned. Additionally, many programs cannot run when flagged Execute Only. Users with Supervisor privileges can assign the Execute Only attribute.

Shareable (S) allows the file to be used by more than one user at a time.

Indexed (I) indicates that the file should be handled in a special way by the NetWare file system to provide quicker access. NetWare automatically sets this attribute when files reach a certain size.

Transactional (T) indicates that the file is protected by the NetWare Transaction Tracking System (TTS).

Delete Inhibit (D) applies to files, preventing erasure even when the user has the Erase right.

Hidden (H) applies to a file, where it cannot be seen by DOS DIR scans, but can be seen by NDIR scans, and it cannot be copied or deleted. If you have the File Scan right, files hidden with this attribute can be seen using NDIR.

Archive Needed (A) applies to files that have been modified since the last backup. Archive Needed is also applied to files that have been copied into another directory. This is DOS's archive bit.

Read-only (Ro) allows a file to only be read; it cannot be written to or deleted. NetWare assigns Delete Inhibit and Rename Inhibit automatically with Read-only.

Read-write (Rw) enables files to be read from and written back to the file. This is the default attribute on newly created files.

NetWare's File Attributes for Macintosh Workstations

Copy Inhibit (C) only restricts the copying ability of Macintosh users.

Delete Inhibit (D) prevents erasure of files and directories even when the user has the Erase right.

Rename Inhibit (R) prevents users from renaming files or directories even if they have the Modify right.

***NOTE:* There were two file attributes, Read audit (Ra) and Write audit (Wa), that were allocated for use in NetWare 3.x but never used. In NetWare 4.x, they were disposed of, and now the whole auditing function is handled by a separate auditing subsystem. *Auditing* is the process of recording events (e.g., file access, creations, deletions, print additions), and using this information to detect violations of the system's or to confirm the correct operation of network procedures. To banter this point — it reminds me of the definition of an auditor, as someone who comes in after the street fight to kill off all those injured during the battle just to make them easier to classify.**

The FLAG command, issued by itself from the command-line, lets you view or change the attributes of a file. In this chapter you will use the FLAG command to view and manipulate NetWare's file attributes.

Directories are useful for grouping and managing logically related files. DOS provides commands to create directories and subdirectories that form virtual hierarchical structures.

With DOS, there are symbols also used in NetWare that represent the root and the parent of the currently active directory. DOS DIR command will often display . and .. in its listing of files and directories. These symbols represent the currently active directory (the .) and the parent (the ..) of the currently active directory, respectively.

The MD (or MKDIR) is used on local workstation hard drives and floppy diskettes. You will also find it useful in this chapter for working in directory structures on the network file server. The CD (or CHDIR) command is used to change to another directory. The RD (or RMDIR) command is used to remove empty subdirectories. For some of the exercises in this chapter you will use MD and CD commands when working with directories.

The DOS ATTRIB command sets, removes, or displays a file (or files) attributes. Use ATTRIB command to change the attribute of a file. You can use the ATTRIB command to change all files to Read-write by reversing the Read-only attribute (reversing the +r to –r). The other attributes DOS recognizes are archive (a), system (s), and hidden (h). Through this chapter, you will use FLAG to manipulate NetWare's attributes and soon realize the limitations of the five attributes DOS offers.

The VER command is used to verify the version of DOS you are working with. The comparable NVER command is used on the network workstation.

Command-line Utilities

NetWare is comprised of command-line utilities and menu utilities.

NDIR is a NetWare command similar to the DOS DIR command. The NDIR command is a powerful command to search through the vast volumes of information in a network directory structure.

This chapter uses the DOS DIR command as well as NetWare's NDIR command-line utility. You will see how the DOS DIR command is somewhat limited in its ability to help you search for files compared to the network command equivalent, NDIR. Through exercises in this chapter, you will see that NDIR can provide vast assistance for locating and searching files on the network server. Though you can use DIR to search the network server for files, these exercises will show you the restriction of using DIR compared to using NDIR.

NDIR can be used to sort files and subdirectories, and can also be used with DOS wildcards. It can be used to list files or directories which have been flagged with a specific attribute. NDIR can be used to search an entire volume by size (GReater, EQual, LEss), owner (OWner EQual), and date (BEFore, EQual, AFter). UPdate can be used to view the last time files were updated. (The boldface characters indicate the proper syntax.)

NCOPY is a NetWare command similar to the DOS COPY command. You will compare the two in this chapter.

FLAG is a NetWare command used in this chapter to view the file attributes on a file or directory. This chapter's exercises will use FLAG and provide you with information to draw similarity to the DOS ATTRIB command.

Now that you have navigated around the NetWare directory structure, you will work with NetWare's security structure as you create, locate and manipulate files stored on the network.

As you learned from the previous chapters, as users are created on the system, they are made members of groups. Rights are then broken into individual accounts and group membership. The individual rights plus the group rights are termed *combined rights* or *trustee rights.*

Directories are useful for grouping and managing logically related files. Rights to directories and/or subsequent subdirectories form a hierarchical rights structure involving network security.

As the user moves down a directory structure, to subsequent subdirectories, these trustee rights (combined rights) travel down the structure with them, unless the rights have been blocked (removed or revoked). Filtering the flow of rights down the directory structure is termed the *inherited rights mask* or *IRM.*

The "obtained" rights a user holds at a specific directory structure location results from their combined and inherited rights, and is termed their *effective rights.*

4.1 NDIR

NetWare's **NDIR** command, comparable to DOS DIR, is used to list information about files and directories. NDIR is also used to search a directory or volume for files, or list specific files in a directory or volume. NDIR listings can also be organized by applying sort specifications.

This exercise assumes you are already logged in to NetWare and at the F:\LOGIN> prompt.

Hands-On Exercise

At your F:\LOGIN> prompt,

    1. **Type** *NDIR*

      Press [Enter]

NDIR
Used for listing file and directory information. NetWare's NDIR command is comparable to DOS DIR.

Your screen displays a listing of files and directory names in the LOGIN directory similar to Figure 4.1. The listing shows the file name, file size, date and time the file was last updated, the attributes/flags applied to the file, and each file's owner. You may need to advance the screen display by pressing the spacebar or the letter C.

***NOTE:* NetWare 3.12, upon installation, creates subdirectories below the LOGIN directory, where NetWare 3.11 does not. If you are working on NetWare 3.11, you may wish to perform this exercise from the root of the volume, at the F:\> prompt.**

To list the files and any directories in the LOGIN directory and subsequent subdirectories,

    2. **Type** *NDIR /SUB*

    Press [Enter]

Your screen now displays a listing of files and directory names in the LOGIN directory. Your screen pauses as it fills with information.
To advance your screen, and control the scrolling one screen at a time,

    3. **Press** [Spacebar] to advance each screen

Pressing the spacebar controls the scrolling of the listed information and thus enables you to view the information without it scrolling past you on screen.
To quickly scroll through the listing and return to the prompt, you can type the letter C and the screen will scroll continuously, without pausing as it fills.
To list just the directory names in the LOGIN directory,

    4. **Type** *NDIR /DO*

    Press [Enter]

Your screen displays just the directory information.
To list just the file information from the F:\LOGIN> prompt,

    5. **Type** *NDIR /FO*

    Press [Enter]

Your screen displays just the file information for the LOGIN directory. You can combine command options to search a larger portion of the volume.
To combine the options within NDIR,

    6. **Type** *NDIR /SUB   FO*

    Press [Enter]

Your screen displays the directory path and lists the files within that directory. To advance your screen quickly,

    Press C

KEY RELATED POINTS

The forward slash (/) is used to apply options to NetWare's command-line utilities. The forward slash can be placed directly after the

FIGURE 4.1

```
MCC\SYS:LOGIN

Files:                  Size      Last Updated       Flags              Owner
-----------             -------   -------------      ------------       -----------
BACK$ERR    000              326  4-10-94  8:38p  [Rw-A------------]  SUPERVISO
BACK$LOG    000            1,686  4-10-94  8:38p  [Rw-A------------]  SUPERVISO
CONSOLE     COM              103  8-25-87  7:57a  [RoS-----------DR]  MCC
EMSNETX     EXE           89,390  2-17-93  1:43p  [RoS-----------DR]  MCC
ETHER       RPL           16,272  4-09-93  8:30a  [RoS-----------DR]  MCC
F1ETH       RPL           12,157  4-09-93  8:34a  [RoS-----------DR]  MCC
LOGIN       EXE          111,625  5-04-93  3:06p  [RoS-----------DR]  MCC
NETX        EXE           77,582  2-17-93  1:41p  [RoS-----------DR]  MCC
PCN2L       RPL           10,607  4-09-93  8:37a  [RoS-----------DR]  MCC
RBOOT       RPL            7,542  4-23-93  3:42p  [RoS-----------DR]  MCC
SLIST       EXE           22,437  4-14-93  5:05p  [RoS-----------DR]  MCC
TOKEN       RPL           17,252  4-27-93  7:48a  [RoS-----------DR]  MCC
XMSNETX     EXE           86,064  2-17-93  1:45p  [RoS-----------DR]  MCC


               Inherited    Effective
Directories:   Rights       Rights        Owner     Created/Copied
-----------    ----------   ----------    -----     --------------
NLS            [SRWCEMFA]   [-R----F-]    MCC       7-19-94   9:46p
OS2            [SRWCEMFA]   [-R----F-]    MCC       7-19-94  10:07p

Strike any key for next page or C for continuous display..._
```

command (NDIR/SUB) or a few spaces after the command (NDIR /SUB). When applying multiple options, only one forward slash is needed (NDIR /SUB FO).

 Where there is nothing to match the option given, NDIR will display:

0 total bytes in   0 files

0 total bytes in   0 blocks

NDIR'S DISPLAY OPTIONS

/DO	Lists directories only.
/FO	Lists files only.
/SUB	Lists files within the current directory and subsequent subdirectories.
/DATES	Lists the file's time and date when last updated, archived, accessed, created, or copied. Defaults to an NDIR listing if there are no files, just directories, at the directory location activated.
/RIGHTS	Lists file attributes, and inherited and effective rights for the owner of the file.

4.2 SORTING WITH NDIR

With NetWare's NDIR, you can restrict displays according to specified conditions. Using NetWare's operators for NDIR, you can sort your listing. Operators can be given as symbols or characters. Operators are used to connect parameters to form specific conditions for NetWare's NDIR to search the directory structure.

This exercise assumes you are already logged in to NetWare and at the F:\LOGIN> prompt.

Hands-On Exercise

Move to the root of the volume using CD\ and then at the F:\> prompt,

> 1. **Type** *NDIR \PUBLIC /SORT SI CR AFT 12-26-93*
>
>   **Press** [Enter]

NetWare first displays the twirling baton on the left side of the screen, opposite the word "Searching...". Then NetWare lists the files in the PUBLIC directory created after 12/26/93. Press C or spacebar to advance your screen display as needed.

To list all the files in the Public directory with a size greater than 300,000 bytes,

> 2. **Type** *NDIR \PUBLIC /SI GR 300000*
>
>   **Press** [Enter]

Your screen displays a listing of the files in the Public directory, larger than 300,000 bytes.

You can specify operators for parameters to form specific conditions for NetWare's NDIR to search the directory structure.

> 3. **Type** *NDIR \PUBLIC /SORT SI CR AFT 12/26/93 UP BEF 12-27-93*
>
>   **Press** [Enter]

You should receive a listing of the files in the Public directory, sorted by size, created after 12/26/93 and updated before 12/27/93.

NOTE: With NDIR, you can use either the dash (–) or forward slash (/) when specifying dates.

NDIR's /SORT option enables you to sort the directory based upon the parameters given. The /REV /SORT reverses the ascending order to descending order for the parameter specified.

From the F:\> prompt,

> 4. **Type** *NDIR \PUBLIC\M*.* /REV /SORT UP*
>
>   **Press** [Enter]

FIGURE 4.2

```
F:\PUBLIC>ndir \login /ow not = supervisor
MCC\SYS:LOGIN

Files:                    Size       Last Updated        Flags              Owner

CONSOLE      COM             103    8-25-87  7:57a  [RoS--------------DR] MCC
EMSNETX      EXE          89,390    2-17-93  1:43p  [RoS--------------DR] MCC
ETHER        RPL          16,272    4-09-93  8:30a  [RoS--------------DR] MCC
F1ETH        RPL          12,157    4-09-93  8:34a  [RoS--------------DR] MCC
LOGIN        EXE         111,625    5-04-93  3:06p  [RoS--------------DR] MCC
NETX         EXE          77,582    2-17-93  1:41p  [RoS--------------DR] MCC
PCN2L        RPL          10,607    4-09-93  8:37a  [RoS--------------DR] MCC
RBOOT        RPL           7,542    4-23-93  3:42p  [RoS--------------DR] MCC
SLIST        EXE          22,437    4-14-93  5:05p  [RoS--------------DR] MCC
TOKEN        RPL          17,252    4-27-93  7:48a  [RoS--------------DR] MCC
XMSNETX      EXE          86,064    2-17-93  1:45p  [RoS--------------DR] MCC

                      Inherited      Effective
Directories:          Rights         Rights        Owner        Created/Copied

NLS                   [SRWCEMFA]     [-R----F-]    MCC           7-19-94  9:46p
OS2                   [SRWCEMFA]     [-R----F-]    MCC           7-19-94 10:07p

       451,031 bytes in     11 files
Strike any key for next page or C for continuous display..._
```

Your screen displays a listing of the files which begin with the letter M in the PUBLIC directory in descending order based upon when the files were last updated. The DOS wildcard symbol (*) can be used with NDIR.

To list files for specific attributes, at the F:\> prompt,

> 5. **Type** NDIR \PUBLIC /S A NOT RO
>
>   **Press** [Enter]

A listing of the files in the Public directory that are flagged Shareable (S) and Archived (A), but not Read-only (Ro), are listed on your screen.

To list files that are not equal to a condition,

> 6. **Type** NDIR \LOGIN /OW NOT = "SUPERVISOR"
>
>   **Press** [Enter]

Your screen displays the files in the LOGIN directory which are not owned by the supervisor account, similar to Figure 4.2.

NDIR PARAMETERS/OPERATORS

	Operator	Description	Operator Symbol
AC Accessed Date	EQ	Equal To	=
AR Archive Date	GR	Greater Than	>
CR Created Date	LE	Less Than	<
OW Owner	NOT	Unequal	NOT =
SI Size	BEF	Before	
UP Update	AFT	After	

KEY RELATED POINTS

 You can search any directory path with NDIR by using the backslash (\) and listing the path after the NDIR command. You can also search separate volumes by listing the volume (e.g., VOL1:DATA\SALES).

4.3 RENAMING DIRECTORIES AND WORKING WITH RENDIR

Directory and subdirectory naming conventions are the same for NetWare as for DOS. With a NetWare network, the path is identified differently from DOS, as: SERVER/VOLUME:DIRECTORY\SUBDIRECTORY.

Directories are useful for grouping and managing logically related files. DOS provides commands to create and delete directories and sub-directories that form virtual, hierarchical structures. However, DOS provides no command for renaming the directory.

RENDIR
NetWare's command-line utility used to rename a directory.

In this exercise, you use NetWare's **RENDIR** command-line utility to rename a directory and will identify the path leading to and including the directory or subdirectory you want to rename. You will also draw upon prior exercise, to use the LISTDIR command to verify your changes to the directory structure.

This exercise assumes you are already logged in to NetWare and at the F:\LOGIN> prompt.

Hands-On Exercise

Move to the USERS\HOME\your home directory using CD\USERS\HOME\your home directory name and then, at the F:\USERS\HOME\your home directory name> prompt,

    1. **Type** *MD TEST*

       Press Enter

You are returned to your home directory prompt.
To list your directories, under your home directory;

    2. **Type** *LISTDIR*

       Press Enter

You see the TEST directory from the listing on your screen.

FIGURE 4.3

```
F:\USERS\HOME\PHARRIS>rendir test best
Directory renamed to BEST.

F:\USERS\HOME\PHARRIS>cd..

F:\USERS\HOME>rendir :/users/home/pharris/best rest
Directory renamed to REST.

F:\USERS\HOME>
```

To rename TEST to BEST,

> 3. **Type** *RENDIR TEST BEST*
>
>   **Press** (Enter)

NetWare confirms with the message listed to your screen, *"Directory renamed to BEST."*

To work with RENDIR and rename the BEST directory from another directory location

> 4. **Type** *CD* .. (2 dots follow CD)
>
>   **Press** (Enter)

You are at F:\USERS\HOME> prompt. This will take you to the parent directory of your home directory.

To rename the BEST directory back to REST

> 5. **Type** *RENDIR :/USERS/HOME/_____/BEST REST*
>   (fill in the blank above with your home directory name)
>
>   **Press** (Enter)

You are returned to F:\USERS\HOME> prompt and NetWare displays the confirmation message on your screen, *"Directory renamed to REST."* Refer to Figure 4.3.

***NOTE:* The :/ is used to represent server and volume name.**

To see the results of this change,

> 6. **Type** *LISTDIR /SUB*
>
>   **Press** (Enter)

Your screen displays your home directory. You see that the subdirectory, BEST, was changed to REST.

To rename a currently active directory, first move to the REST directory.

7. **Type** *CD* _____ *\REST*
(fill in the blank above with your home directory name)

   Press Enter

You are returned to the F:\USERS\HOME\your home directory\REST> prompt.

***NOTE:* After CD, you must use the backslash (\) and not the forward slash (/). When using DOS commands, such as CD, you must adhere to DOS command conventions. NetWare is flexible and relates to directory paths with either the forward slash (/) or backslash (\).**

To rename a currently active directory,

8. **Type** *RENDIR . TEST*

   Press Enter

NetWare confirms your change with the message, *"Directory renamed to TEST,"* and returns you to the changed directory F:\USERS\HOME\your home directory\TEST> prompt.

COMMON CHARACTERS USED IN NETWARE WHEN WORKING WITH DIRECTORIES

Name	Symbol	Description
Colon Forward Slash	: /	Used as a character combination to represent your default server from the volume name, without listing the volume or server name. Example: RENDIR :/LOGIN LOGOUT.
Period or Dot	.	Used to represent the root of your currently active directory.
Dot Dot	..	Used to represent the parent of the currently active directory.
Forward slash	/	Used to separate the volume from the server name. Example: SERVER1/SYS:USERS. Used to separate directories. Example: SERVER1/SYS: USERS/ HOME.
Backslash	\	Used to in separate the volume from the server name. Example: SERVER1/SYS:USERS. Used to separate directories. Example: SERVER1/SYS:USERS/ HOME.

KEY RELATED POINTS

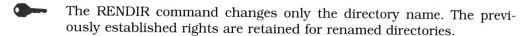

The RENDIR command changes only the directory name. The previously established rights are retained for renamed directories.

You may need to change drive mappings in the LOGIN Script(s) to reflect the change in the directory's name.

There are symbols that represent the root and the parent of the currently active directory. DOS DIR command will often display . and .. in its listing of files and directories. These symbols represent the currently active directory (the **.**) and the parent (the **..**) of the currently active directory, respectively.

The character combination of the colon and forward slash (:/) can be used to represent your default server and volume.

The backslash symbol, after the colon of the drive letter (:\), is used to specify and assure the path begins at the root of the volume.

4.4 WORKING WITH NCOPY AND FLAG

NCOPY
Used to copy files and retain their attributes. Comparable to DOS COPY command.

FLAG
Used to change or view file attributes. Comparable to DOS ATTRIB command.

NetWare's **NCOPY** command works similar to DOS COPY and XCOPY commands. NCOPY has a few advantages over DOS commands since NCOPY retains the file attributes, shows the source and destination directories, and is faster than the DOS commands.

In this exercise, you also work with NetWare's **FLAG** command. The FLAG command is used to change or view file attributes.

This exercise assumes that you have just logged in and your prompt shows F:\LOGIN>. This exercise also assumes that your first search drive, SEARCH1, or S1, is drive letter Z and is mapped to the PUBLIC directory. Use MAP to view and confirm your drive mappings.

Hands-On Exercise

To move to your home directory from the F:\LOGIN> prompt,

  1. **Type** *CD\USERS\HOME*_____
     (fill in the blank with your home directory name)
     Press (Enter)

You should be at the F:\USERS\HOME\your home directory> prompt.

From the F:\USERS\HOME\your home directory> prompt, copy all the .DAT files in the PUBLIC directory to your home directory.

2. **Type** *NCOPY \PUBLIC*.DAT*

   Press Enter

Your screen displays a listing similar to Figure 4.4. All the files in the Public directory with a .DAT extension have been copied into your directory.

To use NetWare's FLAG command to view the files in your home directory,

3. **Type** *FLAG*

   Press Enter

The files in your home directory are displayed on your screen. Notice the attribute flags listed opposite each of the filenames.

To delete all the *.DAT files from the F:\USERS\HOME\your directory> prompt,

4. **Type** *DEL *.DAT*

   Press Enter

Your screen should display an *"Access denied"* message.
From the F:\USERS\HOME\your directory> prompt,

5. **Type** *FLAG*

   Press Enter

You notice that some of the .DAT files were not deleted. The .DAT files remaining in your directory are left because they are flagged with NetWare's Ro, read-only, attribute. Other attributes shown for .DAT files are Delete Inhibit and Rename Inhibit, shown as DI and RI. NetWare automatically assigns DI and RI to files flagged with Ro.

To demonstrate the difference between DOS COPY and NetWare's NCOPY,

6. **Type** *COPY *.DAT *.CAT*

   Press Enter

Your screen displays the files copied and returns you to your home directory prompt, similar to Figure 4.5.

To view the changes,

7. **Type** *FLAG*

   Press Enter

FIGURE 4.4

```
F:\LOGIN>cd\users\home\pharris

F:\USERS\HOME\PHARRIS>ncopy \public\*.dat
From MCC/SYS:\PUBLIC
To   MCC/SYS:\USERS/HOME/PHARRIS
     SYS$MSG.DAT    to SYS$MSG.DAT
     SYS$HELP.DAT   to SYS$HELP.DAT
     SYS$ERR.DAT    to SYS$ERR.DAT
     DIBI$DRV.DAT   to DIBI$DRV.DAT
     NET$LOG.DAT    to NET$LOG.DAT
     REMOTE.DAT     to REMOTE.DAT
     DIBI2$DV.DAT   to DIBI2$DV.DAT
     NET$PRN.DAT    to NET$PRN.DAT

     8 files copied.

F:\USERS\HOME\PHARRIS>_
```

FIGURE 4.5

```
F:\USERS\HOME\PHARRIS>copy *.dat *.cat
SYS$MSG.DAT
SYS$HELP.DAT
SYS$ERR.DAT
DIBI$DRV.DAT
NET$PRN.DAT
        5 file(s) copied

F:\USERS\HOME\PHARRIS>flag
     SYS$MSG.CAT         [ Rw - A - - - - - - - - - - - - - -       ]
     SYS$HELP.CAT        [ Rw - A - - - - - - - - - - - - - -       ]
     TESTIT.BAK          [ Rw - A - - - - - - - - - - - - - -       ]
     TESTIT.BAT          [ Rw - A - - - - - - - - - - - - - -       ]
     TEST.BAT            [ Rw - A - - - - - - - - - - - - - -       ]
     SYS$MSG.DAT         [ Ro S - - - - - - - - - - - -  DI  RI ]
     SYS$HELP.DAT        [ Ro S - - - - - - - - - - - -  DI  RI ]
     SYS$ERR.DAT         [ Ro S - - - - - - - - - - - -  DI  RI ]
     DIBI$DRV.DAT        [ Ro S - - - - - - - - - - - -  DI  RI ]
     SYS$ERR.CAT         [ Rw - A - - - - - - - - - - - - - -       ]
     DIBI$DRV.CAT        [ Rw - A - - - - - - - - - - - - - -       ]
     NET$PRN.CAT         [ Rw - A - - - - - - - - - - - - - -       ]
     NET$PRN.DAT         [ Ro S - - - - - - - - - - - -  DI  RI ]

F:\USERS\HOME\PHARRIS>_
```

Your screen displays the .CAT files flagged as Rw and the .DAT files are flagged Ro. This proves the point that the DOS COPY changes file attributes and NetWare NCOPY retains them.

To delete the .CAT files in your home directory,

> 8. **Type** *DEL *.CAT*
>
> **Press** [Enter]

You are returned to your directory prompt. Use the FLAG command to verify the deletion and view the remaining files in your home directory.

To change the .DAT files from Ro to Rw,

> 9. **Type** *FLAG *.DAT RW*
>
> **Press** [Enter]

The files were displayed on your screen and you see that they were changed to Rw. Use FLAG to view the changes.

To delete the *.DAT files,

> 10. **Type** *DEL *.DAT*
>
> **Press** [Enter]

You are returned to the directory prompt. Your screen should look similar to Figure 4.6. Use FLAG or NDIR commands to verify your deletion.

COMMON FILE ATTRIBUTES USED WITH FLAG

Attribute	Description
A	Archive Needed
ALL	All Attributes
DI **	Delete Inhibit
H	Hidden
N	Normal
P **	Purge
RI **	Rename Inhibit
Ro	Read-only
Rw	Read-write
S	Shareable
Sy **	System
T	Transactional
X	Execute-only

** Indicates attributes that work on files and directories.

FIGURE 4.6

```
F:\USERS\HOME\PHARRIS>del *.cat

F:\USERS\HOME\PHARRIS>flag *.dat rw
     SYS$MSG.DAT                [ Rw  S - - -- -- -- -- -- -- -- -- ]
     SYS$HELP.DAT               [ Rw  S - - -- -- -- -- -- -- -- -- ]
     SYS$ERR.DAT                [ Rw  S - - -- -- -- -- -- -- -- -- ]
     DIBI$DRV.DAT               [ Rw  S - - -- -- -- -- -- -- -- -- ]
     NET$PRN.DAT                [ Rw  S - - -- -- -- -- -- -- -- -- ]

F:\USERS\HOME\PHARRIS>del *.dat

F:\USERS\HOME\PHARRIS>flag
     TESTIT.BAK                 [ Rw  - A - - -- -- -- -- -- -- -- -- ]
     TESTIT.BAT                 [ Rw  - A - : -- -- -- -- -- -- -- -- ]
     TEST.BAT                   [ Rw  - A - - -- -- -- -- -- -- -- -- ]

F:\USERS\HOME\PHARRIS>_
```

KEY RELATED POINTS

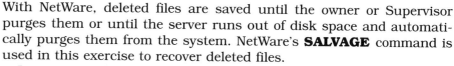 When the Ro flag is applied to files and they are copied using DOS COPY, the flags are changed to Rw. DOS COPY also removes the S, DI, and RI flags, and adds the A flag.

To change individual attributes, use the minus (–) followed by the attribute to be removed (e.g., FLAG *.DAT –RO). In this case, all the .DAT files would be changed to Rw, similar to step 9 of this exercise.

NCOPY and mapped drives work together to make copying files easy. You can use NCOPY *.* G: and find that all the files at your current directory are duplicated to the drive G mapped location.

4.5 USING SALVAGE

SALVAGE
NetWare's menu utility for recovering or purging deleted files.

With NetWare, deleted files are saved until the owner or Supervisor purges them or until the server runs out of disk space and automatically purges them from the system. NetWare's **SALVAGE** command is used in this exercise to recover deleted files.

It is assumed that you have completed exercise 4.3, and logged in, with your cursor active at the F:\LOGIN> prompt.

Hands-On Exercise

To view the files you deleted in exercise 4.3 from the F:\LOGIN> prompt,

1. **Type** *SALVAGE*

    Press [Enter]

The SALVAGE menu utility is shown on your screen and your cursor is active at the View/Recover Deleted Files menu option. At the top of the SALVAGE main menu screen is the banner, which shows your directory path on the second line.

To begin to change your directory path,

2. **Type** *SE* to move the highlight bar to Select Current Directory

Your highlight bar should be on Select Current Directory.

3. **Press** (Enter)

The pop-up window, Current Directory Path is showing the SYS:LOGIN directory location.

4. **Press** (←Backspace) five times to erase LOGIN

Your cursor should be blinking at the colon (:) prompt in the Current Directory Path pop-up window, leaving the server name and volume SYS: showing.

5. **Type** *USERS/HOME/*_____
   (fill in the blank with your home directory location)
   Press (Enter)

The path showing on line 2 of the menu banner shows the path to your home directory and your highlight bar moved to View/Recover Deleted Files menu option.

At the View/Recover Deleted Files menu option,

6. **Press** (Enter)

At the Erase File Name Pattern to Match pop-up window showing the asterisk (*) symbol,

Press (Enter)

The Salvageable Files screen is showing the files you've deleted from your home directory in the last exercise. The asterisk (*) symbol is used to signify a default pattern to indicate all files.

Move the highlight bar downward to the first file in the list. To salvage the file,

7. **Press** (Enter) (highlighted on the first file in the list)

Your screen may look similar to Figure 4.7. In the Recover This File pop-up menu,

8. **Press** (Enter) (highlighted on Yes)

The file disappears from the Salvageable Files screen.

To remove or purge all the remaining files shown in the Salvageable Files screen, move the highlight bar to the file at the top of the list.

FIGURE 4.7

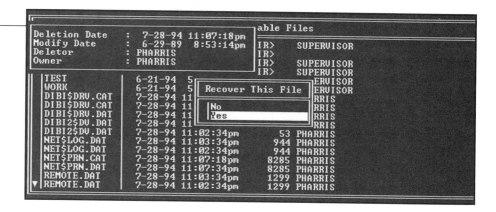

9. **Press** F5 to mark the first file in the list

The file listing begins to blink.

With the first file marked from using F5 and it now blinking on your screen,

10. **Press** Del

With the highlight bar on Yes for Purge This Files pop-up menu,

Press Enter (highlighted on Yes)

The screen should have removed the file from the listing on your screen. To quickly delete all the rest of the files, first exit SALVAGE and then use the PURGE command as follows.

To exit SALVAGE,

11. **Press** Alt F10 simultaneously

Press Enter (highlighted on Yes to exit SALVAGE)

Move to your home directory. Then, at your F:\USERS\HOME\(your home directory)> prompt,

12. **Type** *PURGE*

Press Enter

NetWare displays a listing of all the files that have been removed from the system for your home directory location.

KEY RELATED POINTS

 To purge your deleted files from your current directory and its subdirectories, use the PURGE /ALL command.

- Deleted files are restored with the same attribute assignment they held when they were deleted.

- You can view your files sorted by deletion date, file size, or filename. (The "Default" selection is to view your files sorted by filename.) Using Set SALVAGE Options from the SALVAGE main menu, gives you a choice in the way you view your deleted files.

- You can delete multiple files with F6. NetWare will need you to enter the pattern that matches the entries in the list you want marked for deletion. The default is all, signified by an asterisk (*). If you wanted all the files that began with the letter N marked, you would press F6, and in the Mark Pattern pop-up window, enter either N*.* or N* to mark these files for deletion.

- To recover multiple marked files, you would press Enter and then press Return highlighted on Yes in the Recover ALL Marked Files pop-up window.

- Every file you delete is stored in the directory from which it was deleted. If you delete the directory, the deleted files are then stored in the DELETED.SAV hidden directory. Every volume root has a DELETED. SAV directory. To recover from the DELETED.SAV directory, with the appropriate security rights, you select the first menu option from the SALVAGE main menu, SALVAGE from Deleted Directories.

4.6 CONTROLLING DIRECTORY FILE ATTRIBUTES AND TRUSTEE RIGHTS IN FILER

FILER
NetWare's menu utility for controlling volume, directory, and file information.

NetWare's **FILER** menu utility is a powerful security tool for controlling file information. In this exercise, you work with some of this power, and see how FILER is used to view, add, or delete directory attributes. You also see how FILER can be used for granting or revoking file rights to others.

This exercise assumes that you have logged in and your active prompt is the F:\LOGIN> prompt.

Hands-On Exercise

Move to your home directory prompt. From the F:\USERS \HOME\your home directory> prompt,

    1. **Type** FILER

       Press Enter

You see the FILER main menu, Available Topics, displayed on your screen and the highlight bar is located on Current Directory

FIGURE 4.8

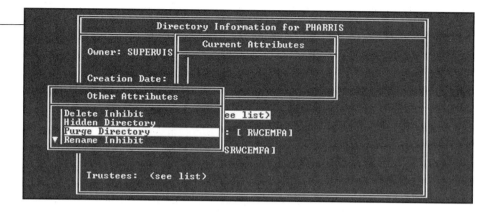

Information. FILER menu header on the second line at the top of your screen displays the directory path to your home directory.

To display information about your current directory path, with the highlight bar on Current Directory Information,

> 2. **Press** Enter

You see FILER'S Directory Information screen for your username and you are highlighted on the Directory Attribute option. The Directory Information screen shows the owner (or creator of the directory) and the creation time and date. The Directory Information screen also displays the effective and inherited rights, the directory attributes, and the directory's trustees (or those users or groups granted access).

To see more information about Directory Attributes,

> 3. **Press** Enter

The double-bar, Current Attributes screen displayed on your screen is empty. As a general rule, where you find a double-bar menu within NetWare, you can press Ins for more options.

To see more options,

> 4. **Press** Ins

The Other Attributes pop-up window shows the other directory attributes you can apply to the directory showing in the menu header.

To select the PURGE directory attribute,

> 5. **Type** *P*
>
> **Press** Enter

You should see the PURGE Directory option listed in the Current Attributes pop-up window. Refer to Figure 4.8. With PURGE applied to the directory, you won't be able to use SALVAGE, for all deletions will be immediately purged from the system.

To remove the PURGE option,

6. **Press** [Del]

Press [Enter] (highlighted on Yes to Delete Attribute)

The Current Attributes pop-up window is empty again.

To look at more directory information,

7. **Press** [Esc]

You are now back at the Directory Information screen.

To look at the trustee information for this directory location, move the highlight bar to Trustees:, and

8. **Press** [Enter] (highlighted on Trustees)

The Trustee Name submenu shown on your screen is blank.

To add a trustee,

9. **Press** [Ins]

The list of usernames and group names is listed on your screen.

To select the Guest user account, move the highlight bar to Guest (User) and

10. **Press** [Enter]

You're back at the Trustee screen, with the Guest (User) account listed after your user account. You have just selected the Guest account to share your directory and have granted them the default rights of read and file scan.

To increase the rights for the Guest account,

11. **Press** [Return]

Press [Ins]

You went from the Trustee Rights pop-up window to the Other Rights pop-up window where you can grant more rights.

To grant the Create right,

12. **Type** C

Press [Enter]

You see the Create Directory/File option displayed in the Trustee Rights screen. Refer to Figure 4.9.

To escape the Trustee Rights screen,

13. **Press** [Esc]

FIGURE 4.9

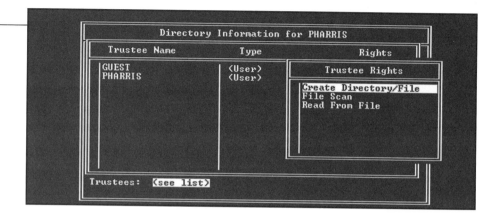

You're back at the Trustee Name screen, the Guest (User) account has been added as a Trustee, and you've increased the rights of the Guest account from Read and File Scan to include Create.

Press [Alt] [F10] to exit *FILER*

KEY RELATED POINTS

Adding trustees to a directory gives them privileges to work in that directory. Access to the directory is controlled by the assignment of rights.

The rights you are granted travel down the directory structure unless they are removed or blocked. The inherited rights mask depicts the rights which have been removed.

The inherited rights mask (IRM), shown in FILER'S Directory Information screen, refers to the rights that are being blocked. Those not listed as inherited rights are the rights being blocked (or removed).

Your effective rights are those you are able to exercise in a directory location. Chapter 5 deals with your access rights.

To FLAG a directory to automatically purge all deleted files either use FLAGDIR . P or you can use FILER since the files will not be held for recovery in NetWare's SALVAGE menu utility when they are deleted. The files in these flagged directories will automatically be completely removed (purged) from the system.

FILE RIGHTS FOR FILER'S DIRECTORY INFORMATION SCREEN: [SRWCEMFA]

(S)   Supervisory right grants all rights to a file or directory. You can grant any other file right(s) to another user with the supervisory right. The supervisory right can only be revoked from the directory location where it was granted.

(R)   Read, or the right to open and read a file, could also be considered the right that provides the ability to launch or execute a program. When applied to a file, the Read right allows you to open and read the file even when the right has been revoked for the directory location.

(W)   Write to a file, could also be considered the right to modify the contents of a file and overwrite the previous contents by saving the edited version, using the same filename. When applied to a file, (W) lets you write to the file even when the right has been revoked for the directory location.

(C)   Create files and subdirectories and lets you salvage deleted files.

(E)   Erase file(s) allows you to delete any file(s) even when the Erase (E) right has been revoked for the directory location.

(M)   Modify a file by renaming it or redefining its file attribute(s), even when the Modify (M) right has been revoked for the directory location.

(F)   File scan, or the right that gives you the ability to view file names, even when the File scan (F) right has been revoked for the directory location.

(A)   Access control or the right that provides the ability for you to modify the file's trustee assignments and can block rights by altering the inherited rights. With the Modify right at a directory location, you may grant any other right, except Supervisory.

4.7 NAVIGATING THE DIRECTORY STRUCTURE IN FILER

In this exercise, you use NetWare's FILER menu utility to navigate the directory structure and view filenames and the subsequent subdirectory names. You will see how FILER displays your directory location and tracks your directory path to show your active directory location in FILER'S menu banner.

This exercise assumes that you have logged in and your active prompt is the F:\LOGIN> prompt.

Hands-On Exercise

From the F:\LOGIN> prompt,

    1. **Type** *FILER*

    Press (Enter)

You are highlighted on Current Directory Information in FILER'S Available Topics main menu. The second line of FILER'S menu banner (at the top of the screen) shows SYS:LOGIN for your directory path.

To view your directory information for the LOGIN directory, while you are highlighted on Current Directory Information,

    2. **Press** (Enter)

The Directory Information for LOGIN screen displays the *"Owner:Supervisor"* message, the creation date, the creation time, and other information about your directory location. Compared to working with FILER in the previous exercise, you should notice that you are only viewing the directory information. With only Read and File Scan rights, as shown in the Current Effective Rights listed on your screen, you have no manipulative ability in this directory, so you can only view and not change the directory's information.

To exit the Directory Information screen,

    3. **Press** (Esc)

You should be back to Available Topics.

To view your rights in another location of the directory structure,

    4. **Type** *S* to move your highlight bar to Select Current Directory

    Press (Enter)

You are at the Current Directory Path pop-up window, with your cursor blinking after LOGIN.

To move to the USERS directory,

    5. **Press** (←Backspace) five times to erase LOGIN

    Type *USERS*

    Press (Enter)

FILER now shows *"SYS:USERS"* near the top of your screen for the directory path listed on the second line of FILER's menu banner.

To view your rights to this directory location,

6. **Type** *C* to move the highlight bar to Current Directory Information

   Press (Enter)

The Directory Information screen is displayed, listing your effective rights and may appear, similar to Figure 4.10.

To use FILER to help you move down the directory structure's path,

7. **Press** (Esc)

   Type *D* to move the highlight to Directory Contents

   Press (Enter)

The Directory Contents screen is displayed.

To view information about the HOME directory,

8. **Type** *HOME*

   Press (Enter)

The Subdirectory Options pop-up windows is displayed. You are highlighted on Copy Subdirectory's Files. You see you are also able to copy or move the subdirectory structure, view/set directory information, or make this your current directory.

To make the HOME directory your current directory,

9. **Type** *M* to move the highlight bar to Make This Your Current Directory

   Press (Enter)

The Directory Contents screen changed to display the contents of the HOME directory. The menu banner displays "SYS:USERS\HOME" for the directory path.

To make your home directory your current directory,

10. **Press** (↓) to move the highlight bar to your home directory name

    Press (Enter) (highlighted on your home directory name)

To make your home directory your current directory,

   Type *M* to move the highlight bar to Make This Your Current Directory

   Press (Enter)

Refer to Figure 4.11. The Directory Contents screen changed to display the contents of your home directory and FILER's menu banner displays the path, ending with your home directory name.

To quickly move back to the HOME directory, while highlighted on .. (parent),

11. **Press** (Enter)

FIGURE 4.10

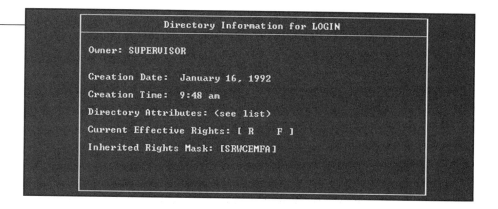

FIGURE 4.11

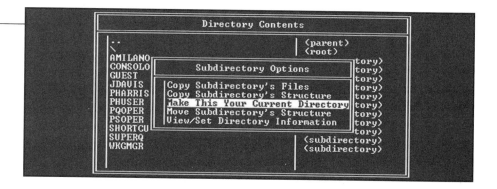

The question posed in the pop-up window asks if you would like to make the PARENT directory the current directory.

Press [Enter] (highlighted on Yes)

The menu banner now displays "SYS:USERS\HOME."

12. To exit FILER,

Press [Alt] [F10].

KEY RELATED POINTS

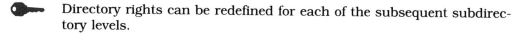 Directory rights can be redefined for each of the subsequent subdirectory levels.

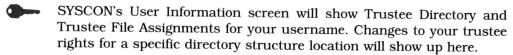 SYSCON's User Information screen will show Trustee Directory and Trustee File Assignments for your username. Changes to your trustee rights for a specific directory structure location will show up here.

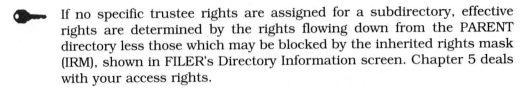 If no specific trustee rights are assigned for a subdirectory, effective rights are determined by the rights flowing down from the PARENT directory less those which may be blocked by the inherited rights mask (IRM), shown in FILER's Directory Information screen. Chapter 5 deals with your access rights.

 Within Filer, as well as other Netware menu utilities, if your account's security responsibility increases for you to administer other user accounts, your access level(s) to certain menu utilities will likely increase/change. One menu utility where expanded privileges would be used is in FILER's Current Directory Information screen where you could change directory security, depending upon the supervisory rights you were granted for a directory location.

4.8 MAKING DIRECTORIES AND COPYING FILES IN FILER

In this exercise, you will make a directory and copy a file to the new directory using NetWare's FILER menu utility.

This exercise assumes that you have completed exercise 3.9 and the TESTIT.BAT file resides in your home directory. This exercise also assumes that you have logged in and changed from the F:\LOGIN> prompt and your current directory prompt to F:\USERS\HOME\your home directory> prompt.

From the F:\USERS\HOME\your home directory> prompt, launch NetWare's FILER menu utility. You are at FILER's Available Topics menu.

Hands-On Exericse

With SYS:\USERS\HOME\your home directory> showing as the directory path in Filer's menu banner, to view the directory contents,

1. **Type** D to move the highlight bar to Directory Contents

   Press Enter

You see the Directory Contents screen, showing the contents of your home directory.

To add a subdirectory under your home directory,

2. **Press** Ins

The New Subdirectory Name prompt is showing in the pop-up window. Refer to Figure 4.12.

   Type WORK

   Press Enter

FIGURE 4.12

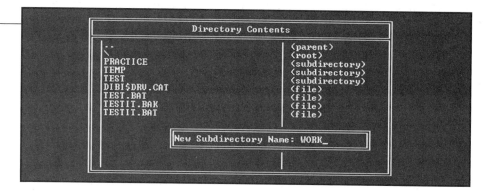

The Directory Contents screen now shows you have added the WORK subdirectory.

To locate the TESTIT.BAT file you created in exercise 3.9,

    3. **Type** *TESTIT* to move the highlight bar to the TESTIT.BAT file

      Press (Enter)

The File Options pop-up window is displayed, where you can move, view, or copy the file.

To select the option to copy the TESTIT.BAT file,

    4. **Type** *C* to select Copy File

      Press (Enter)

In the Destination Directory pop-up window,

      Press (Ins)

In the Network Directories pop-up window,

      Type *W* to move the highlight bar to WORK

      Press (Enter)

The directory path shown has now added the WORK directory to the end. Refer to Figure 4.13.

To validate the path where the file is to be copied,

    5. **Press** (Esc)

Refer to Figure 4.14. With the cursor blinking after WORK in the directory path of USERS/HOME/your home directory/WORK,

      Press (Enter)

To accept the TESTIT.BAT filename for the WORK subdirectory, at the prompt showing the filename TESTIT.BAT,

      Press (Enter)

FIGURE 4.13

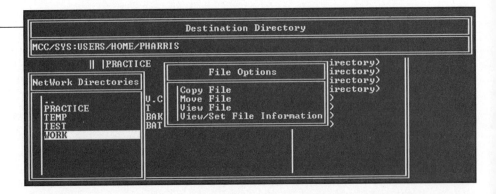

FIGURE 4.14

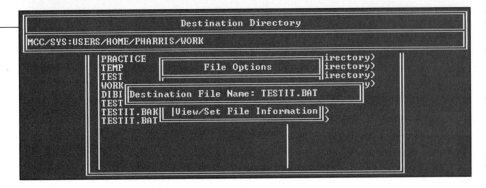

To move to the WORK directory,

>   6. **Press** [Esc] to leave File Options pop-up window
>
>   **Type** *WORK*
>
>   **Press** [Enter] (highlighted on WORK subdirectory)

> In the Subdirectory Options pop-up window,

>   **Type** *M* to highlight Make This Your Current Directory
>
>   **Press** [Enter]

The Directory Contents screen displays the TESTIT.BAT file. The path shown in FILER's menu banner displays you've moved to the WORK directory, beneath your home directory.

To move back to your home directory,

>   7. **Press** [↑] until your highlight bar is on .. (parent)
>
>   **Press** [Enter]

Refer to Figure 4.15.

For the pop-up window asking if you want to make this the current directory,

FIGURE 4.15

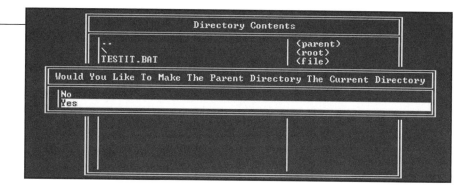

Press Enter (highlighted on Yes)

The path shown in FILER's menu banner displays you've moved to your home directory.

8. To exit FILER

Press Alt F10

COMMON KEYS USED IN FILER'S DIRECTORY CONTENTS SCREEN

Key	Description
Del	With the filename highlighted, press Del to delete a file. Can also be used to delete multiple files, marked with F5.
Enter	With the filename highlighted, press Enter to Copy, View, Move, or Modify file information. When highlighted on the Root (\) or Parent (..) option, this is a quick way to move to that location in the directory structure.
Esc	Used to exit and save your changes.
F2	Brings up the Current Directory Path pop-up window. Used to change to another directory or server. Can be used in combination with Backspace and Ins keys to choose your directory path rather than typing a new one in.
F3	With the filename highlighted, press F3 to Rename a file.
F5	Used to mark files.
F6	Used to mark files meeting a specific pattern or specified criteria, such as all the files which begin with the letter S.
F8	Used with marked files to remove the marking.
Ins	Used to add subdirectories to the current directory location.

4.9 DEALING IN MULTIPLES—MODIFYING ATTRIBUTES FOR MULTIPLE FILES

In this exercise, you will work with FILER to modify the attributes for multiple files. You will work with marking multiple files using the F6 key.

This exercise assumes that you have logged in and your active prompt was changed from the F:\LOGIN> to F:\USERS\HOME\your home directory> prompt.

Hands-On Exercise

From the F:\USERS\HOME\your home directory> prompt, copy a few files to your home directory.

     1. **Type** *NCOPY \PUBLIC*.DAT*

         Press Enter

The .DAT files were copied to your home directory from the PUBLIC directory.

     2. **Type** *FILER* and then press enter from your F:\USERS\HOME\your home directory> prompt to begin working with Filer from your home directory.

From FILER's Available Topics menu, to begin working with the files in your home directory,

     3. **Type** *D*

         Press Enter

You see the files in your home directory listed in the Directory Contents screen.

Move to the first filename listed,

     4. **Type:** *S*

This should have moved your highlight bar to the first filename listed in your directory which begins with the letter S.

To mark all the files that begin with the letter S at once,

     5. **Press** F6

         Press ←Backspace to erase the *

         Type *S** to mark all filenames which begin with S

         Press Enter

You should see all the files that begin with the letter S listed in the Directory Contents screen marked.

With all the letter S files marked, move your highlight bar to the last filename listed that begins with the letter S,

FIGURE 4.16

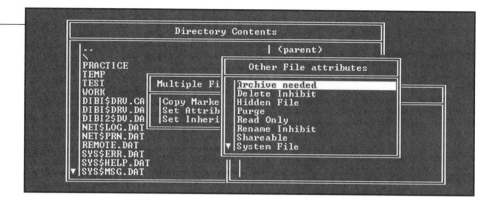

6. **Press** Enter on the last letter S file marked

Your screen displays the Multiple File Options pop-up window.

7. **Type** S

The highlight bar is moved to Set Attributes.

Press Enter (highlighted on Set Attributes)

The File Attributes pop-up window is blank.
To add an attribute,

Press Ins

A listing of attributes is shown and you're highlighted on Archive Needed. Refer to Figure 4.16.

NOTE: Notice that Read-write is not listed as an option in the File Attributes pop-up window. FILER assumes Read-write as a default setting for files.

To add the Archive Needed attribute,

8. **Press** Ins

Press Enter (highlighted on Archive needed)

You see the Archive Needed attribute has been added to the File Attributes pop-up window.

Press Esc

Press Enter (highlighted on Yes to set marked attribute)

You are back at Multiple File Operations pop-up window.

9. To quickly exit

Press Alt F10

FIGURE 4.17

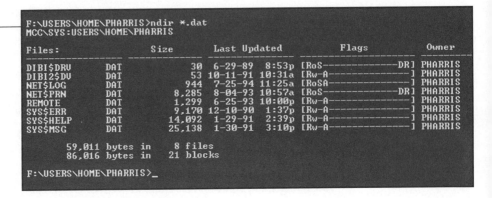

```
F:\USERS\HOME\PHARRIS>ndir *.dat
MCC\SYS:USERS\HOME\PHARRIS

Files:                      Size       Last Updated        Flags              Owner
_____    _____    _____       _____    _____

DIBI$DRU      DAT                30    6-29-89   8:53p  [RoS-------------DR]  PHARRIS
DIBI2$DU      DAT                53   10-11-91  10:31a  [Rw-A------------  ]  PHARRIS
NET$LOG       DAT               944    7-25-94  11:25a  [RoSA------------  ]  PHARRIS
NET$PRN       DAT             8,285    8-04-93  10:57a  [RoS-------------DR]  PHARRIS
REMOTE        DAT             1,299    6-25-93  10:00p  [Rw-A------------  ]  PHARRIS
SYS$ERR       DAT             9,170   12-10-90   1:37p  [Rw-A------------  ]  PHARRIS
SYS$HELP      DAT            14,092    1-29-91   2:39p  [Rw-A------------  ]  PHARRIS
SYS$MSG       DAT            25,138    1-30-91   3:10p  [Rw-A------------  ]  PHARRIS

         59,011 bytes in     8 files
         86,016 bytes in    21 blocks

F:\USERS\HOME\PHARRIS>_
```

When you've returned to F:/USERS/HOME/your home directory>
prompt, to check the changes to the .DAT files whose filename begins
with the letter S,

10. **Type** *NDIR *.DAT*

    Press (Enter)

You see the .DAT files that begin with the letter S are flagged with
both Rw and A. The other .DAT files are flagged Ro. Using NCOPY, as
in Step 1 of this exercise, preserves the file attributes for all files copied.
Changing file attributes assumes Rw as a default. If files are not Rw,
FILER will attempt to change them to Rw. Refer to Figure 4.17.

KEY RELATED POINTS

You saw the File Attributes pop-up window was blank in Step 7. If you do
not make any changes, FILER assumes Rw (Read-write) as the default for
files. Read-write is not listed in the Other File Attribute pop-up window as
an option choice for this reason. For files flagged Read-only, leaving the
File Attributes pop-up window blank, and pressing (Esc) will prompt FILER
to change attributes from Ro to Rw. This explains how the .DAT files
beginning with the letter S changed from Ro to Rw as depicted in Step 10.

4.10 DEALING ONE-ON-ONE—RENAMING, COPYING
AND CHANGING FILE ATTRIBUTES FOR A SINGLE
FILE IN FILER

In this exercise, you rename, copy, and work with changing file attributes for one file using NetWare's FILER menu utility. You can use this

information to compare the difference in the way one file is handled versus multiple files.

This exercise assumes that the TESTIT.BAT file, created in Exercise 3.9, resides in your home directory. This exercise also assumes that you have logged in and your active prompt has been changed from the F:\LOGIN> to F:\USERS\HOME\your home directory> prompt.

Hands-On Exercise

From the F:\USERS\HOME\your home directory> prompt, launch NetWare's FILER menu utility. At FILER's Available Topics menu, with SYS:\USERS\HOME\your directory name showing in the menu banner, to view the directory contents,

1. **Type** *D*

   Press (Enter)

The file and subdirectory names are shown in the Directory Contents screen for your home directory.

To locate the file to be renamed,

2. **Type** *TESTIT*

Your highlight bar is moved to highlight the TESTIT.BAT file.

3. To rename the TESTIT.BAT file to *TESTIT.BAK*,

   Press (F3)

In the Edit File Name: pop-up window,

   Press (←Backspace) once

To make the last letter in the file extension the letter K,

   Type *K*

   Press (Enter)

The renamed file is listed in the Directory Contents screen.

To copy TESTIT.BAK to TESTIT.BAT,

4. **Press** (Enter) (highlighted on TESTIT.BAK) and then,

   Press (Enter) (highlighted on Copy File), next

   Press (Enter) (to accept the same directory path)

In the Destination File Name pop-up window,

   Press (←Backspace) once

To create the filename TESTIT.BAT,

> **Type** *T*
>
> **Press** [Enter]

Refer to Figure 4.18.

To move back to Directory Contents and view your changes,

> **Press** [Esc]

The TESTIT.BAT as well as the TESTIT.BAK files are listed in the Directory Contents screen.

To begin working with File Attributes on the TESTIT.BAK file,

> 5. **Type** *TESTIT* to move the highlight bar to TESTIT.BAK
>
> **Press** [Enter]

In the File Options pop-up window,

> **Press** [↓] three times

This should have moved your highlight bar to View/Set File Information.

> **Press** [Enter] (highlighted on View/Set File Information)

The File Information screen for the TESTIT.BAK file is displayed on your screen.

To initiate changing the TESTIT.BAK file attribute,

> 6. **Press** [Enter] (highlighted on Attributes:)

Refer to Figure 4.19.

The Current File Attributes only displays the *"Archive Needed"* as Read-write is assumed. Refer to Exercise 4.8 for further detail.

To change the TESTIT.BAK file to Read Only,

> 7. **Press** [Ins] at Current File Attributes pop-up window
>
> **Type** *R* to move the highlight bar to Read-only
>
> **Press** [Enter]

Refer to Figure 4.20.

You are returned to the Current File Attributes pop-up window, listing not only the addition of the Read-only attribute. but also when you flag a file Ro, NetWare automatically adds Delete Inhibit and Rename Inhibit.

To apply these new attributes to the TESTIT.BAK file,

> 8. **Press** [Esc]

FIGURE 4.18

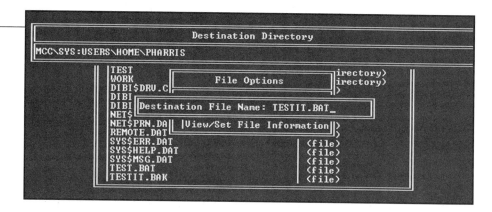

FIGURE 4.19

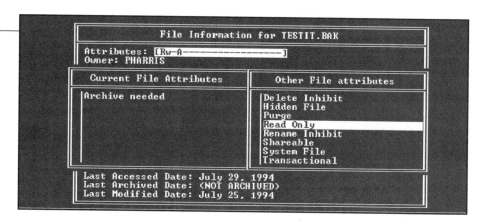

FIGURE 4.20

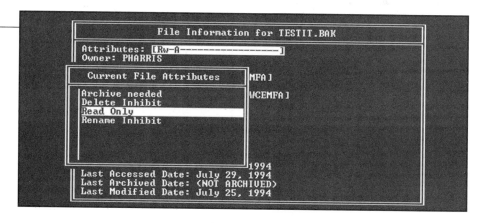

The Attributes: listing now shows that the Ro, DI, and RI attributes were added.

9. To quickly exit *FILER*

   Press Alt F10

KEY RELATED POINTS

 NetWare automatically adds the DI and RI attributes when Ro is applied to a file.

4.11 USING GRANT AND TLIST—CHANGING TRUSTEE RIGHTS; USING RIGHTS AND ALLOW—CHANGING EFFECTIVE RIGHTS

In this exercise, you will manipulate directory and file rights using NetWare's command-line utilities: GRANT, TLIST, RIGHTS, and ALLOW. You will use FILER to view changes in trustee assignments.

This exercise assumes that you have logged in and your active prompt was changed from F:\LOGIN> to F:\USERS\HOME\your home directory> prompt.

Hands-On Exercise

To begin manipulating rights, at your F:\USERS\HOME\your home directory> prompt,

1. **Type** *GRANT R W C F M TO GUEST*

   Press Enter

NetWare confirms your change by displaying *"Rights set to [RWC MF]"* on your screen.

To view others who have Trustee rights granted in your home directory,

2. **Type** *TLIST*

   Press Enter

TLIST is the command-line utility for listing Trustees and their rights at a directory location. NetWare provides a listing similar to 4.15, showing the User trustees: GUEST.

To revoke the M or Modify right from the Supervisor account,

3. **Type** *REVOKE M FOR GUEST*

   Press Enter

FIGURE 4.21

```
F:\USERS\HOME\PHARRIS>grant r w c f m to guest

MCC/SYS:USERS\HOME\PHARRIS
PHARRIS                                    Rights set to [ RWC MF ]


F:\USERS\HOME\PHARRIS>tlist

MCC\SYS:USERS\HOME\PHARRIS
User trustees:
   PHARRIS                                         [ RWCEMFA ]
   GUEST                                           [ RWC MF ]
No group trustees.

F:\USERS\HOME\PHARRIS>revoke m for guest
MCC/SYS:USERS\HOME\PHARRIS
Trustee's access rights set to [ RWC  F ]

Rights for 1 directories were changed for GUEST.


F:\USERS\HOME\PHARRIS>_
```

NetWare responds, telling you the rights for one directory were changed for GUEST. Use TLIST to view and list the changes. Refer to Figure 4.21.

To use FILER to view the changes,

    4. **Type** *FILER*

       Press Enter

From the Available Topics menu,

    5. **Press** Enter (highlighted on Current Directory Information)

       Move The highlight bar to Trustees: and then

       Press Enter

Refer to Figure 4.22.

You will see the Guest account has been granted the RWCF rights. As demonstrated earlier in this chapter, FILER is the menu utility for granting rights to directories and files.

To go back to the Directory Information screen,

    6. **Press** Esc

To go back to Available Topics,

    7. **Press** Esc

       Type *SET* to move to Set Filer Options

       Press Enter

       Type *Y* highlighted on Confirm Deletion

       Press ↓ once

       Type *Y* highlighted on Confirm File Copies

To save your changes and then leave FILER,

    8. **Press** [Esc] twice

    Press [Alt] [F10] to exit *FILER*

At your home directory prompt, to view your effective rights,

    9. **Type** *RIGHTS*

    Press [Enter]

Your effective directory rights are displayed. These are the same as the effective rights listed in FILER's Directory Information screen.

To revoke all rights for the Guest account,

    10. **Type** *REVOKE ALL FROM GUEST*

    Press [Enter]

NetWare responds to confirm the changes for the Guest account with the message, *"Rights for 1 directories were changed for GUEST."* Use TLIST to view the changes.

To remove Guest from the trustee assignment for this directory location,

    11. **Type** *REMOVE GUEST FROM SYS:USERS/HOME/_____*

(The blank line is to be filled in with your home directory name.)

    Press [Enter]

NetWare confirms with the message *"Trustee GUEST removed from 1 directories."*

To view the changes,

    12. **Type** *TLIST*

    Press [Enter]

You see that the Guest account has been removed from the trustee assignments for this directory location.

To use allow to change inherited rights, fill in the blank below with your home directory name:

    13. **Type** *ALLOW SYS:\USERS\HOME_____\WORK R F A C*

    Press [Enter]

NetWare responds to confirm and show your changes listed on your screen. Since you hold the S, or Supervisory right, NetWare adds this to your assignment. Once the Supervisory right has been granted, it can only be removed from the directory location where granted.

FIGURE 4.22

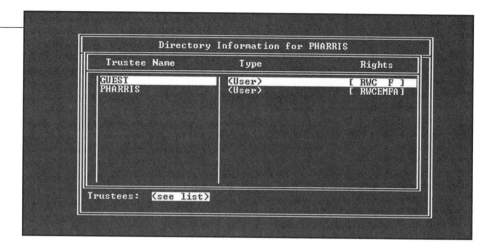

```
              Directory Information for PHARRIS
     Trustee Name            Type              Rights
    GUEST                   <User>          [ RWC   F ]
    PHARRIS                 <User>          [ RWCEMFA ]




    Trustees:   <see list>
```

To move to the WORK directory and view your changes,

    14. **Type** *CD WORK*

       Press Enter

To check your changes,

    15. **Type** *RIGHTS*

       Press Enter

You see that NetWare has responded and listed your effective rights.

KEY RELATED POINTS

- The Supervisory right can only be removed from the directory location where it was granted.

- The effective rights are rights you can exercise for a given file or directory location.

- Trustee rights are often thought of as combined rights because they are the rights you obtain from your username and from belonging to groups.

- The inherited rights control which rights users can inherit. Inherited rights control which directory rights can be exercised on the file and which can be exercised on the directory. The ALLOW command is used to set or modify the inherited rights.

4.12 DELETING AN ENTIRE DIRECTORY STRUCTURE WITH FILER

FILER is a menu utility used to control volumes, directories, and files. One of FILER'S most useful and powerful capabilities is the ability to delete an entire subdirectory structure or delete exclusively the files in a subdirectory structure. In this exercise you will mark the subdirectory and then delete the directory and its contents.

This exercise assumes that you have logged in and your active prompt was changed from F:\LOGIN> to F:\USERS\HOME\your home directory> prompt.

Hands-On Exercise

To begin, at your F:\USERS\HOME\your home directory> prompt,

   1. **Type** *MD DELETION*

      Press (Enter)

      Type *CD DELETION*

      Press (Enter)

Your directory prompt changed to be F:\USERS\HOME\your home directory/DELETION> directory prompt.

To copy some files from the directory prompt,

   2. **Type** *COPY .. *.** (make sure you add two dots after copy)

      Press (Enter)

You are returned to the DELETION directory prompt. You have copied the files in your home directory, or the PARENT directory (..) into the DELETION directory.

To work with FILER, from the DELETION directory prompt,

   3. **Type** *FILER*

      Press (Enter)

From Filer's Available Topics main menu,

      Type *D* to move the highlight bar to Directory Contents

      Press (Enter)

You are highlighted on .. (parent) directory selection.

      Press (Enter) (highlighted on parent)

      Press (Enter) (highlighted on Yes)

FIGURE 4.23

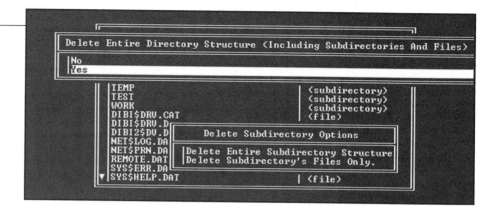

You made the parent your current directory, and you are back at your home directory.

To delete the DELETION directory,

> **Type** *D* (to move the highlight bar to DELETION subdirectory)
>
> **Press** Del

Your screen displays the Delete Subdirectory Options pop-up window, and you're highlighted on Delete Subdirectory's Files Only. If you wanted to delete just the files and keep the directory structure, this would be the choice.

To delete the entire subdirectory structure,

> 4. **Press** ↑ (once)

Your highlight bar is now on Delete Entire Subdirectory Structure.

> **Press** Enter

The pop-up window displayed on your screen is asking a serious question *"Delete Entire Directory Structure (Including Subdirectories And Files)."* You are highlighted on No.

To move the highlight bar to Yes in the pop-up window,

> 5. **Type** *Y* to highlight *YES*

You are highlighted on Yes, and you pause to look at FILER'S menu banner to see you're at your home directory, but you cannot see the directory structure you are about to delete for the pop-up windows are covering the Directory Contents screen, as shown in Figure 4.23.

To delete the directory structure and files,

> 6. **Press** Enter (highlighted on Yes)

You are at the Delete Default Directory pop-up window. This is NetWare's life preserver, for you began FILER from the DELETION directory prompt, and you may look upon this pop-up window as your way of knowing the correct subdirectory, the DELETION subdirectory, has been selected.

Highlighted on Yes to Delete Default Directory and its subdirectories,

7. **Press** ⌨Enter⌨

You are back at Directory Contents, and the DELETION directory is not listed.

To exit FILER,

8. **Press** ⌨Alt⌨ ⌨F10⌨

With answering Yes to exit FILER, your screen may display your cursor at the Current drive is no longer valid> prompt. If so, type *F:* and if your screen displays *"Invalid drive specification"*, chances are very good FILER deleted the mapping to your default drive location, drive F.

To see if you lost drive F, use MAP. NetWare returns your drive mappings, and you will see that drive F is deleted. Your default drive pointer was using drive F to point to the DELETION subdirectory, thus FILER deleted not only the subdirectory, DELETION, but also the mapping for the drive pointing to this directory location. Use MAP F:=SYS:USERS/ HOME/your home directory name to remap drive F. You can then type F: and use NDIR to view your changes.

KEY RELATED POINTS

 Throughout this chapter, you have seen that many of the functions performed through FILER may also be carried out at the command-line prompt by using various NetWare command-line utilities.

A user who has appropriate security rights can use FILER to:

1. View information about volumes, directories, and subdirectories.

2. List and view information about the files for a subdirectory.

3. Delete, rename, and copy files.

4. Change a file's attributes.

5. Alter the current directory path.

6. List, add, delete and rename subdirectories.

7. View storage information about the volume where the current directory is located.

There are symbols that represent the root and the parent of the currently active directory. The DOS DIR command will often display . and .. in its listing of files and directories. These symbols represent the currently active directory (the .) and the parent (the ..) of the currently active directory.

END OF CHAPTER REVIEW

Important Terms

FILER   NDIR
FLAG   RENDIR
NCOPY   SALVAGE

Matching

_____1. Drawer   A. Subdirectory
_____2. File Cabinet   B. Directory
_____3. Hanging Folder   C. Hard disk
_____4. Report or Letter   D. Volume
_____5. Manila Folder   E. File

True/False Questions

1. When using FILER to delete a subdirectory, you must first delete all the files in that subdirectory.

2. Special rights are needed in order to carry out many of the filing tasks available in FILER.

3. To access FILER, type FILER at any directory prompt. Assume a search drive is mapped to PUBLIC.

4. Only a Supervisor can change file attributes.

5. You cannot use FILER to find out how much free space is available on a network volume.

6. The FLAG command is used for network security.

7. File attributes will need to be changed from the default setting to allow multiple uses to read files.

8. If a file is Flagged Read–write, trustee rights for users may read, write, copy, or delete that file.

9. The RIGHTS command lists the permissions granted to a particular user for directories and files in NetWare.

10. The TLIST command is used for listing the trustee assignments granted for a user.

11. You can use NDIR/SUB from F:\> to search the entire server volume.

ON YOUR OWN—HANDS-ON

Displaying Security Information on the NetWork.

Directions: For this exercise, you will need to have a formatted diskette located in drive A on your local workstation. You will use the DOS redirector (>) and the DOS append (>>) symbols to store files containing listings of information about your network. You will be given instruction for making changes where noted with PERFORM: and where noted with TYPE: you will redirect and store output of these changes to the SECURITY file, much as you did with Chapter 3 and the mapping file.

1. Use LOGIN to log in to NetWare. At the F:\LOGIN> prompt,
   PERFORM: FLAG command listed to your screen. Then, when you are sure your output is ready to be stored,
   TYPE: FLAG > A:SECURITY
   You should have been returned to your F:\LOGIN> drive prompt. Nothing appears on your screen, so use the DOS DIR to check that the SECURITY file was created on the disk you have in drive A. If the SECURITY file did not save, check to see that the diskette is formatted. Then,
   TYPE: ECHO LISTING for 1>>A:SECURITY and
   PRESS Enter. This will add the label "LISTING for 1" to your SECURITY file.

2. Use the DOS TYPE command to check the contents of the SECURITY file. At the F:\LOGIN> prompt,
   TYPE: TYPE A:SECURITY
   You should see the contents of the SECURITY file displayed on your screen.

3. Move to your home directory, and at the F:\USERS\HOME\your home directory> prompt, add to the SECURITY file,
   PERFORM: NDIR/SUB command listed to your screen. Then, when you're sure your output is ready to be stored,
   TYPE: NDIR/SUB >>A:SECURITY If your screen pauses and does not return to the prompt, you may need to press the letter C to help scroll the output continuously to the file.

This will add the NDIR/SUB command information, output to the previous file, SECURITY. Then,
TYPE: ECHO LISTING for 3 >>A:SECURITY and
PRESS [Enter]. This will add the label "LISTING for 3" to your SECURITY file.
Use DOS TYPE command, TYPE A:SECURITY, to check your output.

4. To make a printout of this file, at the F:\LOGIN> prompt,
   TYPE: TYPE A:SECURITY>LPT1
   This output will work, assuming you have been given instructions on how to capture a network printer or have captured a network printer upon logging in. You could also use this on any computer, networked or not, that has a locally attached printer.

5. To begin displaying information, the following assumes you have your formatted diskette in drive A and have either gone through or read through the instructions for steps 1–4, above, as this assignment refers back to them.

6. *PERFORM:* Change the attributes of the TESTIT.BAT file in your home directory to Read only.
   TYPE: FLAG command listed to your screen. Then, when you're sure your output is ready to be stored,
   Use FLAG >>A:SECURITY once you have completed this task. Then,
   TYPE ECHO LISTING for 6 >>A:SECURITY and
   PRESS [Enter]. This will add the label "LISTING for 6" to your SECURITY file.

7. Make a TEMP directory under your home directory. Change to your TEMP directory.
   PERFORM: Use NCOPY to copy all the *.DAT files from the PUBLIC directory.
   TYPE: FLAG command listed to your screen. Then, when you are sure your output is ready to be stored,
   TYPE: FLAG >>A:SECURITY once you have completed this task. Then,
   TYPE ECHO LISTING for 7 >>A:SECURITY and
   PRESS [Enter]. This will add the label "LISTING for 7" to your SECURITY file.

8. From the USERS/HOME/your home directory/TEMP> prompt,
   PERFORM: Delete all the files that begin with the letter N.
   TYPE: FLAG >>A:SECURITY once you have completed this task.
   PERFORM: FLAG command listed to your screen. Then, when you are sure your output is ready to be stored,
   TYPE: ECHO LISTING for 8 >>A:SECURITY and
   PRESS [Enter]. This will add the label "LISTING for 8" to your SECURITY file.

9. From the USERS/HOME/your home directory/TEMP> prompt, use DOS COPY to
PERFORM: Copy the SYS$MSG.DAT file to TEMPFILE. Then use NCOPY to copy SYS$MSG.DAT file to TEMPFILL.
PERFORM: FLAG command listed to your screen. Then, when you are sure your output is ready to be stored,
TYPE: FLAG >>A:SECURITY once you have completed this task. Then,
TYPE: ECHO LISTING for 9>>A:SECURITY and
PRESS Enter. This will add the label "LISTING for 9" to your SECURITY file.

10. From the USERS/HOME/your home directory/TEMP> prompt, delete all the .DAT files.
PERFORM: FLAG command listed to your screen. Then, when you are sure your output is ready to be stored,
TYPE: FLAG >>A:SECURITY once you have completed this task. Then,
TYPE: ECHO LISTING for 10 >>A:SECURITY and
PRESS Enter. This will add the label "LISTING for 10" to your SECURITY file.

11. From the USERS/HOME/your home directory/TEMP> prompt,
PERFORM: FLAGDIR . P to flag the directory PURGE.
PERFORM: FLAGDIR command listed to your screen. Then, when you are sure your output is ready to be stored,
TYPE: FLAGDIR >>A:SECURITY once you have completed this task. Then,
TYPE: ECHO LISTING for 11>>A:SECURITY and
PRESS Enter. This will add the label "LISTING for 11" to your SECURITY file.

12. From the USERS/HOME/your home directory/TEMP> prompt,
PERFORM: FLAG all the .DAT files with the Rw attribute.
PERFORM: FLAG command listed to your screen. Then, when you are sure your output is ready to be stored,
TYPE: FLAG >>A:SECURITY once you have completed this task. Then,
TYPE: ECHO LISTING for 12 >>A:SECURITY and
PRESS Enter. This will add the label "LISTING for 12" to your SECURITY file.

13. From the USERS/HOME/your home directory/TEMP> prompt,
PERFORM: Delete all the .DAT files.
PERFORM: FLAG command listed to your screen. Then, when you are sure your output is ready to be stored,
TYPE: FLAG >>A:SECURITY once you have completed this task. Then,
TYPE: ECHO LISTING for 13>>A:SECURITY and
PRESS Enter. This will add the label "LISTING for 13" to your SECURITY file.

14. From the USERS/HOME/your home directory/TEMP> prompt,
    TYPE: PURGE>>A:SECURITY
    Your screen will not display anything to view. You will be returned to your directory prompt when the writing of the PURGE listing to your diskette is completed. Then,
    TYPE: ECHO LISTING for 14 >>A:SECURITY and
    PRESS [Enter]. This will add the label "LISTING for 14" to your SECURITY file.

15. From the USERS/HOME/your home directory/TEMP> prompt,
    PERFORM: GRANT all rights to the GUEST account.
    PERFORM: TLIST command listed to your screen. Then, when you are sure your output is ready to be stored,
    TYPE: TLIST>>A:SECURITY once you have completed this task. Your screen will not display anything to view. You will be returned to your directory prompt when the writing of the TLIST listing to your diskette is completed. Then,
    TYPE: ECHO LISTING for 15>>A:SECURITY and
    PRESS [Enter]. This will add the label "LISTING for 15" to your SECURITY file.

16. From the USERS/HOME/your home directory/TEMP> prompt,
    PERFORM: REVOKE the E and W rights from GUEST.
    PERFORM: TLIST command listed to your screen. Then, when you're sure your output is ready to be stored,
    TYPE: TLIST >>A:SECURITY once you have completed this task. Again, your screen will not display anything to view. You will be returned to your directory prompt, as before, when the writing of the TLIST listing to your diskette is completed. Then,
    TYPE: ECHO LISTING for 16 >>A:SECURITY and
    PRESS [Enter]. This will add the label "LISTING for 16" to your SECURITY file.

17. *PERFORM:* Make a printout of the SECURITY file. Refer to Step 4 as needed.
    TYPE: TYPE A:SECURITY>LPT1

18. From the main menu of FILER, Available Topics, highlight Current Directory Information and press [Enter].

Available Topics
Current Directory Information
Directory Contents
Select Current Directory
Set Filer Options
Volume Information

Select Current Directory Information.
PERFORM: Write down the following information:

OWNER:
Creation DATE:
Creation TIME:
Current EFFECTIVE RIGHTS:
IRM:

19. Press [Esc] once, until you reach the Available Topics menu again. Highlight Volume Information from the Available Topics menu and press [Enter].
PERFORM: Write down the information displayed:

File Server Name:
Volume Name:
Volume Type:
Number of total KBytes:
Number of Kilobytes available:
Maximum number of directory entries:
Number of directory entries available:

IN YOUR OWN WORDS

1. What are the differences you noticed between NDIR and LISTDIR?

2. On a separate sheet of paper,
    a. Explain File and Directory rights.
    b. Explain NetWare Security.
    c. List and Define NetWare's Directory and File Attributes.
    d. Define Trustee Rights.
    e. Define Effective Rights.
    f. Define Inherited Rights.

3. From the drawing of the directory structure you completed in Chapter 3 for all users working on wordprocessing in the MicroView company,
    a. add usernames and supply directory rights for each username.
    b. group the users and provide a list of the Group names and members.
    c. within the groups, designate one username to be the Workgroup.
    d. add a manager for that group.
    e. make sure you have got a Shared Data directory for all users as well as a Shared Data directory for each group.

Access Rights— NetWare's Users and Groups in SYSCON and FILER

OBJECTIVES

- Create a new user.

- Add a user to a group.

- Assign access rights for a new user.

- Examine NetWare's Operator and Manager security assignments.

- Enforce User Account Restrictions.

- Enact Disk, Time, and Station Restrictions for a user account.

- Modify Trustee Directory Assignments for a user account.

- Modify the Inherited Rights Mask in FILER.

CHAPTER INTRODUCTION

Netware Security—Users, Groups and Rights

Upon installation of a NetWare 3.x server, two Users and one Group are created. The two users created are Supervisor and Guest and the Group is named Everyone. The *Supervisor* account is granted full access to all resources of NetWare where the Guest account is granted very limited access.

Passwords for the Supervisor or Guest account do not exist and are neither required nor established when a NetWare server is first created. However, once installed, NetWare can be configured by the Supervisor to require passwords.

As each new user on the network is added, NetWare automatically assigns them as members of the group *Everyone*. User accounts can be removed from the group Everyone, but risk losing privileges of command-line and menu utilities as well as other features to service their connection.

The *Guest* account is given limited access on the network and can be deleted from the server/operating system. On the other hand, if the Supervisor account is deleted, big problems will eventually ensue, even if there are *Supervisor Equivalent* accounts established.

If the Supervisor account were deleted, recopying an older set of the bindery files is one way of restoring the account. The *bindery files* are files where objects, properties, and other resource information is kept about the network. These files are located in the SYS:SYSTEM subdirectory and should be backed up regularly.

As users are created on the system, you learned from the previous chapters that they are made members of groups. The bindery files hold the group member information and upon logging in are activated to associate the user account with the groups they belong to.

You learned from the previous chapters that directory rights are then broken into individual accounts and group membership. The individual rights plus the group rights are termed *combined rights* or *trustee rights*. In this chapter, you work with assigning trustee rights.

Directories are useful for grouping and managing logically related files. Rights to directories and/or subsequent subdirectories form a hierarchical rights structure involving network security. As the user moves down a directory structure, to subsequent subdirectories, these trustee rights (combined rights) travel down the structure with them, unless the rights have been blocked (removed or revoked). Filtering the flow of rights down the directory structure is termed the *inherited rights mask* or *IRM*. The "obtained" rights a user holds at a specific directory structure location, results from their combined and inherited rights, and is termed their *effective rights*.

Managers and Operators

A Manager is a designated user or group account that is a subset of the Supervisor account. NetWare uses the title Manager for those with user account maintenance responsibility and uses Operator for those charged with managing operational tasks on the network. Management responsibility over network printing tasks is designated as either *Print Server Operator* or *Print Queue Operator*. For management of the file server, a *Console Operator* is given limited responsibility.

SYSCON's managers include a *Workgroup Manager*, *User Account Manager*, or *Supervisor Equivalent*. Username accounts with Manager status are created in SYSCON and take responsibility over certain aspects of system management using SYSCON to manage user accounts.

The Supervisor, Supervisor Equivalent, or Workgroup Manager create users in NetWare. The Supervisor and Supervisor Equivalent account have full access privileges over all users throughout the file server, whereas the Workgroup Manager does not.

Workgroup managers assist the network Supervisor, but cannot create other Workgroup managers. They do not automatically acquire rights to the directory and file structure; the SUPERVISOR account or SUPERVISOR equivalent account(s) must grant directory structure access to Workgroup managers.

A Workgroup Manager is one of NetWare's system managers responsible for adding and deleting users. Workgroup managers can view, add, and delete User Account managers. Workgroup managers usually hold the Supervisory directory right for the directory structure(s) they manage.

A User Account Manager can be designated by a Workgroup Manager to manage specific user accounts that the Workgroup Manager administers. The User Account Manager cannot create users or groups and primarily assists Workgroup managers in handling routine tasks (e.g., assigning users to new groups, changing drive mappings or account restrictions). A user account can be managed by more than one User Account Manager.

In this chapter, you work with increased security rights, that of Workgroup Manager or greater, to accomplish creating and managing security rights for users and groups. You will work with SYSCON, NetWare's system configuration menu utility, to create and establish security rights for a new user. You will work with groups to see how simplifying network administration is done by dealing with user accounts collectively. You then will work with user account restriction to see limitations that can be implemented. By imposing time restrictions, you can limit the hours of the day users can log in. Limiting disk space is one way to assure storage space is evenly allocated.

5.1 CREATING NEW USES WITH NETWARE

You will work with SYSCON, NetWare's system configuration menu utility in this exercise to create and establish security rights for a new user.

You will use the WGMGR username to log in or you will need to be given a user account with minimum of **Workgroup Manager** privileges on the network to complete this exercise.

This exercise assumes you are already logged in to NetWare at the F:\LOGIN> prompt.

Hands-On Exercise

Once logged in and at the F:\LOGIN> prompt,

> 1. **Type** *SYSCON*
>
>   **Press** Enter

The main menu of NetWare's system configuration menu utility, SYSCON, shows the Available Topics menu.

To position yourself in SYSCON for creating your new user,

> 2. **Type** *U* to move the highlight bar to User Information
>
>   **Press** Enter

You are at the User Names pop-up window and all the users of this file server are listed.

From the User Names pop-up window, to create a new user,

> 3. **Press** Ins

You are at the pop-up window that displays, *"User Name:."*

In the User Name window,

> 4. **Type** *xxxUSER* (replace the xxx with your initials)
>
>   **Press** Enter

***NOTE:* If you get the message, "You have insufficient rights to add User xxxUSER to Group EVERYONE <Press ESCAPE to continue>,"**

> **Press** Esc

This just means that the group Everyone is not available for you to add users to or work with on your server.

To clear the path showing, and enter SYS:USERS\NEWUSER\xxxUSER,

> 5. **Press** Backspace until the path shown is erased
>
>   **Type** *SYS:USERS/NEWUSER/xxxUSER*

Workgroup Manager
One of NetWare's system managers. Responsible for adding and deleting users. Can also view, add, and delete User Account managers, but cannot create other workgroup managers.

FIGURE 5.1

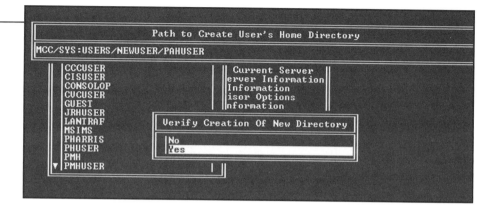

The pop-up window, Path to Create User's Home Directory, is showing *"SYS:USERS/NEWUSER/xxxUSER."*

NOTE: **Remember that the forward slash (/) or backslash (\) can be used when creating a directory path in NetWare.**

NOTE: **You could erase the path by using the Backspace key and retype the SYS:USERS/NEWUSER/XXXUSER path or use the Backspace key to erase the path and navigate the directory structure using the Ins key.**

To accept the path showing, and enter the path you typed, SYS:USERS/NEWUSER/xxxUSER,

6. **Press** Enter

The pop-up window, Verify Creation of New Directory is showing and your highlight bar is on No. Your screen should look similar to Figure 5.1.

NOTE: **You do not have to create a home directory to create a new user. If you misspelled the directory name, you can specify No and edit the entry for the Path to Create User's Home Directory. If you specify Yes, you accept the path listed, create the home directory and allow NetWare to automatically create the directory and specify trustee directory rights.**

To accept verification of creating the new directory,

7. **Type** Y to move the highlight bar to Yes

Press Enter

Your new user is now added to the system. You are highlighted on xxxUSER, your new username, in the User Name window.

To exit from the User Names window,

8. **Press** (Esc)

You are back at the Available Topics menu, highlighted on User Information. If you are going on to the next exercise, remain highlighted on User Information, otherwise, to exit SYSCON from Available Topics menu,

9. **Press** (Esc)

Press (Enter) (highlighted on Yes to exit SYSCON)

You are back at F:\LOGIN> where you can log out.

CHART OF ACCOUNTS WITHIN NETWARE

Supervisor: Created upon installation of a NetWare server. The username for the network Supervisor or System Administrator. Has all rights throughout the NetWare server.

Supervisor Equivalent: An account designated with security equivalence equal to the Supervisor account.

Workgroup Manager: A user account identified to have supervisory rights to manage certain user accounts and groups. Can be given rights to modify file and directory rights, volume restrictions, and disk space restrictions.

User Account Manager: A user or group account identified to have routine maintenance rights to manage certain user accounts and groups.

Group membership: Provides a way to collectively deal with users. Only one group, Everyone, is system-created. All other groups are created to simplify network administration.

Everyone Group: Created upon installation of a NetWare server. All users are included in this group when first created. The system-created accounts of Guest and Supervisor also belong to this group.

Guest Account: Created upon installation of a NetWare server. The username for anyone needing temporary, restricted access to the server.

Print Server Operator: An account designated as a Printing Supervisor over print servers.

Print Queue Operator: An account designated as a Printing Supervisor over print queues.

File Server Console Operator: An account designated as a Manager over the file server.

KEY RELATED POINTS

🔑 You don't have to create a home directory to create a new user.

🔑 User accounts are created with the Workgroup Manager, Supervisor Equivalent or Supervisor account status.

🔑 When users are created, they are automatically made members of the group Everyone. NetWare is designed so the manager accounts can change rights to this group. For a Manager account, taking away the group Everyone also takes away management ability over Everyone and narrows down the jurisdiction of user management for a Workgroup Manager to just those users assigned or created by the Workgroup Manager.

🔑 SYSCON's managers include a Workgroup Manager, User Account Manager, or Supervisor Equivalent. Username accounts with manager status are created in SYSCON and take responsibility over certain aspects of system management using SYSCON to manage user accounts.

🔑 A Manager is a designated user or group account that is a subset of the Supervisor account. NetWare uses the title Manager for those with user account maintenance responsibility and uses Operator for those charged with managing operational tasks on the network.

🔑 The Supervisor, Supervisor Equivalent, or Workgroup Manager create users in NetWare. The Supervisor and Supervisor Equivalent account have full access privileges over all users throughout the file server, while the Workgroup Manager does not.

5.2 ASSOCIATING NEW USERS WITH GROUPS AND MANAGERS

Groups are used in NetWare as a means of simplifying network administration by dealing with user accounts collectively. In this exercise you will use SYSCON to use the new user account you created from Exercise 5.1 and make them a member of the NEWUSERS group.

You will use the WGMGR username to log in or you will need to be given a user account with a minimum of Workgroup Manager privileges on the network to complete this exercise.

This exercise assumes you are already logged in to NetWare and at the SYSCON Available Topics menu, highlighted on User Information.

Hands-On Exercise

Highlighted on User Information in SYSCON, to locate your new, xxxUSER, username in the list of users,

> 1. **Press** Enter (highlighted on User Information)

From the User Name window,

> **Type** *xxxUSER* (replace xxx with your initials)

Highlighted on the username you created in Exercise 5.1,

> **Press** Enter

You are at the User Information menu for this account, highlighted on Account Balance.
To make your new user a member of the NEWUSERS group,

> 2. **Type** G
> **Press** Enter

At the Groups Belonged To window,

> **Press** Ins

Your screen should look similar to Figure 5.2.
To select NEWUSERS group from the Groups Not Belonged To window,

> **Type** *N* to move the highlight bar to NEWUSERS group
> **Press** Enter

Back at the Groups Belonged To window, highlighted on NEWUSERS,

> **Press** Esc

You are back at the User Information window.
To check the groups your new user belongs to,

> 3. **Type** *S* to highlight Security Equivalences
> **Press** Enter

You should see the NEWUSERS (Group) in the Security Equivalences window. This verifies you have added your new user to the NEWUSERS group.
To see that NetWare automatically placed the account you logged in with as the Manager of this newly created account,

> 4. **Press** Esc to leave Security Equivalences window
> **Type** *MANAGERS* to move to Managers in the User Information window

FIGURE 5.2

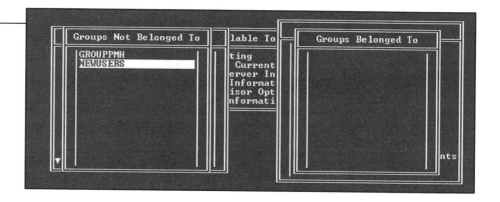

          Press Enter (highlighted on Managers)

At the Managers window, you see your LOGIN account name or WGMGR (User) if you are using this account name.

To view your account and see that NetWare has identified your LOGIN name as the Manager of this user account,

          5. **Press** Esc twice from Managers window to get to User Names window

From the User Names window, notice that the second line of SYSCON'S menu banner, at the top of your screen reads *"User _____ On File Server _____"* and gives you the names of your LOGIN user-name and file server.

          Type _____ (your LOGIN name)

(Replace the blank line with the name of the LOGIN username shown in SYSCON's menu banner.)

Highlighted on your LOGIN username shown in SYSCON's menu banner,

          Press Enter

You are at User Information window for your LOGIN username.

To check who you manage,

          6. **Type** *M* to move the highlight to Managed Users and Groups

          Press Enter

You will see the new xxxUSER account you just created listed in the Managed Users and Groups window, with the designation *"(User/Direct)."* This means you directly, or specifically, manage this account.

To exit to the Available Topics menu, from the Managed Users and Groups window,

          7. **Press** Esc three times

You are back at Available Topics, SYSCON's main menu, highlighted on User Information. If you are going on to the next exercise, remain highlighted on User Information, otherwise, to exit SYSCON from Available Topics,

8. **Press** [Esc]

   Press [Enter] (highlighted on Yes to exit SYSCON)

You are back at F:\LOGIN> where you can log out.

KEY RELATED POINTS

The Managers option in SYSCON's User Information window is used to show the user's Manager(s), listing the accounts which are responsible for assisting with network administration for this username. You can modify this option if you are a Manager.

The designation of Direct management vs. Indirect management is to be a direct account management designation for the usernames showing (Direct/User) or group names showing (Direct/Group). Indirect managed users and groups are assigned by the network so the Manager(s) can change the rights to the group Everyone and share the administrative responsibility of each user in this group. Where shared management is not needed, Everyone is removed from a Manager's responsibility by removing the Manager account from belonging to this group.

Not all accounts are assigned to a Workgroup Manager. If users are created by a Workgroup Manager, then the Workgroup Manager can handle those accounts. The Supervisor and Supervisor Equivalent automatically manage all user accounts.

A User Account Manager can be designated by a Workgroup Manager to manage specific user accounts the Workgroup Manager administers. The User Account Manager cannot create users or groups and primarily assists Workgroup managers in handling routine tasks (e.g., assigning users to new groups, changing drive mappings or account restrictions).

A user account can be managed by more than one User Account Manager.

Workgroup managers assist the network supervisor, but cannot create other Workgroup managers. Workgroup managers do not automatically acquire rights to the directory and file structure, the SUPERVISOR account or SUPERVISOR equivalent account(s) must grant directory structure access to Workgroup managers.

Workgroup managers usually hold the Supervisory directory right for the directory structure(s) they manage.

5.3 WORKING WITH NETWARE'S ACCOUNT RESTRICTIONS

User accounts can be restricted by disk storage space, number of concurrent connections, hours of the day to log in, and by physical locations; or they can be restricted by the station (computer) which they can log in from.

In this exercise, you will work with NetWare's account restrictions for the username account you created in Exercise 5.1.

This exercise assumes you are already logged in to NetWare and at the SYSCON Available Topics menu, highlighted on User Information.

Hands-On Exercises

Highlighted on User Information in SYSCON, to locate your new, xxx USER, username in the list of users,

  1. **Press** Enter from User Information

     Move the highlight bar to your new xxxUSER from Exercise 5.1.

     Press Enter (highlighted on your xxxUSER account)

You are at the User Information window, highlighted on Account Balance.

To work account restrictions, highlighted on Account Balance,

  2. **Press** ↓ to highlight Account Restrictions

     Press Enter (highlighted on Account Restrictions)

You are at the Account Restrictions For User xxxUSER screen.

To give the xxxUSER an account expiration date,

  3. **Press** ↓ to highlight Account Has Expiration Date

     Type Y

     Press Enter

NetWare provides a default date.

Highlighted on Date Account Expires:, to change this to Christmas,

     Type 12/25/xx (replace xx with this calendar year)

The field cleared when you began typing.

NOTE: If your cursor is blinking in the field, backspace to erase, then type 12/12/xx. If the cursor is not blinking in the field, yet your cursor is highlighted on the field, you can begin typing and the previous entry will clear automatically.

When you are finished typing the entry,

     Press Enter

NetWare will automatically convert the account expiration date to December 25, 19xx. You are now highlighted on Limit Concurrent Connections.

To limit concurrent connections,

> 4. **Type** Y (in the Limit Concurrent Connections field)
>
> **Press** [Enter]

NetWare provides one (1) as the default.

> **Type** 4 (in the Maximum Connections field)
>
> **Press** [Enter]

This user can now be logged in from four different stations. You are now highlighted on Allow User to Change Password.

While highlighted on Allow User to Change Password, look at the date the password and the account expire. The date shown in the Date Password Expires: is NetWare's default.

To change the date the password expires,

> 5. **Move** the highlight bar to Date Password Expires:

Highlighted on here, to change the date,

> **Type** 11/24/xx (replace xx with this calendar year)

The field cleared when you began typing. When you are finished typing the entry,

> **Press** [↓]

You are now highlighted on Limit Grace Logins.

NOTE: You can use either the Enter or Down Arrow key to move down the list and save your changes.

To limit the Grace LOGINS, with the highlight bar on Limit Grace LOGINS:, since the default is already set to Yes,

> 6. **Press** [↓] to highlight Grace Logins Allowed:

NOTE: The default is six Grace LOGINs. The Supervisor or Supervisor Equivalent account can change the default system-wide and their change would show up here.

> **Type** 7 (highlighted on Grace LOGINS Allows:)
>
> **Press** [Enter]

You are highlighted on Remaining Grace LOGINS:, which changed from six to seven automatically from entering seven in Limit Grace LOGINS. Your screen should look similar to Figure 5.3.

FIGURE 5.3

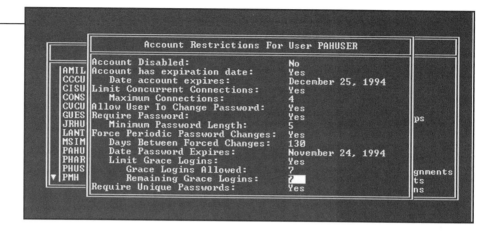

Since the last field listed, Require Unique Passwords:, is by default set to Yes, to leave the unique password at the default and save your changes to the other fields,

7. **Press** Esc

You should be back at the User Information window. To change passwords for this user,

Type *C* to move to Change Password

At Enter New Password: window, since the account restriction for this user is set to a minimum of five characters,

Type *JULIA* (or another 5 character password you can easily remember)

The password does not echo to the screen for security reasons as you type it, but NetWare asks you to verify the password at the Retype New Password: prompt, so enter the password again.

NOTE: Passwords are 1–20 characters long, if required.

Highlighted on Change Password, to get back to Available Topics,

8. **Press** Esc two times

You are now back at the Available Topics menu, highlighted on User Information. If you are going on to the next exercise, remain highlighted here, otherwise, to exit SYSCON from the Available Topics menu,

9. **Press** Alt F10

Press Enter (highlighted on *Yes* to exit SYSCON)

You are back at F:\LOGIN> where you can log out.

NETWARE'S USER ACCOUNT RESTRICTIONS

Account Disabled: If set to No, user cannot log in. Account expiration date passing and Grace LOGINS expiring automatically set this to No. Supervisor, Supervisor Equivalent, Workgroup or User Account managers can set to No to keep user from also logging in.

Account Has Expiration Date: Used to designate if the account will have a date set to expire.

Date Account Expires: Displays the account expiration date.

Limit Concurrent Connections: Used to designate if an account will be limited in the number of stations the account can simultaneously log in. Default is No limitation.

Maximum Connections: If Limit Concurrent Connections is Yes, displays the number of stations the account can simultaneously log in. Default is one.

Allow User to Change Password: Used to designate if user can change their own password. Default is Yes.

Require Password: Used to designate if a password for this account is required.

Minimum Password Length: If password is required, minimum length value must be set from 1–20 characters.

Force Periodic Password Changes: Used to designate if password changes will be activated.

Days Between Forced Changes: If force periodic password is set to Yes, the number of days between changes must be specified. Forty (40) days is the default, but the Supervisor can change the default system-wide, for all users.

Date Password Expires: Displays the date when the password will expire. The account will expire at 12:01 the next day.

Limit Grace Logins: If set to Yes, this is the number of chances the user has to change their password when it expires. NetWare will prompt the user to change their password and list the number of Grace LOGINS remaining before they will no longer be able to log in. The default is six Grace LOGINS, but the Supervisor can change this system-wide, for all users.

Grace Logins Allowed: Used to designate the number of times a user can log in with an expired password.

Remaining Grace Logins: Figure shows the number of times remaining that a user can log in with an expired password.

Require Unique Passwords: Used to designate if differentiating passwords must be set. Default is set to rotate 10 different passwords before the same password can be used again, and each password must be in effect for 24 hours.

5.4 OTHER ACCOUNT RESTRICTIONS—STATION, TIME, AND DISK

Station Restrictions
Set to limit the physical location a user can log in from.

Time Restrictions
Set to limit the hours of the day users can log in.

Disk Restrictions
Set to limit volume storage space.

In this exercise you will work with other restrictions that can be placed upon user accounts. **Station restrictions** are set to limit the physical location a user can log in from. By imposing **time restrictions**, you can limit the hours of the day users can log in. Limiting disk space is one way to assure storage space is evenly allocated, known as **disk restrictions**.

In this exercise, you will work with NetWare's account restrictions for the username account you created in Exercise 5.1.

This exercise assumes you are already logged in to NetWare and at the SYSCON Available Topics menu, highlighted on User Information.

Hands-On Exercies

Highlighted on User Information in SYSCON, to locate your new, xxxUSER, username in the list of users,

    1. **Press** ⌈Enter⌉ (highlighted on your xxxUSER)

You should be at the User Information window, highlighted on Account Balance.

To work with the disk storage space for this user account,

    2. **Type** *V*

      Press ⌈Enter⌉

From Volume/Disk Restrictions, you are at the pop-up window, Select A Volume.

To restrict disk space on volume SYS, highlighted on Volume/Disk Restrictions,

    3. **Press** ⌈Enter⌉ (highlighted on SYS)

At the Select A Volume window,

      Press ⌈Enter⌉ (highlighted on SYS)

At the User Volume/Disk Restrictions window, you are highlighted on Limit Volume Space showing No.

      Type *Y*

      Press ⌈Enter⌉

You are at Volume Space Limit: field and need to enter a value.

      Type *10* (highlighted on Volume Space Limit:)

      Press ⌈Enter⌉

Your xxxUser now has a whole 10K bytes to run with! Obviously, this is not a marathon disk user and likely you would need to establish much more disk space than the example given here.

You need to exit SYSCON and find the network address for you to use with station restrictions,

4. Use [Alt] [F10] to exit SYSCON and then, at the command-line prompt,

   Type *USERLIST/A* from the command-line prompt

   Press [Enter]

USERLIST/A is used to obtain the network and node address information. From this listing, your station is represented with an asterisk (*) in front of your LOGIN username. The node address and network address are important numbers, so write them down—exactly—as they appear in the listing.

5. Once you have written down the network and node address numbers from USERLIST, at the prompt,

   Type *SYSCON*

Then from the Available Topics menu,

6. Move to highlight User Information, find your xxxUSER in the list and press [Enter].

You're back at the User Information window, highlighted on Account Balance.

To work with station restrictions, from the User Information window for the user you created in Exercise 5.1,

7. **Type** *ST* to move your highlight bar to Station Restrictions

   Press [Enter]

At the Allowed Login Addresses pop-up window,

8. **Press** [Ins]

   Type _____ (Type the network address from USERLIST)

Once you have added the network address number, and you are sure you have checked the number carefully,

9. **Press** [Enter]

At the Allow Login From All Nodes pop-up window, highlighted on No,

10. **Press** [Enter] (highlighted on No)

At the Node Address: pop-up window,

11. **Type** _____ (Type the node address from USERLIST)

FIGURE 5.4

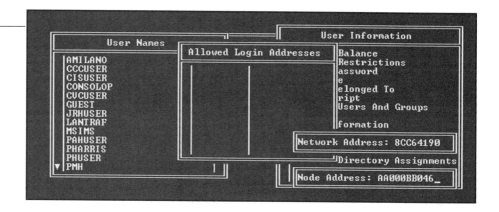

FIGURE 5.5

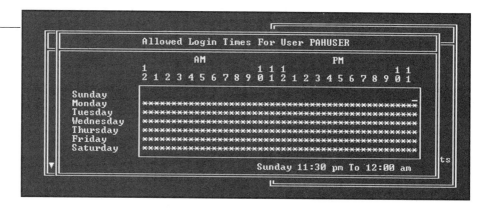

Your screen may resemble Figure 5.4

When you are sure you have checked the number carefully,

    12. **Press** [Enter]

The network and node address appear in the Allowed Login Addresses window.

To work with time restrictions, highlighted on Allowed Login Addresses,

    13. **Press** [Esc] to return to User Information window

       Type *T* to move highlight bar to Time Restrictions

       Press [Enter] (highlighted on Time Restrictions)

Your screen shows the timetable, in half-hour blocks of time, similar to Figure 5.5. You can remove a block of asterisks (*) to indicate times when users cannot log in.

To remove a block of asterisks (*) and restrict log ins on Sunday,

13. **Press** F5
    Press End

The entire line for Sunday is now marked.

Press Del to remove the asterisks for Sunday

The asterisks (*) are removed from the Sunday line, and xxxUSER will not be able to log in on Sunday. Your screen should look similar to Figure 5.6.

To exit and save your changes to the Allowed Login Times window,

14. **Press** Esc three times

You are back at the Available Topics menu, highlighted on the User Information option. If you are going on to the next exercise, remain highlighted on User Information, otherwise, to exit SYSCON from Available Topics,

15. **Press** Esc

Press Enter (highlighted on *Yes* to exit SYSCON)

You are now back at F:\LOGIN> where you can log out.

KEY RELATED POINTS

 The network address is determined by the System Administrator(s) to define a cabling scheme upon which the workstation is attached. The node address is a 12-digit hexadecimal standard which is defined by the NIC manufacturer that uniquely identifies your workstation's NIC.

FIGURE 5.6

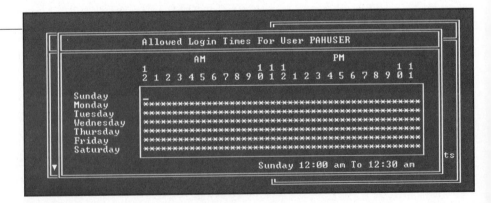

5.5 ESTABLISHING TRUSTEE DIRECTORY AND TRUSTEE FILE ASSIGNMENTS

Directory rights are then broken into individual accounts and group membership. Effective rights are those resulting from the combined rights and Inherited rights. The filtering of rights as they flow to subsequent subdirectories is termed the inherited rights mask or IRM. The individual rights plus the group rights are termed combined rights or trustee rights. In this exercise, you work with assigning trustee rights.

In this exercise, you will work with NetWare's account restrictions for the username account you created in Exercise 5.1.

This exercise assumes you are already logged in to NetWare and at the SYSCON, Available Topics menu, highlighted on User Information.

Hands-On Exercises

Highlighted on User Information in SYSCON'S Available Topics Menu, press ⏎Enter⏎ to locate your new, xxxUSER, username in the list of users and press ⏎Enter⏎ again. From User Information window for your new xxxUSER from Exercise 5.1,

Trustee Directory Assignment
The rights which a user or group trustee rights have been granted. The trustee rights are extended to each subdirectory of the directory structure location where they are granted, unless they are changed in a subsequent subdirectory.

1. **Type** *TR* to move to Trustee Directory Assignments

   Press ⏎Enter⏎

At the Trustee Directory Assignments window,

   Press ⏎Ins⏎

For the Directory in Which Trustee Should be Added pop-up window,

   Press ⏎Ins⏎

Your screen shows the list of servers on your network.
   From the list of servers shown in the File Servers window,

2. **Move** the highlight bar to the file server name from the list of file servers that matches the file server name on the second line of SYSCON's menu banner.

   Press ⏎Enter⏎ (highlighted on your file server name)

From the Volumes window,

   Type *SYS*

   Press ⏎Enter⏎ (highlighted on SYS)

At NetWork Directories window,

> **Type** *USERS*
>
> **Press** ⌷Enter⌷ (highlighted on USERS)

At NetWork Directories window showing subdirectories of USERS,

> **Type** *NEWUSER*
>
> **Press** ⌷Enter⌷ (highlighted on NEWUSER)

At NetWork Directories window showing subdirectories of NEWUSER,

> **Press** ⌷Esc⌷

Your directory path showing in the Directory in Which Trustee Should Be Added window displays your server name followed by /SYS:USERS/NEWUSER and then, with the directory path showing your server name followed by /SYS:USERS/NEWUSER,

> 3. **Press** ⌷Enter⌷

Back at Trustee Directory Assignments window, the SYS:USERS\NEWUSER directory location has been added and automatically given the default rights of Read and File Scan.

Highlighted on SYS:USERS\NEWUSER in the Trustee Directory Assignments window, to increase the directory rights,

> 4. **Press** ⌷Enter⌷

For the Trustee Rights Granted window,

> **Press** ⌷Ins⌷

From the Trustee Rights Not Granted window,

> **Type** *C* to highlight Create
>
> **Press** ⌷F5⌷ to mark Create
>
> **Type** *E* to highlight Erase
>
> **Press** ⌷F5⌷ to also mark Erase
>
> **Press** ⌷Enter⌷

Your screen should look similar to Figure 5.7.

Both Create and Erase have been added to Read and File Scan in the Trustee Rights Granted window.

To add these rights to the directory assignments,

> 5. **Press** ⌷Esc⌷

Back at Trustee Directory Assignments, you see the addition of the C and E, or Create and Erase rights added to the R and F or Read and File Scan rights.

FIGURE 5.7

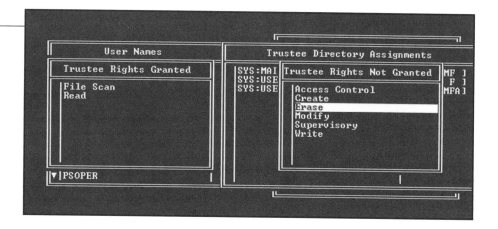

To exit SYSCON,

    6. **Press** [Alt] [F10] and then highlighted on *Yes*, press [Enter] in the exit
       SYSCON pop-up window.

KEY RELATED POINTS

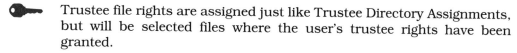

Trustee file rights are assigned just like Trustee Directory Assignments, but will be selected files where the user's trustee rights have been granted.

Trustee Directory Assignments can also be viewed or changed in FILER. From FILER's Current Directory Information, the Directory Information screen will show Trustees:, highlight that field and press [Enter]. Highlighting the Trustee Name and pressing [Enter] shows the Trustee Rights window. In the Trustee Rights window you can press Ins to highlight and add rights from the Other Rights window. From FILER's Directory Information screen, the IRM shows you the inherited rights where you can change them.

5.6 ESTABLISHING THE INHERITED RIGHTS MASK IN FILER

SYSCON is used for managing users and FILER is used for managing directories and files. In this exercise, you hold the Supervisory directory right in the NEWUSER directory structure, and you can see that access to change the directory structure and subsequent subdirectories is now available in FILER.

Hands-On Exercises

From F:\USERS\NEWUSER\xxxUSER> (where xxx is replaced with your initials) directory prompt,

   1. **Type** *COPY \PUBLIC*.DAT*

    Press [Enter]

You have copied all the .DAT files from the Public directory to work with assigning trustee file assignments in this exercise.
To verify copying,

   2. **Type** *NDIR*

    Press [Enter]

You notice from the listing that these files are flagged Rw (Read-write) and A (Archive).
To begin working with FILER,

   3. **Type** *FILER*

    Press [Enter]

From FILER's Available Topics menu,

    Press [Enter] (highlighted on Current Directory Information)

You see the IRM is allowing all rights for the SYS:USERS\ NEWUSER\xxxUSER directory location.
To switch directory locations,

   4. **Press** [Esc] (from Directory Information for xxxUSER screen)

    Type *S* to move the highlight to Select Current Directory

    Press [Enter]

From the Current Directory Path window,

    Press [Backspace] to remove \xxxUSER

From the Current Directory Path window, now showing your file server name followed by /SYS:USERS\NEWUSER,

   5. **Press** [Enter]

You are back at Available Topics, with your file server name followed by /SYS:USERS\NEWUSER showing in FILER's menu banner.
To change the IRM for this directory location,

   6. **Type** *C* to move to Current Directory Information

    Press [Enter]

FIGURE 5.8

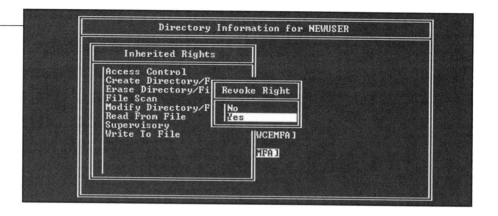

Move highlight bar to Inherited Rights Mask: option

Press Enter (highlighted in the field for Inherited Rights Mask:)

You are now at the Inherited Rights window.
At the Inherited Rights window, highlighted on Access Control,

Press Ins

7. **Type** *M* to highlight Modify Directory/File

Press F5 to mark Modify Directory/File

Press Enter

To revoke a right,

Type *M* to highlight Modify Directory/File

Press Del

Your screen should resemble Figure 5.8.
From the Revoke Right window, highlighted on Yes,

Press Enter (highlighted on Yes)

Press Esc

Back at the Directory Information for NEWUSER directory, you see that Modify (M) has been removed from the rights for this directory. Highlighted on Inherited Rights Mask: showing [SRWCE FA],

8. **Press** ↓ to move to Trustees:

Press Enter (highlighted on Trustees:)

You see your xxxUSER from Exercise 5.5 has RCEF rights. You added the C and E rights in Exercise 5.5, Step 4, and see the change for xxxUSER show up in FILER.

To change the trustee rights assignment for your xxxUSER in the USERS\NEWUSER directory location,

> 9. **Move** the highlight bar to xxxUSER
>
> **Press** Enter

From the Trustee Rights window,

> **Type** *E* to move to Erase Directory/File
>
> **Press** Del

Your screen may resemble Figure 5.9.
From Revoke Right window, highlighted on *Yes*,

> **Press** Enter (highlighted on *Yes*)

Back at the Trustee Rights window, you see the Erase Directory/File right has been removed.

To save your changes, from the Trustee Rights window, showing Create Directory File, File Scan, and Read From File,

> 10. **Press** Esc

Back at the Trustee Name listing, you see that the rights for your xxxUSER are now Read (R), Create (C), and File Scan (F).

> 11. To exit FILER,
>
> **Press** Alt F10

Go to SYSCON and check the xxxUSER's Trustee Directory Assignments from the User Information menu to view the changes. Trustee Rights changed in FILER will be shown in SYSCON.

FIGURE 5.9

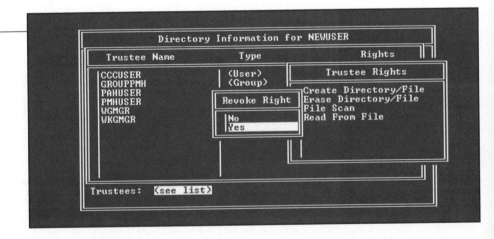

5.7 LOGGING IN AS XXXUSER—VIEWING ESTABLISHED RIGHTS

In this exercise, you will log in as your xxxUSER to view the rights you set for this user and experience what a new user experiences when they log in the first time.

Hands-On Exercises

At the F:\LOGIN> directory prompt,

> 1. **Type** *LOGIN xxxUSER* (replace xxx with your initials or the user account you created in exercise 5.1)
>
> **Press** Enter

NetWare allows the first log in, but wants the user to change their password by placing the message listed on your screen:

> *"Password for user xxxUSER on server _____ has expired.*
>   *You have 6 grace login(s) left to change your password.*
> *Would you like to change your password? (Y/N) Y"*

Refer to Figure 5.10.

***NOTE:* Though you changed the password for the xxxUSER account in Exercise 5.3, NetWare now wants the password changed when the account is activated.**

With the question posed to change your password showing on screen, and the default NetWare given for this response as Yes, and with the Y prompt showing,

> 2. **Press** Enter to accept Y for Change Password prompt

NetWare responds with the Enter your new password: prompt.
    At the Enter your new password: prompt,

> 3. **Type** (a password you will remember for the xxxUSER)
>
> **Press** Enter

At the Retype your new password: prompt,

> **Type** (the password typed previously)
>
> **Press** Enter

You are now at the F:\> prompt.
    From the F:\> prompt, to move to the xxxUSER HOME directory,

> 4. **Type** *CD \USERS\NEWUSER\xxxUSER* (replace xxx with your initials)
>
> **Press** Enter

You are at the F:\USERS\NEWUSER\xxxUSER> prompt.
From the F:\USERS\NEWUSER\xxxUSER> prompt,

> 5. **Type** *RIGHTS*
>
>   **Press** [Enter]

You see the effective directory rights listed.
To check the rights from the NEWUSER directory,

> 6. **Type** *CD ..*
>
>   **Press** [Enter]

You are at the F:\USERS\NEWUSER> prompt.
From the \USERS\NEWUSER directory prompt,

> 7. **Type** *RIGHTS*
>
>   **Press** [Enter]

TLIST . GROUPS
Used to view the trustee rights granted at a specific directory location resulting from Group membership.

You see that the trustee rights you placed at this directory location from Exercise 5.6 are in effect.
To verify whether user or group trustee rights are activated,

> 8. **Type** *TLIST . GROUPS*
>
>   **Press** [Enter]

TLIST . USERS
Used to view the trustee rights granted at a specific directory location resulting from User assignment.

NetWare provides no listing for the NEWUSER directory for a group trustee rights assignment.

> 9. **Type** *TLIST . USERS*
>
>   **Press** [Enter]

FIGURE 5.10

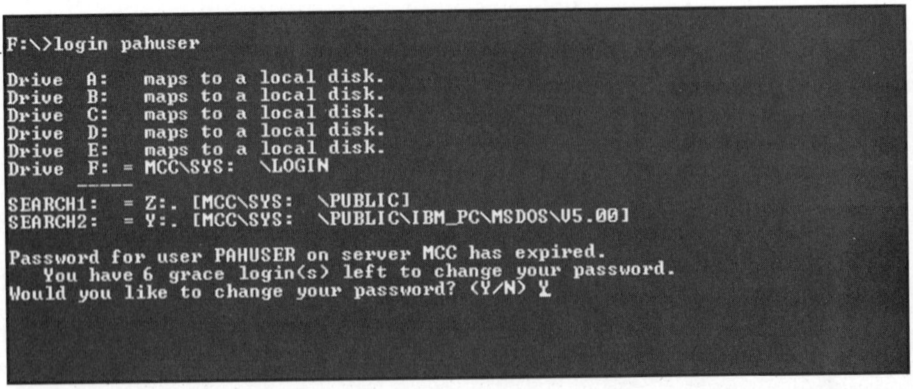

```
F:\>login pahuser

Drive  A:      maps to a local disk.
Drive  B:      maps to a local disk.
Drive  C:      maps to a local disk.
Drive  D:      maps to a local disk.
Drive  E:      maps to a local disk.
Drive  F: = MCC\SYS:   \LOGIN

SEARCH1:  = Z:. [MCC\SYS:   \PUBLIC]
SEARCH2:  = Y:. [MCC\SYS:   \PUBLIC\IBM_PC\MSDOS\V5.00]

Password for user PAHUSER on server MCC has expired.
    You have 6 grace login(s) left to change your password.
Would you like to change your password? (Y/N) Y
```

FIGURE 5.11

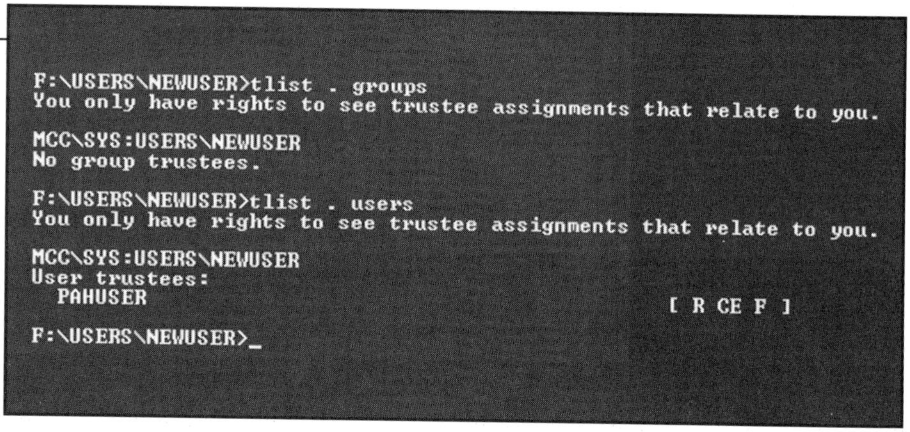

```
F:\USERS\NEWUSER>tlist . groups
You only have rights to see trustee assignments that relate to you.

MCC\SYS:USERS\NEWUSER
No group trustees.

F:\USERS\NEWUSER>tlist . users
You only have rights to see trustee assignments that relate to you.

MCC\SYS:USERS\NEWUSER
User trustees:
   PAHUSER                                                  [ R CE F ]

F:\USERS\NEWUSER>_
```

You can see that the trustee rights granted at this specific location in the directory structure equal the effective rights. Refer to Figure 5.11.

To check all your rights, logged in as xxxUSER,

   10. **Type** *WHOAMI /A*

       Press Enter

All rights you have established for your xxxUSER are listed on your screen. Your user as well as group security equivalency should be listed on your screen.

KEY RELATED POINTS

🔑 NetWare wants the password changed when the account is activated. Grace LOGINS were changed from six to seven for this user, so Netware uses one Grace LOGIN the first time the account is activated. If the log ins continue, and the password is not changed within the Grace LOGIN remaining, NetWare will disable LOGINS. NetWare does not require passwords unless the Supervisor has authorized passwords as such. Even though the account password is set when the account is created, when the user activates the account and logs in under their username, the password needs to be set again.

🔑 For any trustee rights granted at a specific location within the directory structure, the trustee rights assignment equals the effective rights.

END OF CHAPTER REVIEW

Important Terms

Disk Restrictions   TLIST . USERS
Station Restrictions   Trustee Directory Assignment
Time Restrictions   Workgroup Manager
TLIST . GROUPS

True/False Questions

1. Limit Password is the account restriction that keeps track of a user's most recently used passwords to prevent reuse.

2. The account restriction which prevents a user from logging in from more than one workstation is Limit Grace Logins.

3. The command-line utility used for obtaining a station's node and network address is USERLIST/A.

4. The Volume/Disk Restriction option controls the amount of space a user has available in Kbytes.

5. Where trustee rights are granted for a specific directory location, trustee rights equal effective rights.

6. Passwords set upon account creation do not need to be changed when the user first utilizes their new username account to log in.

7. When a log in time restriction is enforced, NetWare uses one-hour increments to block and disable LOGINs.

8. Supervisory rights on a directory allow full privileges over that portion of the directory structure where granted.

9. Passwords are required with NetWare.

10. Workgroup managers can create other workgroup managers.

ON YOUR OWN—HANDS-ON

1. Upon creating a new user, write the default setting for your system in the Default column beside each Account Restriction listed below. (The default settings for your system will be shown when you create a new user.) For those restrictions which are changed from the NetWare Default, write these settings in the NW Default column.

DEFAULT USER ACCOUNT RESTRICTIONS

Account Restrictions for User _____

	Default	NW Default
Account Disabled:	___	___
Account Has Expiration Date:	___	___
Date Account Expires:	___	___
Limit Concurrent Connections:	___	___
Maximum Connections:	___	___
Allow User to Change Password:	___	___
Require Password:	___	___
Minimum Password Length:	___	___
Force Periodic Password Changes:	___	___
Days Between Forced Changes:	___	___
Date Password Expires:	___	___
Limit Grace Logins:	___	___
Grace Logins Allowed:	___	___
Remaining Grace Logins:	___	___
Require Unique Passwords:	___	___

2. A. Use SYSCON to create USER1xxx (where xxx is replaced with your initials). For their home directory, use USERS/ NEWUSER/USER1xxx for the directory path.
    B. Create a new group, GROUPxxx (where xxx is replaced with your initials). Add USER1xxx to GROUPxxx.
    C. Make a directory under USERS/NEWUSER using the name DIRxxx.
    D. Give USER1xxx the Manager status for GROUPxxx.
    E. Give your USER1xxx account supervisory trustee directory rights to the USERS/NEWUSER/DIRxxx directory location.
    F. Create another user, USER2xxx. For their home directory, use USERS/NEWUSER/USER2xxx. Place USER2xxx as a member of your GROUPxxx group.
    G. For the USER1xxx account, make them a Manager of your GROUPxxx group. Place the USER2xxx account as a Managed User for the GROUPxxx group.
    H. Make both USER1xxx and USER2xxx members of the NEWUSERS group.
    I. Give the GROUPxxx group the Trustee Directory Assignment of Read (R) and File Scan (F) for the USERS/NEWUSER directory location.
    J. Use FILER to set the Options for the USERS/NEWUSER/DIRxxx directory to Confirm Deletions and Confirm File Copies.
    K. Log in as USER1xxx.

IN YOUR OWN WORDS

1. Describe the difference between a Workgroup Manager and a User Account Manager.

2. Envision one separate circumstance for each of the account restrictions that you feel would demand changing from NetWare's default setting. On a separate piece of paper, write the circumstance and the setting change you feel appropriate to fit the circumstance.

3. For the MicroView company's wordprocessing group, provide account restrictions appropriate for an 8–5 work week. For the username designated as Workgroup Manager from Chapter 4, designate the username(s) accounts which assist this individual. List the User Account responsibilities and suggested changes to account restrictions for these individuals.

Working with Network Printing

OBJECTIVES

- Establish network printing using CAPTURE.

- Control print jobs with PCONSOLE.

- Manipulate print jobs in print queues.

- Delete print job entries using PCONSOLE.

CHAPTER INTRODUCTION

NetWare printing is a process, with the print queue at the heart of the process. Think of the queue as where the print jobs are collected and held prior to being printed. Print jobs are sent to print queues rather than sent directly to the network printer(s). The print queue is actually allocated directory space on the file server's hard disk. There is a numbered directory, corresponding to the print queue's ID number, under the SYS:SYSTEM directory. This is the exact location where the queue holds and services the print jobs prior to being printed.

PCONSOLE is NetWare's menu utility that is used to set up the print server and print queue, control network printing, and display information about network printing.

CAPTURE

NetWare's command-line printing utility used to re-route your print jobs to a specified print queue.

CAPTURE is NetWare's command-line utility designed to capture your printer port and re-route your print jobs to a specified print queue. CAPTURE controls either printing from applications or printing from screen. The CAPTURE command has many option settings to configure the print job. In this chapter you will use CAPTURE and some of these other options.

NPRINT is NetWare's command-line utility for printing outside of an application and is equal to the DOS PRINT command. NPRINT is designed to send *text files* to be printed from the command-line. Like capture, NPRINT has many options to choose from to configure your print job. You will work with some of these options in this chapter.

ENDCAP

Used to re-route printing to LPT1, reassigning the captured network printer for LPT1. ENDCAP must be used when CAPTURE's NoAutoendcap option is chosen.

ENDCAP re-routes your printer port to the printer attached directly to the workstation. The default for ENDCAP is LPT1, but other LPT ports can be specified if the local workstation has been configured for printer ports other than LPT1. ENDCAP does not send print jobs to a print queue, but rather, directly to the workstation's locally attached printer.

6.1 GETTING STARTED WITH CAPTURE

In this exercise you will use NetWare's PCONSOLE to learn about print queues. You will first use CAPTURE to re-route your print jobs to the PQ1 print queue.

This exercise assumes that PQ1 has already been set up for your use.

This exercise also assumes that you are already logged in to NetWare and at the F:\LOGIN> prompt.

Once you are logged in and at the F:\LOGIN> prompt,

Hands-On Exercise

To capture the PQ1 print queue,

> 1. **Type** *CAPTURE Q=PQ1*
>
> **Press** Enter

NetWare displays *"Device LPT1: re-routed to queue PQ1 on server your server name."*

To verify the change,

CAPTURE SH
CAPTURE SHow is
used to list the
current status of
your LPT ports and
how they are
configured if
captured.

> 2. **Type** *CAPTURE SH*
>
> **Press** Enter

Your screen shows that LPT1 is captured to PQ1 print queue, and lists the default capture settings for LPT1.

To re-route printing to your locally attached printer,

> 3. **Type** *ENDCAP*
>
> **Press** Enter

Your screen displays, *"Device LPT1: set to local mode,"* which means that no network printers are currently being used for LPT1.

To view the changes,

> 4. **Type** *CAPTURE SH*
>
> **Press** Enter

The assignment for LPT1, LPT2, and LPT3 is displayed on your screen, with *"Capturing is Not Currently Active"* shown after each listing. The CAPTURE SHow command is used to list the status of your LPT ports, and how the ports are configured.

To capture your printing again,

> 5. **Type** *CAPTURE QUEUE=PQ1 L=2*
>
> **Press** Enter

Your screen displays that your CAPTURE command was accepted and printing is now re-routed for LPT2 to print queue PQ1. With NetWare's CAPTURE options, you can either spell the option out or use the abbreviated form. In this example you spelled out queue, rather than use the appreviated version, Q, as before. You can also specify which LPT port by using the letter L followed by the equal sign and then the number of the LPT port (such as L=2).

NOTE: **CAPTURE's option commands are not case sensitive, so upper or lower case letters will work. The uppercase letter L is used here to add definition to the character and distinquish it from the number 1.**

To view your changes,

    6. **Type** *CAPTURE SH*

       Press [Enter]

Your screen displays that network printing has been established for LPT2, serviced by print queue PQ1. Refer to Figure 6.1.

NOTE: **If LPT2 were not established in the application or at the command, using ENDCAP by itself will not terminate captured printing for LPT2. To terminate network printing for LPT2,**

    7. **Type** *ENDCAP L=2*

       Press [Enter]

Your screen displays, *"Device LPT2: set to local mode."* Use CAPTURE SH to view your changes.

COMMAND CONVENTIONS USED IN EXERCISE 6.1

Command	Option	Description
CAPTURE	Q= or QUEUE=	Specifies a network printing queue to send print jobs to. Assumes LPT1 unless otherwise specified.
CAPTURE	L= or LPT=	Used to specify which LPT port, other than the default of LPT1, will be re-routed for network printing. Must be used in conjunction with Q=, to re-route to a print queue.
CAPTURE	Q= or QUEUE=	Used to establish network printing, specifying which print queue to send your print jobs to for servicing.
CAPTURE	SH or SHOW	To view the configuration for network printing.
ENDCAP	L= or LPT=	Used to specify which LPT port will no longer be serviced by a network print queue.

FIGURE 6.1

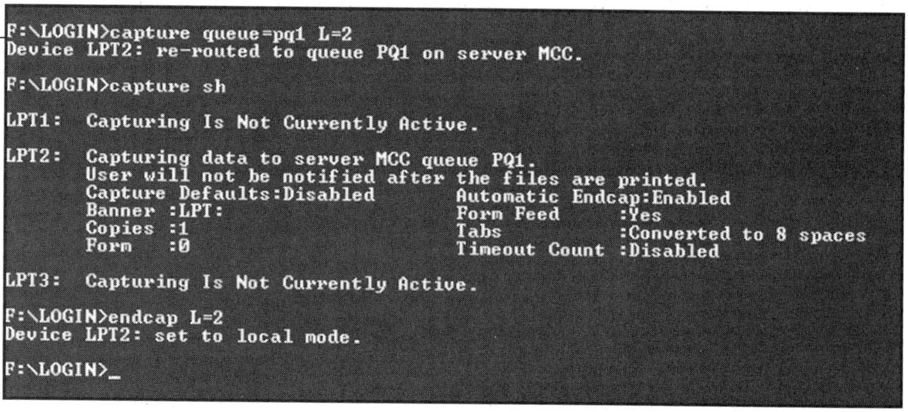

```
F:\LOGIN>capture queue=pq1 L=2
Device LPT2: re-routed to queue PQ1 on server MCC.

F:\LOGIN>capture sh

LPT1:  Capturing Is Not Currently Active.

LPT2:  Capturing data to server MCC queue PQ1.
       User will not be notified after the files are printed.
       Capture Defaults:Disabled        Automatic Endcap:Enabled
       Banner :LPT:                     Form Feed        :Yes
       Copies :1                        Tabs             :Converted to 8 spaces
       Form   :0                        Timeout Count :Disabled

LPT3:  Capturing Is Not Currently Active.

F:\LOGIN>endcap L=2
Device LPT2: set to local mode.

F:\LOGIN>_
```

KEY RELATED POINTS

- Using CAPTURE re-routes your print jobs to a network queue.

- Unless otherwise specified, the default port for CAPTURE is LPT1.

- Use CAPTURE L=n (CAPTURE command followed by L=*number* of LPT port) to specify an LPT port other than the default, LPT1 (e.g., CAPTURE L=2). In this example, LPT2 would be captured.

- Unless otherwise specified, ENDCAP terminates captured printers for LPT1.

- Use ENDCAP L=n (ENDCAP command followed by L=*number* of LPT port) to specify an LPT port other than the default, LPT1 (e.g., ENDCAP L=2). In this example, LPT2 would no longer be serviced by a network print queue.

6.2 CONTROLLING NETWORK PRINTING WITH PCONSOLE

PCONSOLE
Menu utility for controlling network printing.

PCONSOLE is NetWare's menu utility to control network printing. In this exercise you will use the CAPTURE command and explore the PCONSOLE menu utility for controlling printing. The NoAutoendcap option is used with CAPTURE to let you control and work with your print job entries in PCONSOLE.

This exercise assumes you are already logged in to NetWare and moved from the F:\LOGIN> prompt to F:\USERS\HOME\your home directory> prompt.

This exercise also assumes that PQ1 has already been set up for your use.

Hands-On Exercise

Once you are logged in and at the F:\USERS\HOME\your home directory> prompt,

    1. **Type** *CAPTURE Q=PQ1 NA*

    Press Enter

Your screen displays *"Automatic ENDCAP has been Disabled"* and that LPT1 is captured to PQ1 on your server. Disabling automatic END-CAP will allow you to work with your print job entries in PCONSOLE.
    To create a print job entry,

    2. **Type** *ECHO This is a great day for printing! > LPT1*

    Press Enter

You should return to your home directory prompt. You have disabled output to LPT1 with CAPTURE's NoAutoendcap (NA) option and are ready to work with PCONSOLE.
    To begin working with PCONSOLE,

    3. **Type** *PCONSOLE*

    Press Enter

You should be at the Available Options menu of PCONSOLE.
    To view information about your print job, first select the Print Queue Information option from PCONSOLE's Available Options menu.

    4. **Type** *P* to move your highlight bar to Print Queue Information

    Press Enter

You are now at the Print Queues pop-up window, which lists the print queues on your file server.
    To select PQ1,

    5. **Type** *PQ1* to move your highlight bar to PQ1

    Press Enter

Your screen displays the Print Queue Information pop-up window and you are highlighted on Current Print Job Entries.
    While highlighted on Current Print Job Entries,

    6. **Press** Enter

Your screen displays PCONSOLE print job entries screen, and you are highlighted on your print job. Notice that the Status column near the right of your screen displays *"Adding."* The Adding condition specifies a print job that is still in the process of being sent by the user.

FIGURE 6.2

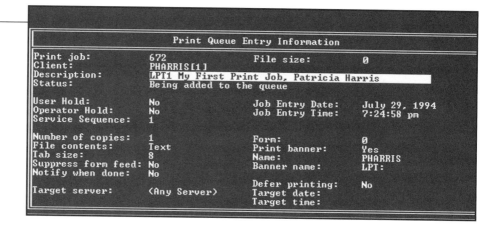

Although you have sent your job, Adding is waiting for you to issue ENDCAP to force the Status column to Ready so the queue can send your print job to a network printer. For now, you can think of your print job as being placed on hold.

Highlighted on your print job entry,

7. **Press** Enter

Your screen displays the Print Queue Entry Information screen and you are highlighted on Description: LPT1 Catch. The Description field either shows the filename or LPT*n* Catch, depending upon how the print job was submitted. This is a changeable field, and can be used for adding comments.

To add a comment to the Description field,

8. **Press** Enter

With your cursor blinking in the Description field,

Press ←Backspace five times to erase the word, *Catch*, and then

Type *My First Print Job*, (type your first and last name here)

Your screen displays LPT1 followed by My First Print Job, and your first and last name. You are highlighted after the last character in your last name. Refer to Figure 6.2.

With your cursor blinking after the last letter in your last name, to leave the Print Queue Entry Information screen and view your changes,

9. **Press** Esc to enter your typed entry

Press Esc to return to the listing of your print job

Your screen displays your new description. Refer to Figure 6.3.

FIGURE 6.3

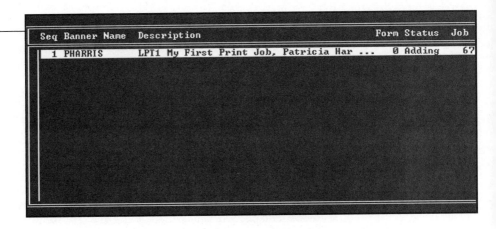

Seq Banner Name	Description	Form Status	Job
1 PHARRIS	LPT1 My First Print Job, Patricia Har ...	0 Adding	67

PRINT QUEUE ENTRY INFORMATION SCREEN

Left Screen Specifications:

Type*	Item	Description
V	Print Job	Lists the arbitrary job number NetWare assigns.
V	Client	LOGIN name.
C	Description	Changeable comment field.
V	Status	Lists a designation describing the print job's situation. Status could be listed as Adding, Active, Ready, Held, or Waiting for the Queue Entry screen. Refer to the table on page 198.
C	User Hold	Used to hold the job in the queue until taken off hold by the user, where field displays No.
P	Operator Hold	Used to hold the job in the queue until taken off hold by the Queue Operator, where field displays No.
P	Service Sequence	Queue Operator changes the order in which the job is serviced by the printer.
C	Number of copies	Value indicates the number of copies to be printed.
C	File contents	Based upon Tabs/No Tabs option specified in CAPTURE or NPRINT. Tabs indicates Text, whereas No Tabs indicates Byte Stream. Field choices are either Byte Stream or Text. Byte stream is used for applicaton printing.

Type*	Item	Description
C	Tab size	Value represents the number of spaces NetWare will recognize when a Tab character is encountered. Available only when File Contents field displays Text option.
C	Suppress form feed	Answer Yes/No to whether you want the printer to automatically advance a sheet of paper at the end of the print job.
C	Notify when done	Answer Yes/No to whether or not the Client (user) is notified when the job has finished printing.
C	Target server	Lists which valid Target Print Server to send the print job.

Right Screen Specifications:

V	File size	Lists the size of the file in number of bytes.
V	Job Entry Date	Lists the date the job entered the queue.
V	Job Entry Time	Lists the time the job entered the queue.
C	Form	Lists the number of the form established in PRINTDEF, one of NetWare's printing configuration menu utilities.
C	Print banner	Yes/No option to indicate whether a Banner page will print.
C	Name	Shows the LOGIN name of the print job's submitter. Prints field contents in large type on the Banner page, in the middle section of the Banner.
C	Banner name	Prints field contents in large type on the Banner page, in the last section of the banner. Specified in NPRINT or CAPTURE. The LST: output indicates a CAPTURE submission, a filename output indicates an NPRINT submission.
C	Defer printing	Answer Yes/No to whether you want a later time and/or date specified to delay printing.
C	Target date	If defer printing set to Yes, this is the date for printing.
C	Target time	If defer printing set to Yes, this is the time for printing.

*Type field categories:
C—User or Print Queue Operator can **C**hange
V—This field is **V**iew only
P—**P**rint Queue Operator or Supervisor must change

To exit PCONSOLE,

10. **Press** Alt F10

   Press Enter (highlighted on *Yes to exit PConsole*)

To allow the queue to send your job to the printer, from your home directory prompt,

11. **Type** *ENDCAP*

   Press Enter

NetWare confirms that LPT1 is set to local mode.

12. Go over to the printer and pick up your print-out. You will easily find your printout from the Banner page listing *your name* after Description: at the top of the first Banner page. Your actual output will be on the second page.

PCONSOLE'S STATUS FIELD ENTRIES

Print Queue Information Screen	Print Queue Entry Information Screen
Status Field	*Status Field*
Active	Being serviced by print server *server name*
Adding	Being added to the queue
Ready	Ready to be serviced, waiting for server
Held	Operator hold on job
Held	User hold on job
Waiting	Waiting for target execution date & time

6.3 INSERTING PRINT JOBS INTO THE QUEUE—CONTROLLING ENTRIES

In this exercise you will insert a text file, TESTIT.BAT, located in your home directory to PQ1's print job listings by using the Current Print Job Entries screen. Once the job is submitted to the queue, by displaying the configuration options in the Print Queue Entry Information screen, you then make a change which affects the Status field. Through working with print job entries in this exercise, you will learn more about controlling print jobs entries.

   This exercise assumes you are already logged in to NetWare and moved from the F:\LOGIN> prompt to F:\USERS\HOME\your home directory> prompt.

This exercise also assumes that PQ1 has already been set up for your use. Once logged in, from your F:\USERS\HOME\your home directory> prompt it is assumed you have typed PCONSOLE to begin working with NetWare's PCONSOLE menu utility.

Hands-On Exercise

After accessing PCONSOLE from your F:\USERS\HOME\your home directory prompt, at PCONSOLE's Available Options menu,

   1. **Type** *P* to move the highlight bar to Print Queue Information

      Press Enter

This displays the Print Queues pop-up window.

   2. **Type** *PQ1* to move your highlight bar to PQ1

      Press Enter

Your screen displays the Print Queue Information pop-up window and you are highlighted on Current Print Job Entries.
While highlighted on Current Print Job Entries menu selection,

   3. **Press** Enter

Your screen displays PCONSOLE's Current Print Job Entries screen, or those print jobs waiting to be printed in the print queue.
To insert a text file into the print queue,

   4. **Press** Ins

Your home directory path shows in the Select Directory to Print From. You could use the backspace and retype the entry to show your home directory path if needed.
With your home directory path USERS\HOME\YOUR DIRECTORY showing,

   5. **Press** Enter

The Available Files pop-up window appears.
To select the TESTIT.BAT file,

   6. **Type** *TESTIT.BAT* to move your highlight bar to this entry

      Press Enter

Your screen displays the Print Job Configurations pop-up window, highlighted on (PConsole Defaults). Refer to Figure 6.4.
While highlighted on (PConsole Defaults),

   7. **Press** Enter

Your screen displays the *"New Print Job TO BE Submitted"* screen. You haven't entered the job into the print queue yet, so
With your highlight bar on Description,

8. **Press** [Enter]

   Type *by* (type your first and last name)

The Description: field now reads TESTIT.BAT followed by your first and last names. With your cursor blinking after the last letter in your last name,

   Press [Enter]

This will move your active field to User Hold.
To put the job on hold so you can work with it,

9. **Type** Y while your highlight bar is on User Hold:

Refer to Figure 6.5.
To save your changes,

   Press [Esc] twice to bring up Save Changes pop-up window

   Press [Enter] (highlighted on Yes to Save Changes)

The print job entries screen is showing on your monitor. You are highlighted on your new print job entry, showing Held in the Status column.
While highlighted on your print job entry,

10. **Press** [Enter]

The Print Queue Entry Information screen is displayed, showing the settings you selected when this print job entry was saved. Notice NetWare added a print job number and file size. For the fields you can

FIGURE 6.4

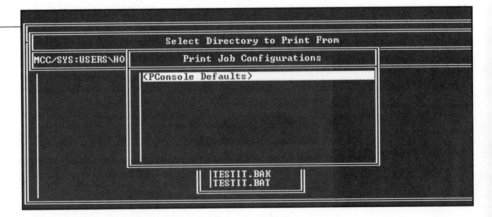

FIGURE 6.5

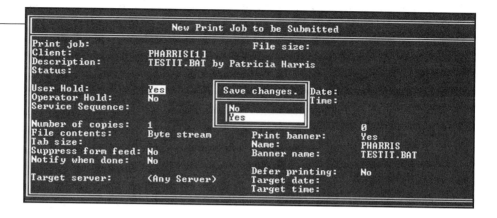

access, you could alter these field entries now, but you will work with altering these in the next exercise.

    11. **Press** ⬇ until highlighted in the User Hold Field

       Type *N* to switch User Hold from Yes to No.

The status field will switch to display User Hold on Job. You're holding this job to work with it prior to printing it in Exercise 6.4.

Exit PCONSOLE or press Esc twice to remain highlighted on your new print job in the Current Print Job Entries screen.

To exit PCONSOLE, if you are not going on to the next exercise,

    12. **Press** Alt F10 to go to the command-line and log out.

6.4 WORKING WITH PRINT JOBS HELD IN THE QUEUE— CONTROLLING ENTRIES

In this exercise, you will work with controlling the print job entry created in Exercise 6.3. You will also make some alterations to the entry which will show up on on the Banner page when this job is printed.

This exercise assumes you are already logged in to NetWare and moved from the F:\LOGIN> prompt to F:\USERS\HOME\your home directory> prompt. This exercise also assumes that you have completed Exercise 6.3.

Once logged in, from your F:\USERS\HOME\your home directory> prompt it is assumed you have typed PCONSOLE to begin working with NetWare's PCONSOLE menu utility.

After accessing PCONSOLE from your F:\USERS\HOME\your home directory prompt, then at PCONSOLE's Available Options menu, it is assumed that you have moved to PCONSOLE's Current Print Job

Entries screen and highlighted on the print job with the description showing TESTIT.BAT (followed by your first and last name).

Hands-On Exercise

With your highlight bar on your TESTIT.BAT print job entry in PCONSOLE's Current Print Job Entries,

    1. **Press** (Enter) (highlighted on your TESTIT.BAT listing)

Your screen displays PCONSOLE's Print Queue Entry Information screen and you are highlighted on the Description field.
To move the highlight bar to Defer printing:,

    2. **Press** ⬇ six times

    Press ➡ once

Your highlight bar moved to the Defer printing: field.
To activate deferred printing,

    3. **Type** Y

    Press (Enter)

Your highlight bar moved to the Target date: field.
To change the target date to the date of Christmas,

    4. **Press** (Enter) highlighted in the Target Date field

    Press (←Backspace) until the field is blank

    Type December 25

    Press (Enter)

You are highlighted on Target time: and it is showing *"2 a.m."* This is the default time NetWare places in this field when you select Yes to activate deferred printing.
To change the time to something a bit more reasonable,

    5. **Press** (Enter) highlighted in the Target Time field

    Press (←Backspace) until the field is blank

    Type *4 P*

    Press (Enter)

Your screen displays *"4:00:00 pm"* for the target time field.
To take the print job off hold,

    6. Use your arrow keys to move the highlight bar to the User Hold field and then,

FIGURE 6.6

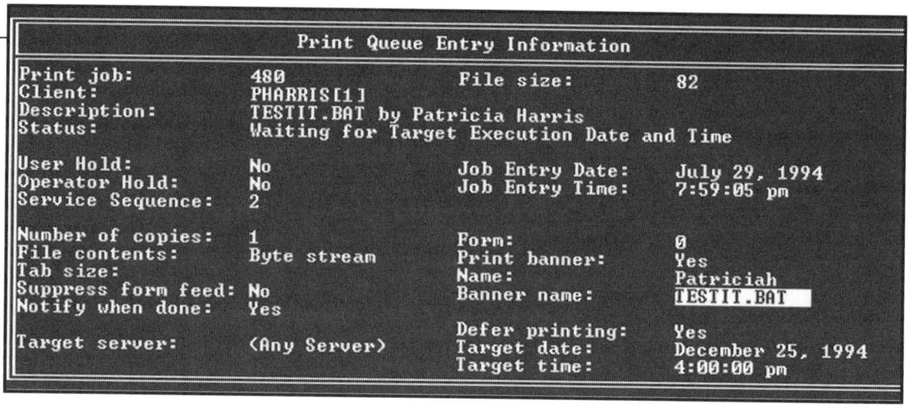

```
╔═══════════════════════════════════════════════════════════════════╗
║                  Print Queue Entry Information                      ║
║ Print job:         480           File size:        82               ║
║ Client:            PHARRIS[1]                                       ║
║ Description:       TESTIT.BAT by Patricia Harris                    ║
║ Status:            Waiting for Target Execution Date and Time       ║
║                                                                     ║
║ User Hold:         No            Job Entry Date:   July 29, 1994    ║
║ Operator Hold:     No            Job Entry Time:   7:59:05 pm       ║
║ Service Sequence:  2                                                ║
║                                                                     ║
║ Number of copies:  1             Form:             0                ║
║ File contents:     Byte stream   Print banner:     Yes              ║
║ Tab size:                        Name:             Patriciah        ║
║ Suppress form feed: No           Banner name:      TESTIT.BAT       ║
║ Notify when done:  Yes                                              ║
║                                  Defer printing:   Yes              ║
║ Target server:     <Any Server>  Target date:      December 25, 1994║
║                                  Target time:      4:00:00 pm       ║
╚═══════════════════════════════════════════════════════════════════╝
```

Type *N* highlighted opposite User Hold:

Press Esc

Your Status field now shows *"Waiting for Target Execution Date and Time."*

To Notify you when your printout is ready,

7. Move the highlight bar opposite Notify when done:.

Type *Y* to change the field entry to Yes

Press Enter

Your highlight bar moved to to the Form: field.

To change the name on the Banner's print-out,

8. **Press** ↓ twice to move the highlight bar to Name:

Press Enter to activate your cursor in the Name field

Press ←Backspace until the field is blank

Type your first name followed by the first initial of your last name

Press Enter

Refer to Figure 6.6.

To save your changes,

9. **Press** Esc

You are now back at the Current Print Job Entries screen and the Status field shows *"Waiting."* The Banner name shows your first name followed by the first initial of your last name. Refer to Figure 6.7.

To exit PCONSOLE,

10. **Press** Alt F10

FIGURE 6.7

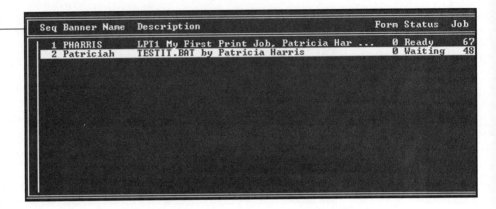

```
Seq Banner Name  Description                          Form Status  Job
  1 PHARRIS      LPT1 My First Print Job, Patricia Har ...  0 Ready    67
  2 Patriciah    TESTIT.BAT by Patricia Harris             0 Waiting   48
```

THE ANATOMY OF A BANNER PAGE

User name:	LOGIN name	Queue: Servername/Queue Name
File name:	FILENAME	Server: Print Server name
Directory:	PATH	
Description: contents of Description field		
Entry Date		Entry Time

Name: Field Contents

Banner name: Field Section

6.5 A BIT OF CAPTURE, PCONSOLE, AND LEARNING TO DELETE PRINT JOBS

In this exercise, you will work with controlling the print job entry you placed on hold in Exercise 6.4. You will also work with sending a print job using CAPTURE and deleting a print job in PCONSOLE.

This exercise assumes you are already logged in to NetWare and at the F:\LOGIN> prompt.

Hands-On Exercise

From the F:\LOGIN> prompt,

1. **Type** *CAPTURE Q=PQ1 NA NB NFF*

   Press Enter

Your screen shows Automatic ENDCAP has been disabled and device LPT1 has been re-routed to PQ1.

To verify your CAPTURE setting,

2. **Type** *CAPTURE SH*

   Press Enter

Your screen displays *"(None)"* for the Banner: option you set in your CAPTURE statement using NB (no banner). The Form Feed option shows No for using NFF (no form feed). Automatic ENDCAP is listed as Disabled since you used NA (NoAutoendcap). If your screen does not show these option settings, repeat Step 1. Refer to Figure 6.8.

To create a print job,

3. **Type** *ECHO This is the best day for Printing! > LPT1*

   Press Enter

You should return to the F:\LOGIN> prompt.

4. Move to your home directory prompt.

   Type *CD\USERS\HOME_____*

   (fill in the blank above with your home directory name)

   Press Enter

Your screen displays F:\USERS\HOME\your home directory> prompt.

At your home directory prompt,

5. **Type** *PCONSOLE*

   Press Enter

   Type *P* to move the highlight bar to Print Queue Information

   Press Enter

   Type *PQ1* to select PQ1

   Press Enter

   Press Enter (highlighted on Current Print Job Entries)

FIGURE 6.8

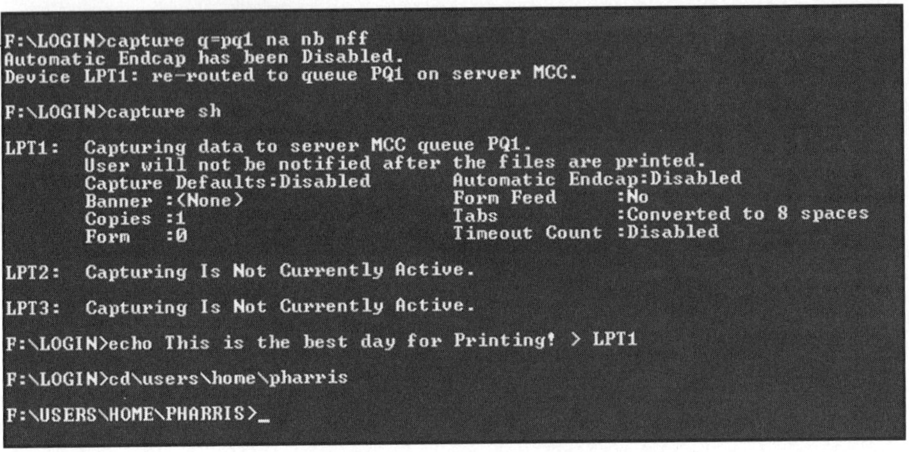

```
F:\LOGIN>capture q=pq1 na nb nff
Automatic Endcap has been Disabled.
Device LPT1: re-routed to queue PQ1 on server MCC.

F:\LOGIN>capture sh

LPT1:   Capturing data to server MCC queue PQ1.
        User will not be notified after the files are printed.
        Capture Defaults:Disabled      Automatic Endcap:Disabled
        Banner :<None>                 Form Feed       :No
        Copies :1                      Tabs            :Converted to 8 spaces
        Form   :0                      Timeout Count :Disabled

LPT2:   Capturing Is Not Currently Active.

LPT3:   Capturing Is Not Currently Active.

F:\LOGIN>echo This is the best day for Printing! > LPT1

F:\LOGIN>cd\users\home\pharris

F:\USERS\HOME\PHARRIS>_
```

Your highlight bar is on the first print job in the list.

6. Move your highlight bar to your print job

You will find it by looking for your first name in the Banner name column, LPT1 Catch in the Description column, and Adding in the Status column. Refer to Figure 6.9.

Once you have found your print job entry in the list and placed the highlight bar on your print job entry,

7. **Press** Enter

Your screen displays the Print Queue Entry Information screen for this print job. Notice the Print banner shows No and the Supress form feed shows Yes. This was from using NB and NFF in Step 1. Refer to Figure 6.10.

To delete this job from the queue,

8. **Press** Esc to get back to the listing of print jobs

While highlighted on your print job,

Press Del

Press Enter (highlighted on *Yes* for Delete Queue Entry window)

Refer to Figure 6.11.

9. To exit PCONSOLE,

Press Alt F10

FIGURE 6.9

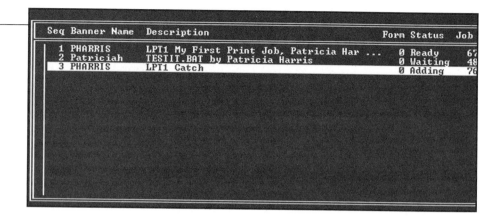

FIGURE 6.10

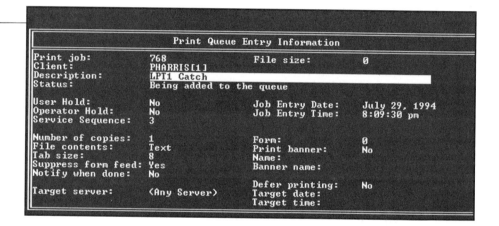

FIGURE 6.11

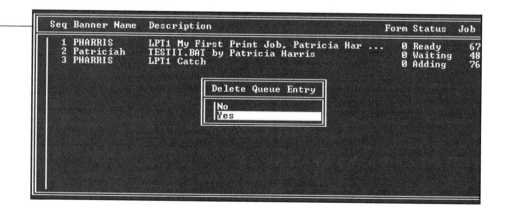

CAPTURE AND NPRINT OPTIONS

CAPTURE	NPRINT	Flag	Default	Description
Y	N	SH	None	SHow current CAPTURE settings
Y	Y	J=	Default	Use print Job configuration established in PRINTCON
Y	Y	Q=	None or Spool 0*	Send print job to a valid print Queue
Y	Y	S=	Default	Send print job to a valid print Server
Y	N	L=	1	Used to specify LPT port (1, 2, or 3.
Y	Y	F=	0	Use a valid Form name or number
Y	N	CR=	None	CReate and send output to a filename
Y	Y	C=	1	Specify number of Copies to print
Y	N	TI=	8	Identify TImeout period before printing
Y	N	A	On	Represents Autoendcap
Y	N	NA	Off	Specifies NoAutoendcap
Y	N	K	Off	Keep or preserve jobs that have been received
Y	Y	T=	8	Specify characters in one Tab stop
Y	Y	NT	Off	No Tabs may need to be used with Byte Stream
Y	Y	B=	LST:	Specify up to 12 characters for a Banner
Y	Y	NB	Off	Omit printing a Banner page
Y	Y	NAM=	Username	Specify up to 12 characters for upper part of Banner page
Y	Y	FF	On	Advance next job to top of next sheet of paper
Y	Y	NFF	Off	Disables Form Feed
Y	Y	NOTI	Off	NOTIfy username when job is done
Y	Y	NNOTI	On	Disable Notify
N	Y	D	No	Delete file after it is printed
Y	Y	/? or ?		List Available Options

6.6 USING NPRINT

NPRINT
NetWare's command-line utility for printing text files.

NPRINT is NetWare's command-line utility for printing text files outside an application, and can be correlated to DOS PRINT command. NPRINT can be used with a wildcard to print several files at once, as with NPRINT *.DAT.

This exercise assumes you are already logged in to NetWare and at your home directory prompt, F:\USERS\HOME\your home directory> prompt.

Hands-On Exercise

To work with NPRINT, from the F:\USERS\HOME\your home directory> prompt,

1. **Type** *NPRINT*

    Press Enter

The options or flags associated with NPRINT are listed on your screen.

To use NPRINT, from the F:\USERS\HOME\your home directory> prompt,

2. **Type** *NPRINT TESTIT.BAT Q=PQ1 NAM=_____ B=_____*
    (fill in the NAM= blank line above with your first name and the B= blank line with as much of your last name as you can fit in the 12 character limitation)

    Press Enter

NetWare responds with *"Queuing data to Server ___, Queue PQ1"* with your server name appearing after the server.

If you look quickly, you can see the print job in PCONSOLE.

3. To start PCONSOLE, select PQ1, and find your print job listed in the Current Print Job Entries screen. Look for the banner with your last name. You may not find it if it has already printed.

4. You can use wildcards with NPRINT to send multiple text files to the printer. At F:\USERS\HOME\your home directory> prompt,

    Type *NCOPY TESTIT.BAT TEST.BAT*

    Press Enter

    Type *NPRINT *.BAT Q=PQ1*

NetWare responds by listing the filenames it sent to the print queue. Refer to Figure 6.12.

FIGURE 6.12

```
F:\USERS\HOME\PHARRIS>nprint *.bat q=pq1
Queuing data to Server MCC, Queue PQ1.
MCC\SYS:USERS\HOME\PHARRIS
        Queuing file TESTIT.BAT
        Queuing file TEST.BAT

F:\USERS\HOME\PHARRIS>_
```

END OF CHAPTER REVIEW

Important Terms

CAPTURE   PCONSOLE
CAPTURE SH   NPRINT
ENDCAP

Multiple Choice

1. For a workstation that has been set up for network printing, where does a print job go before printing?
   A. To the printer.
   B. To the print server.
   C. To the print queue.
   D. To the local printer.

2. Where is the print queue located?
   A. On the printer.
   B. On the file server.
   C. On the print server.
   D. None of the above.

3. Which of the following is an incorrect CAPTURE statement?
   A. CAPTURE l=VOYAGER2 C=O CR=SYS:MYTEST.TXT
   B. CAPTURE S:VOYAGER2 Q=DOT_1 NT NB NFF
   C. CAPTURE NB NAM=MO NFF QU AU MB
   D. All of the above are incorrect.
   E. None of the above are incorrect.

4. Which of the following specifies information that appears in the lower section (panel) of the Banner page?
   A. local
   B. name
   C. banner
   D. job
   E. None of the above.

5. Which of the following specifies information that appears in the upper section (panel) of the Banner page?
   A. local
   B. name
   C. banner
   D. job
   E. None of the above.

6. Which of the following can be combined with ENDCAP?
   A. local
   B. all
   C. cancel
   D. All of the above.
   E. None of the above.

7. Who can delete a print job from a print queue?
   A. The originator of the print job.
   B. The user Supervisor.
   C. The Print Queue Operator.
   D. All of the above
   E. None of the above.

ON YOUR OWN—HANDS-ON

1. From PCONSOLE, view the print servers and print queues on your LAN and draw a map of your network's printing environment, listing:
   A. the names of the print queues and the print servers.
   B. the names of the Print Queue Operators and Print Server Operators.
   C. the printer queues and print servers you can use, either because you belong to a group or are individually assigned.
   D. the currently attached servers.
   E. for the print queues, do any take away the privilege of users placing entries in the queue? If so, list the queue name(s).

2. Check your printing environment.
   When you log in, is default printing assigned? Check your environment with CAPTURE Show.

3. Write CAPTURE statements for the following.
   A. CAPTURE a print server named "Lazy," DOT1 print queue, to notify you when the job has printed, and direct the output to LPT2.

B. CAPTURE to laser queue, with no banner, supress form feed, timeout of 15, and no autoendcap.

C. CAPTURE with a banner name of Charlie, a name of Chan, specify three copies to be printed, queue named "deskjet."

IN YOUR OWN WORDS

1. What does a Print Queue Operator do? Explain their purpose in network printing. How many Print Queue Operators do you think one queue should have?

2. What does a Print Server Operator do? Explain their purpose in network printing. How many Print Server Operators do you think one print server should have?

Setting up
Print Services

OBJECTIVES

- Create a print queue.

- Create a print server.

- Assign a print queue to a print server.

- Assign a printer to a print server.

- Establish remote printing for a workstation.

CHAPTER INTRODUCTION

A print job is either directed to a locally attached printer or to a network printer. A local print job goes directly from the workstation to the locally attached printer, using no network resources. The network print job goes from the workstation to the print queue and then is delivered to the network printer assigned to the print queue.

A print queue is where the print jobs are collected and held prior to being printed. It is a numbered directory, corresponding to the print queue's ID number, under the SYS:SYSTEM directory. This is where the queue holds and services the print jobs prior to being printed.

Print jobs "stand in line" when they reach the print queue to be sent to a network printer. The jobs can be expedited by increasing the priority or can be re-routed to be serviced by other print queues.

The print server is a program which controls the printers and receives jobs from the print queue(s). It does not store the print job, the print queue does this. The print server is not to be thought of so much as a physical device, but more as a logical process.

The print server can exist (1) as a process running on a dedicated workstation using PSERVER.EXE, (2) as a non-dedicated process on top of the NetWare file server using PSERVER.NLM, or (3) as a non-dedicated process on a workstation using RPRINTER.EXE. Each print server can support up to 16 printers and service queues on up to eight file servers.

With RPRINTER.EXE, a printer, directly attached to a user's workstation, can be set up as a network printer. When the local printer is established as a network printer, the print server sends jobs to the printer. A network printer is also known as a remote printer. With NetWare, the network printer can be directly attached to the file server, or attached to where the print server program is running.

PCONSOLE is NetWare's menu utility that is used to create and set up the print server and the print queue, to define printers, control network printing, and to display information about network printing. In this chapter, you will use PCONSOLE to set up network print services.

RPRINTER is a program which runs on the local workstation that allows you to connect a locally attached printer to the network for the local workstation and others to use for printing.

7.1 ESTABLISHING A PRINT QUEUE

In this exercise you will create a print queue. A print queue is where the print jobs are collected and held prior to being printed.

It is assumed that you are logged in with the Supervisor Equivalent status.

This exercise also assumes you are already logged in to NetWare and at the F:\LOGIN> prompt.

Hands-On Exercise

Once logged in and at the F:\LOGIN> prompt,

1. **Type** *PCONSOLE*

You are at PCONSOLE's Available Options menu.

2. **Type** *P* to move to Print Queue Information

   Press ⸢Enter⸣

At the Print Queues window, to initiate creating a print queue,

3. **Press** ⸢Ins⸣

At New Print Queue Name: pop-up window, to create a new queue,

4. **Type** *Q1xxx* (replace xxx with your initials)

   Press ⸢Enter⸣

You are now back at the Print Queues window, highlighted on your new Q1xxx queue name.
At the Print Queues window, to configure the queue,

5. **Press** ⸢Enter⸣ (highlighted on Q1xxx)

At the Print Queue Information window,

6. **Press** ⸢Pg Dn⸣ to highlight Queue Users

   Press ⸢Enter⸣

You see the group EVERYONE. All queues created are automatically assigned to the group EVERYONE.
To add users, at the Queue Users window,

7. **Press** ⸢Ins⸣

   Type *GUEST* to move to GUEST user

   Press ⸢Enter⸣

You are now back at Queue Users and see the Guest User has been added. Refer to Figure 7.1.
To view the current Queue Operator,

8. **Press** ⸢Esc⸣ to leave Queue Users menu

   Press ⸢↑⸣ twice to highlight Queue Operators

   Press ⸢Enter⸣ (highlighted on Queue Operators)

The Supervisor account is shown in the Queue Operators. The Supervisor account is automatically added as a Queue Operator when a queue is created.

To add a Queue Operator,

9. **Press** [Ins]

You are at the Queue Operator Candidates window. Move the high-light bar down the list using the down arrow to highlight your LOGIN name. You will find your LOGIN name after User on the second line of PCONSOLE's menu banner at the top of your screen.

Highlighted on your LOGIN name in the Queue Operator Candidates window,

10. **Press** [Enter]

You should be back at the Queue Operators window and your LOGIN name has been added.

11. If you have completed Exercise 5.1 to add your xxxUSER account (where xxx was replaced with your initials),

Press [Ins] at the Queue Operators window and scroll the highlight bar through the list in the Queue Operator Candidates to select and add your xxxUSER account as a Queue Operator.

PRINT QUEUE INFORMATION SCREEN DEFINED

Current Print Job Entries	Used to provide a list of all jobs being held in the queue.
Current Queue Status	Used to display the number of entries in the queue, the number of servers being serviced by the queue, and the operator flags.
Currently Attached Servers	Used to display a list of print servers able to service a print queue.
Print Queue ID	Used to display the eight-digit numbered .QDR subdirectory under SYS:SYSTEM assigned to a queue.
Queue Operators	Provides a list of assigned operators and can be used to establish others with Operator status.
Queue Servers	Used to display a list of print servers able to service a print queue.
Queue Users	Used to display a list of user accounts able to send a print job to a queue.

FIGURE 7.1

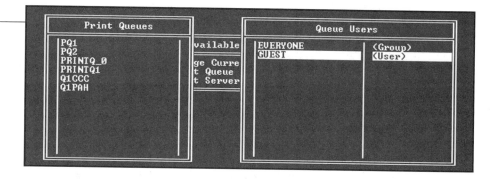

To go on to the next exercise,

   12. **Press** [Esc] until you are at the Available Options menu or,

to exit,

   13. **Press** [Alt] [F10]

KEY RELATED POINTS

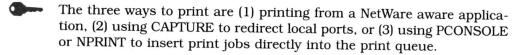 The three ways to print are (1) printing from a NetWare aware application, (2) using CAPTURE to redirect local ports, or (3) using PCONSOLE or NPRINT to insert print jobs directly into the print queue.

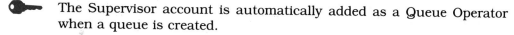 The Supervisor account is automatically added as a Queue Operator when a queue is created.

7.2 ESTABLISHING A PRINT SERVER

In this exercise you will create a print server. A print server is a program which controls the printers and receives jobs from the print queue(s).

It is assumed that you are logged in with the Supervisor Equivalent status.

This exercise also assumes you are already logged in to NetWare and at the Available Options menu within PCONSOLE.

Hands-On Exercise

Once logged in and at PCONSOLE's Available Options menu,

   1. **Press** [Pg Dn] to highlight Print Server Information

      Press [Enter] (highlighted on Print Server Information)

You are at the Print Servers window, with the list of the current print servers on your network shown.

At the Print Servers window, to add a print server,

>   2. **Press** [Ins]

At the New Print Server Name: window,

>   **Type** *PSxxx* (replace *xxx* with your initials)
>
>   **Press** [Enter]

You are back at Print Servers, highlighted on your new PS*xxx* print server name.

To configure your print server, highlighted on your new PS*xxx* print server,

>   3. **Press** [Enter]

You are now at the Print Server Information pop-up window.

At the Print Server Information window, to view current users of your print server,

>   4. **Press** [Pg Dn] to highlight Print Server Users
>
>   **Press** [Enter] (highlighted on Print Server Users)

You are at the Server Users window, highlighted on the group EVERYONE. The group EVERYONE is automatically added as Server Users when a print server is created.

To add new users to your print server,

>   5. **Press** [Ins]

At the Print Server User Candidates window,

>   **Type** *GUEST*
>
>   **Press** [Enter]

You are now back at the Server Users window, highlighted on GUEST. Refer to Figure 7.2.

To view the current Print Server Operators, from the Server Users window,

>   6. **Press** [Esc] to move to Print Server Information window

From the Print Server Information window,

>   **Press** [↑] to move to Print Server Operators
>
>   **Press** [Enter] (highlighted on Print Server Operators)

You are at Print Server Operators window, highlighted on SUPERVI-SOR. The Supervisor account is automatically assigned as a Print Server Operator when the print server is created.

FIGURE 7.2

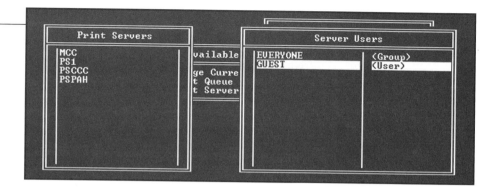

To add a print server operator, from the Print Server Operators pop-up window,

7. **Press** [Ins] from the Print Server Operators window

You are now at the Print Server Operator Candidates window. Move the highlight bar down the list using the down arrow to highlight your

PRINT SERVER INFORMATION SCREEN DEFINED

Change Password	Used by the Supervisor or Supervisor Equivalent to assign or change the passwords to print servers.
Full Name	Used by the Supervisor or Superivor Equivalent to display a descriptive name for the print server.
Print Server Configuration	Used by the Supervisor or Supervisor Equivalent to configure the print server's printers, startup queues, and notify list.
Print Server ID	Displays the Object ID of the print server, which is not used by any other NetWare configuration.
Print Server Operators	Displays the list of users and groups who are Operators for the Print Server Users.
Print Server Status/Control	This option is *only* available when the print server is currently running. Used to display the status of the print server.
Print Server Users	Used to list the users or groups who can use the print server.

LOGIN name. You will find your LOGIN name after *"User"* on the second line of PCONSOLE's menu banner. PCONSOLE's menu banner at the top of your screen reads *"User _____ On File Server ____ Connection ___,"* where the blank lines are filled in with your LOGIN name, your file server name, and your connection number.

Highlighted on your LOGIN name in the Print Server Operator Candidates window,

 8. **Press** [Enter]

You are back at the Print Server Operators window. You have added your LOGIN name to SUPERVISOR as a Print Server Operator.

 9. If you have completed Exercise 5.1 to add your xxxUSER account (where xxx was replaced with your initials),

 Press [Ins] at the Print Server Operators window and scroll the highlight bar through the list in the Print Server Operator Candidates to select and add your xxxUSER account as a Server Operator.

To go on to the next exercise,

 10. **Press** [Esc] until you move back to the Available Options menu or,

to exit,

 11. **Press** [Alt] [F10]

KEY RELATED POINTS

- The group EVERYONE is automatically added as Server Users when a print servers is created.

- The Supervisor account is automatically assigned as a Print Server Operator when the print server is created.

7.3 ASSIGNING YOUR PRINT QUEUE TO YOUR PRINT SERVER

You assign print queues to authorize print servers to service the queues. Print queues can be serviced on the file server, using the printers attached to the file server, or you can bring up print servers on your network to service the printers.

It is assumed that you are logged in with the Supervisor Equivalent status.

This exercise also assumes you are already logged in to NetWare and at the Available Options menu within PCONSOLE.

Hands-On Exercise

Once logged in and at PCONSOLE's Available Options menu,

1. **Type** *P* to move to Print Queue Information

   Press Enter (highlighted on Print Queue Information)

You are at the Print Queues pop-up window, listing the print queues for this file server.

To associate your print queue with your print server, from the Print Queue Information window,

2. **Type** *Q1xxx* (replace xxx with your initials)

This was the queue you created in Exercise 7.1.

   Press Enter

You are back at the Print Queue Information window.

At the Print Queue Information window,

3. **Press** Pg Dn and then,

   Press ↑ to highlight Queue Servers

Highlighted on Queue Servers,

   Press Enter

You are at the Queue Servers window.

At the Queue Servers windows, now shown with no entries, to add a queue to this print server,

4. **Press** Ins

From the Queue Server Candidates window,

   Type *PSxxx* (replace xxx with your initials)

You are highlighted in the Queue Servers pop-up window on the print server, PSxxx, you created in Exercise 7.2.

Highlighted on your PSxxx print server, in the Queue Server Candidates window,

5. **Press** Enter

FIGURE 7.3

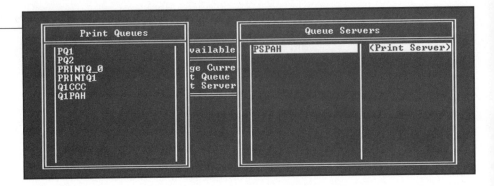

You are highlighted on PSxxx (Print Server) in the Queue Servers window. Refer to Figure 7.3.

> **Press** ⌷Esc⌷ three times to return to Available Options

You are back at the Available Options menu.

7.4 ASSIGNING PRINTER TO YOUR PRINT SERVER

Defining printers and configuring them for the print server is what you will work with in this exercise.

It is assumed that you are logged in with the Supervisor Equivalent status.

This exercise also assumes you are already logged in to NetWare and at the Available Options menu within PCONSOLE.

Hands-On Exercise

Once logged in and at PCONSOLE's Available Options menu,

> 1. **Press** ⌷Pg Dn⌷ to highlight Print Server Information
>
> **Press** ⌷Enter⌷

You are at the Print Servers window, listing all the print servers on the network.

To locate your print server,

> 2. **Type** PSxxx (replace xxx with your initials)

This was the print server you created in Exercise 7.2.
To select your print server,

> 3. **Press** ⌷Enter⌷ (highlighted on PSxxx)

You are now at the Print Server Information window.

To select the configuration option,

4. **Type** *P* to highlight Print Server Configuration

   Press [Enter]

You are at the Print Server Configuration menu.

To print to your print server,

5. **Type** *P* to move the highlight to Printer Configuration

   Press [Enter]

You should be at the Configure Printers menu, highlighted on Not Installed 0.

At the Configure Printers menu, highlighted on Not Installed 0, to configure your printer,

6. **Press** [Enter] highlight on Not Installed 0

You are at the Printer 0 configuration screen, highlighted on Name: Printer 0.

Highlighted on Printer 0 in the Printer 0 configuration screen, to define this printer,

7. **Press** [↓] to move to Type:

   Press [Enter] (highlighted on Type:)

You are at the Printer Types window, highlighted at the bottom of the window on Defined elsewhere.

To select Parallel, LPT1 from the Printer types window,

8. **Press** [Pg Up] to highlight Parallel, LPT1

   Press [Enter] (highlighted on Parallel, LPT1)

PRINT SERVER CONFIGURATION MENU DEFINED

File Servers to be Serviced	Used to specify which file server the print server will utilize when activated.
Notify List for Printer	Used to specify which users and groups will be notified when a printer needs attention.
Printer Configuration	Used to define network printers.
Queues Serviced by Printer	Used to specify which print queues will be serviced by each printer.

Refer to Figure 7.4.

You are now back at the Printer 0 configuration screen with Parallel, LPT1 showing and including other information automatically added for the printer interrupts, buffer size, and queue service mode.

To accept the defaults added as well as your changes to the Printer 0 configuration screen,

9. **Press** [Esc]

Press [Enter] (highlighted on Yes to Save changes)

You are back at Configured printers, highlighted on Printer 0.

10. **Press** [Esc]

You are back at Print Server Configuration menu.

At the Print Server Configuration menu, to add your print queue to be serviced by your print server,

11. **Type** *Q* to move the highlight to Queues Serviced by Printer

Press [Enter] (highlighted on Queues Serviced by Printer)

At the window of Defined Printers, showing your highlight on Printer 0,

Press [Enter] (highlighted on Printer 0)

At the Queue screen,

Press [Ins]

Type *Q1xxx* (replace xxx with your initials)

This was the queue you created in Exercise 7.1.

Press [Enter]

FIGURE 7.4

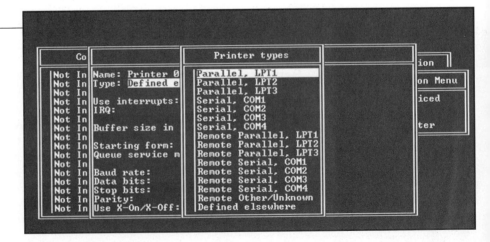

FIGURE 7.5

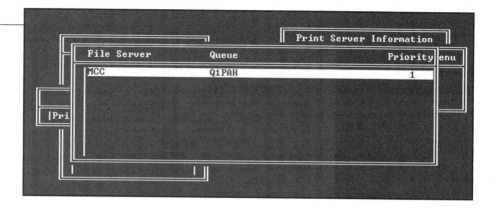

At the Priority: window showing 1,

> **Press** Enter

You have added your Q1xxx print queue to your PSxxx print server and the queue users will print with a top priority, priority 1, status. Refer to Figure 7.5.

To exit PCONSOLE, use Alt F10 or use Esc to return to PCONSOLE's available options main menu.

7.5 ESTABLISHING A REMOTE PRINTER FOR YOUR WORKSTATION

Remote printing allows printing to be distributed throughout the network. In this exercise you will work with defining and configuring a remote printer.

It is assumed that you are logged in with the Supervisor Equivalent status.

This exercise also assumes you are already logged in to NetWare and at the Available Options menu within PCONSOLE.

Hands-On Exercise

Once logged in and at PCONSOLE's Available Options menu,

> 1. **Press** Pg Dn to highlight Print Server Information
>
>   **Press** Enter

You are at the Print Servers pop-up window.

At the Print Servers window, to select your print server,

> 2. **Type** *PSxxx* where *xxx* is replaced with your initials
>
>   **Press** Enter (highlighted on PSxxx)

You are now at the Print Server Information window.

To configure the remote printer, from the Print Server Information window,

> 3. **Type** *P* to highlight Print Server Configuration
>
>   **Press** (Enter)

At the Print Server Configuration menu,

> **Type** *P* to highlight Printer Configuration
>
> **Press** (Enter)

You are at the Configured Printers, highlighted on Printer 0.

At the Configured Printers window to configure Printer 1,

> 4. **Press** (↓) to highlight Not Installed 1
>
>   **Press** (Enter)

You are at the Printer 1 configuration screen.

To configure Printer 1 as a remote printer, from the Printer 1 configuration screen, highlighted on Name:,

> 5. **Press** (Enter)
>
>   **Press** (←Backspace) to erase Printer 1
>
>   **Type** *xxx PRINTER* in the Name: field
>   (replace *xxx* with your initials)
>
>   **Press** (↓) to highlight the Type: field

You are highlighted on Type:, now showing Defined elsewhere.

To change Defined elsewhere to a remote printer,

> **Press** (Enter)

You should be highlighted on Defined elsewhere in the Printer types window. To select Remote Parallel, LPT1,

> **Type** *R* to highlight Remote Parallel, LPT1
>
> **Press** (Enter)

The default printer configuration settings for interrupts, etc., for Remote Parallel, LPT1 is displayed. Refer to Figure 7.6.

To save your changes,

> 6. **Press** (Esc)
>
>   **Press** (Enter) (highlighted on Yes to Save changes window)

FIGURE 7.6

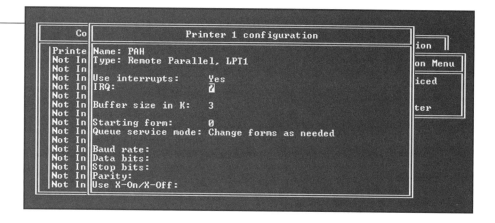

You are now at Configured Printers window, highlighted on xxx Printer 1.

To select a queue for your remote printer, at the Configure Printers window,

>   7. **Press** [Esc]

At the Print Server Configuration Menu,

>   **Type** Q
>   **Press** [Enter]   (highlighted on Queues Serviced by Printer)

Move the highlight bar to xxx Printer 1

>   **Press** [Enter]

At the blank screen, to bring up a listing of queues,

>   **Press** [Ins]

From the Available Queues window,

>   **Type** Q / xxx
>   **Press** [Enter]

At the Priority: window showing 1,

>   **Press** [Enter]

>   8. To exit PCONSOLE,

>   **Press** [Alt] [F10]

KEY RELATED POINTS

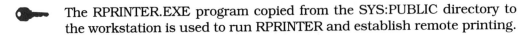 The RPRINTER.EXE program copied from the SYS:PUBLIC directory to the workstation is used to run RPRINTER and establish remote printing.

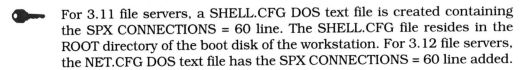 For 3.11 file servers, a SHELL.CFG DOS text file is created containing the SPX CONNECTIONS = 60 line. The SHELL.CFG file resides in the ROOT directory of the boot disk of the workstation. For 3.12 file servers, the NET.CFG DOS text file has the SPX CONNECTIONS = 60 line added.

To begin RPRINTER on the local workstation, once the SHELL.CFG or NET.CFG file is created and the workstation (re)booted,

> **Type** *RPRINTER PSxxx 1* (where *xxx* is replaced with your initials)
>
> **Press** Enter

Printer 1 is configured as REMOTE, LPT1 in our example. Substitute the number with the printer number configured as a remote printer. Hence, the syntax for RPRINTER is:

> RPRINTER *print server name   printer number*

To run RPRINTER on the workstation, the psxxx server must be operational and properly running.

7.6 CONTROLLING A PRINTER FROM PCONSOLE

To control a printer from PCONSOLE is primarily what a Print Server Operator is responsible for. In this exercise you will work with PCON-SOLE to pause and restart a printer.

It is assumed that you are logged in with the Print Server Operator or Supervisor Equivalent status.

This exercise also assumes you are already logged in to NetWare and at the Available Options menu within PCONSOLE.

Hands-On Exercise

Once logged in and at PCONSOLE's Available Options menu,

> 1. **Press** Pg Dn to highlight Print Server Information
>
>   **Press** Enter

You are at the Print Servers window.

   2. Select your PS*xxx* print server or one that is operational on your network where your LOGIN name is recognized as Print Server Operator or higher security status. Once highlighted on the print server you will be using for this exercise,

     Press Enter

At the Print Server Information window,

   3. **Press** Pg Dn and then,

     Press ↑ to highlight Print Server Status/Control

     Press Enter

You are now at the Print Server Status and Control window.

***NOTE:* If you don't see Print Server Status/Control listed in the Print Server Information Window, the Print Server you have selected is not mounted and is unable to be used for this exercise.**

PRINTER CONTROL OPTIONS

Abort print job	Used to stop current print job from printing.
Form Feed	Used to advance a single sheet of paper through the printer. This option can be used when the printer is stopped.
Mark top of form	Used to mark, with a line of asterisks, the top of the form to assist you in aligning paper in the printer. This option can be used when the printer is stopped.
Pause printer	Used to temporarily halt printing. Start printing will resume printing where the print job left off.
Rewind printer	Used with Pause Printer, issued to back up the print job a certain number of bytes.
Start printer	Used to resume or start sending print jobs to the printer.
Stop printer	Used to stop the printer from printing. If the printer was printing when stopped, when the printer resumes service with Start Printer, the previously active print job will be printed from the beginning.

From the Print Server Status and Control window,

    4. **Type** *P*

       Press [Enter] (highlighted on Printer Status)

In the Active Printers window,

       Press [Enter] on the active printer showing

At the Status of the Printer screen, you are highlighted on Printer Control.

NOTE: If you have a single bar menu and unable to access Printer Control, your account is not a Printer Server Operator status and must obtain this security equivalence for this exercise.

Highlighted on Printer Control, in the Status of the Printer screen,

    5. **Press** [Enter]

A pop-up window, similar to Figure 7.7 is showing on your screen. This is where you control the printer.

To pause printing,

    6. **Type** *P*

       Press [Enter] (highlighted on Pause printer)

The Status: field shows *"Paused."* Refer to Figure 7.7

To restart printing,

       Press [Enter] to display the Printer Control pop-up window options

       Type *S* to highlight Start printer

       Press [Enter]

The Status: field shows the server is again active, displaying *"Waiting for job."* The server may show *"Printing job"* if there were jobs waiting when you selected pause printer.

FIGURE 7.7

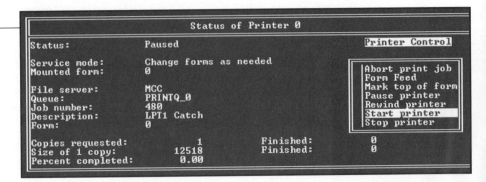

KEY RELATED POINTS

 Common Status Field First Line Entries for Status of Printer Screen:

Mark/Eject
Online
Offline
Paused
Printing job
Stopped
Waiting for job
Waiting for form to be mounted

 Common Status Field Second Line Entries for Status of Printer Screen:

Not Ready
Out of paper
[Blank]

END OF CHAPTER REVIEW

True/False Questions

1. Supervisor is automatically added as a Print Server Operator when the print server is first created.

2. The group EVERYONE is always added as queue users when the print queue is first created.

3. NPRINT is used to redirect local ports where CAPTURE and PCONSOLE are used to insert jobs directly into the print queue.

4. The Supervisor account is automatically added as a Queue Operator when a queue is created.

5. Current Print Job Entries is used to display the number of entries in the queue, the number of servers being serviced by the queue, and the operator flags.

6. Current Queue Status is used to provide a list of all jobs being held in the queue.

7. Print Queue ID is used to display the eight-digit numbered .QDR subdirectory under SYS:SYSTEM assigned to a queue.

8. The group EVERYONE is automatically added as Server Users when a print servers is created.

9. Print Server ID is used to display the Object ID of the print server, which is not used by any other NetWare configuration.

10. The RPRINTER.EXE program copied from the SYS:SYSTEM directory to the workstation is used to run RPRINTER and establish remote printing.

ON YOUR OWN—HANDS-ON

1. Begin PCONSOLE. From Print Server Status and Control, select Printer Status. At the Status of the Printer Screen, use the Mark top of form option to align the paper. Explain what operations you performed to use the Mark top of form option and what you had to do after using it.

IN YOUR OWN WORDS

1. Explain what happens to the print job when Abort print job is used.

2. Explain what happens to the print job when Pause printer is used.

3. Explain what happens to the print job when Stop printer is used.

4. Which printer control options can be used with Stop printer?

Automating The Workstation: Working with LOGIN Scripts and Custom Menus

OBJECTIVES

- Create LOGIN Scripts.

- Describe the types of LOGIN Scripts.

- Learn various LOGIN Script commands.

- Create, test and debug LOGIN Scripts.

- Use LOGIN/S to create a simulated system script.

- Create Custom Menus.

- Create and compile a NetWare 3.12 Menu.

- Test and debug a NetWare 3.12 Menu.

- Use NMENU and MENUMAKE commands.

CHAPTER INTRODUCTION

LOGIN Scripts are similar to DOS Batch files with added configuration options for automating and customizing the workstation's operating environment. You will work with LOGIN Scripts in this chapter to view how they are executed as part of the log in procedures for network workstations.

After you initiate a LOGIN request and supply a valid username and password, the LOGIN program executes the LOGIN Script(s). The first script is the System LOGIN Script, which is created as a system-wide, global setting of variables to set and control the user community's network environment. The Supervisor user account, or Supervisor Equivalent user account(s) sets and revises the System LOGIN Script.

NetWare has a default LOGIN Script which is enacted when the file server is first set up. This script is the only one that exists until the System script or a User script is created. The Default LOGIN Script cannot be revised.

You will first work with the User LOGIN Script to create and specify individual environment variable settings for your personal LOGIN Script. The User (personal) LOGIN Script is changed through SYSCON's User Information submenu. You will create a typical user LOGIN Script that contains drive mappings and other features to customize your personal operating needs and preferences.

After working with the user's personal LOGIN Script, you will work with bypassing the System LOGIN Script to gain a larger perspective of customizing logging in to the file server for all users and groups.

There are a few conventions to consider with LOGIN Scripts and this chapter discusses these as well as supplies you with proper syntax for keywords, variables, and parameters. Proper spacing in commands, delimiters, and in other characters and punctuation are also discussed as you work with specifying proper command format. You will see that LOGIN Scripts are not case-sensitive; but identifier variables enclosed in quotation marks must be preceded by the percent sign (%) and typed using uppercase letters. You will also see that the remark statement can be given in a variety of ways and is commonly used to document your LOGIN Script.

Some of the general LOGIN Script conventions you will work with in this chapter center on the following:

Command-lines cannot exceed 150 characters.

Allow long commands to wrap text to the next line. Do not break the line by entering a return to designate a new line.

Enter only one command for each line and press Enter at the end of each command-line.

Commands can be issued in either upper- or lowercase letters, but pay attention to command conventions as case-sensitivity is somewhat variable.

Identifier variables enclosed in quotation marks must be preceded by a percent sign (%) and typed using uppercase letters.

Remark or comment statements can be issued using either the asterisk (*) or the semicolon (;) punctuation marks. Otherwise, REMARK or REM is used for comment lines within a LOGIN Script.

Use conditional variables with only the IF...THEN condition.

Command-line utilities can be executed in a LOGIN Script if preceded by the pound sign (#).

Use the EXIT command to end the LOGIN Script, otherwise use the # to start another program or process in the middle of the LOGIN Script. Use # to run a command-line utility like CAPTURE and use EXIT to run a program or start a menu, like NMENU.

Near the end of the chapter, you will work with creating menus. NetWare contains the ability to work with creating on-screen menus to simplify the use of the network. You will see that a good menu can be an important security and training device on the network. With limiting the set of options and implementing a menu interface for network workstations, you are given examples in this chapter to see how you can lessen both the security and training hazards that are notorious for creating havoc amid network administration.

8.1 GETTING STARTED WITH LOGIN SCRIPTS

The User LOGIN Script can also be called a personal LOGIN Script. Either the system manager account(s) or individual users can create the personal LOGIN Scripts, used to customize and set individual user account's working environment upon logging in.

In this exercise you will create a User LOGIN Script using NetWare's menu utility for system configuration, SYSCON.

This exercise also assumes you are already logged in to NetWare and at the F:\LOGIN> prompt.

Hands-On Exercises

1. **Type** *SYSCON*

   Press Enter

You are at SYSCON's Available Options menu.

  2. **Type** *U* to move to User Information

Highlighted on User Information,

  Press ⌷Enter⌸

At the User Names menu, move your highlight bar to find your user name list.
  Highlighted on your user name,

  3. **Press** ⌷Enter⌸

You are now at the User Information window, highlighted on Account Balance.
  To move to the screen to type your LOGIN Script,

  4. **Type** *L* to move the highlight bar to LOGIN Script

  Press ⌷Enter⌸

NOTE: If you receive the "LOGIN Script does not exist" Window, press [Enter] when prompted to "Read LOGIN Script from User: (your username)." This will enable and advance you to the Blank LOGIN Script Screen for your username.

Once you are at the LOGIN Script for User {your LOGIN name} screen, to create a simple LOGIN Script for testing,

  5. **Type** *REM This is a LOGIN Script for {your user name}*

  Press ⌷Enter⌸

This places a remark statement at the top of your screen. A remark statement is used for documenting purposes. Refer to Figure 8.1.
  On the second line, to create a simple, one-line greeting as you log in,

  6. **Type** *WRITE "Good %GREETING_TIME, %LOGIN_NAME"*

  Press ⌷Enter⌸

You are at the third line of the LOGIN Script. Refer to Figure 8.1.
  To save your script,

  7. **Press** ⌷Esc⌸

  Press ⌷Enter⌸ (highlighted on Yes to save changes)

You are now back at the User Information window.
  To test your LOGIN Script,

  8. **Press** ⌷Alt⌸ ⌷F10⌸

  Press ⌷Enter⌸ (highlighted on Yes to exit SYSCON)

FIGURE 8.1

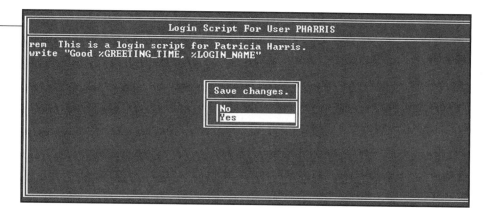

At the F:\LOGIN> prompt,

Type *LOGOUT*

Press Enter

COMMON USER LOGIN SCRIPT COMMANDS

EXIT	Commonly used to terminate the execution of the System LOGIN Script and prevent further commands or scripts from executing. EXIT can be used to terminate the LOGIN Script execution and launch a ".COM, .EXE or .BAT file (e.g., EXIT "Filename").
REM	REM, REMARK, asterisk (*), or semicolon (;) are used in LOGIN Scripts to insert explanatory comments that are ignored as the script commands are interpreted and executed.
WRITE	Considered to be an environment variable used in LOGIN Scripts to display information about the workstation, date, time, network, or user information.
GREETING_TIME	Identifier variable for displaying morning, afternoon, or evening.
LOGIN_NAME	Identifier variable for displaying the LOGIN name.
%	Identifier variables, such as GREETING_TIME and LOGIN_NAME are preceded by the percent sign (%) and typed in uppercase if enclosed in quotes (e.g., WRITE "Welcome, %USER_ID").

At the F:\LOGIN> prompt, having logged out,

9. **Type** *LOGIN {your username}*
   Press [Enter]

At the password prompt, supply your password and watch for the 1-line message, *"Good greeting time, LOGIN name."* Depending on the time of day, greeting time will be replaced with *"Good morning," "Good afternoon,"* or *"Good evening."* The LOGIN name displayed is just that—the name you supply after you type LOGIN.

NOTE: If you did not see your Good Greeting-time message at all, the system LOGIN Script might contain the EXIT command which would prevent your personal, username script from ever executing.

KEY RELATED POINTS

- The personal or user LOGIN Script is contained in the SYS:MAIL directory in a numbered subdirectory under the filename of LOGIN. The LOGIN file is a text file written in LOGIN Script syntax.

- Each user's numbered subdirectory in SYS:MAIL was established when their User Account was created and is checked upon log in. The numbered subdirectory in MAIL is the User ID number, which is listed in SYSCON's User Information, Other Information menu option.

- The User LOGIN Script is executed after the System LOGIN Script.

- If no LOGIN Script exists, the Default LOGIN Script executes.

- If no User LOGIN Script exists, the System script executes, followed by the Default script. If a User script exists, the System script executes, followed by the User script, bypassing the Default LOGIN Script.

- A suite of identifier variables are used in LOGIN Scripts to display the date, time, workstation, network, or user information.

8.2 USING MAP AND DRIVE IN LOGIN SCRIPTS

MAP is commonly used in LOGIN Scripts as a way to program or permanently write drive mapping assignments to define your working environment. The **DRIVE** command is used after the MAP command to position the entry point or default directory for you when you log in. In

FIGURE 8.2

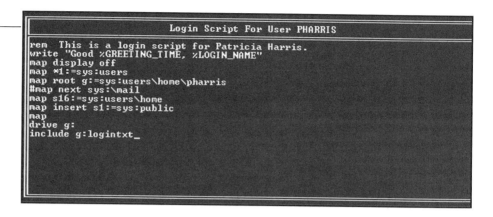

```
                   Login Script For User PHARRIS
rem  This is a login script for Patricia Harris.
write "Good %GREETING_TIME, %LOGIN_NAME"
map display off
map *1:=sys:users
map root g:=sys:users\home\pharris
#map next sys:\mail
map s16:=sys:users\home
map insert s1:=sys:public
map
drive g:
include g:logintxt_
```

this exercise, you will work with placing both the MAP and DRIVE commands in your LOGIN Script.

This exercise also assumes you are already logged in to NetWare and at the LOGIN Script for User {your LOGIN name} screen within SYSCON.

DRIVE
Specifies your default drive as you exit the LOGIN Script. Used in LOGIN Scripts to set your default drive so you will not have to change your preferred drive specification every time you log in. (See page 238.)

Hands-On Exercises

From the previous exercise, at the LOGIN Script for User LOGIN name screen within SYSCON,

1. Move to the third line and begin your new entries in your LOGIN Script with a line to turn the display of your drive mapping off as you log in.

    Type *MAP DISPLAY OFF*

    Press (Enter)

Refer to Figure 8.2.

You are at the fourth line of your LOGIN Script and ready to begin adding some drive mappings.

To add a drive mapping to the USERS directory,

2. **Type** *MAP *I:=SYS:USERS*

    Press (Enter)

On the next line of your LOGIN Script, create a fake root drive mapping to your home directory in the USERS directory structure.

3. **Type** *MAP ROOT G:=SYS:USERS\HOME\%LOGIN_NAME*

    Press (Enter)

On the next line,

#
Used in LOGIN
Scripts to call and
execute external
programs.

4. **Type** *#MAP NEXT SYS:\MAIL*

   Press [Enter] to map the *next available* drive letter to the MAIL directory.
   The # sign is used to execute the MAP command as an external command
   to the LOGIN Script, as if you had typed it at the command-line prompt.

Map the next available search drive to the users\home directory
location.

5. **Type** *MAP S16:=SYS:USERS\HOME*

   Press [Enter]

Next, use MAP INSERT to map S1 search drive to the PUBLIC directory.

6. **Type** *MAP INSERT S1:=SYS:PUBLIC*

   Press [Enter]

Use the MAP and DRIVE command at the end of your LOGIN Script
to show your LOGIN Script drive mappings and position you at your
home directory.

7. **Type** *MAP*

   Press [Enter]

   Type *DRIVE G:*

   Press [Enter]

COMMON DATE- AND TIME-RELATED IDENTIFIER VARIABLES

DAY	Day of the month, numbered from 01 to 31.
DAY_OF_WEEK	Day of the week, such as Monday, Tuesday, etc.
NDAY_OF_WEEK	Numbered day of the week, Sunday is 1 and Saturday is 7.
MONTH	Month as a number, from 01 to 12.
MONTH_NAME	January, February, etc.
YEAR	Four-digit format for the year, 1994, 1995, etc.
SHORT_YEAR	Two-digit, shortened format for the year, 94, 95, etc.
AM_PM	Day or night, am or pm depending upon time of day.
GREETING_TIME	Morning, afternoon, evening.
HOUR	The hour of day or night, 12-hour format, hour 1 to 12.
HOUR24	24-hour, military time format.
MINUTE	Minute, 00 to 59.
SECOND	Second, 00 to 59.

Refer to Figure 8.2.
Save your script.

8. **Press** Esc

Press Enter (highlighted on Yes to save changes)

You are now back at the User Information window.
To test your LOGIN Script,

9. **Press** Alt F10

Press Enter (highlighted on Yes to exit SYSCON)

At the F:\LOGIN> prompt,

Type *LOGOUT*

Press Enter

At the F:\LOGIN> prompt, having logged out,

10. **Type** *LOGIN {your username}*

Press Enter

At the password prompt, supply your password and watch for flaws or bask in the glory of flawlessness from your typing the script syntax correctly the first time.

Go back and turn the MAP DISPLAY ON to notice the difference in being able to watch your drive mappings execute as you test your LOGIN Script.

KEY RELATED POINTS

Mapping a fake root and then using the DRIVE command is commonly used to position users at their home directory location.

LOGIN Scripts contain commands that initialize variables, map network drives, and control the user's program execution.

The EXIT command in a LOGIN Script terminates the script at the point where EXIT is used. The # will execute the external program and return to complete and finish executing the LOGIN Script file(s).

8.3 ADDING PERSUASION TO YOUR LOGIN SCRIPTS

LOGIN Scripts are often perpetrated as a tool of logging in to capture someone's attention in an attempt to prompt or stimulate them.

WRITE
Used to customize LOGIN Scripts by displaying text or identifier variables to screen as you log in.

WRITE, **FIRE PHASERS**, and **PAUSE** commands are used in this exercise as a means of using the LOGIN Script as a persuasive messaging tool. You will also use the LOGIN Script—**INCLUDE** command—to incorporate a text file you create in your home directory, written in LOGIN Script syntax, to execute as you log in.

This exercise assumes you have successfully completed the first two exercises in this chapter, and are at the G: prompt, root drive mapping for your home directory created in the previous exercise.

Hands-On Exercises

At the G:\> prompt,

> 1. **Type** COPY CON LOGINTXT
>
>   **Press** Enter

Your cursor is blinking under the letter G of the G:\> drive prompt.

> 2. With the cursor blinking under the drive letter G,
>
>   **Type** WRITE "This is a file included in my LOGIN Script."
>
>   **Press** Enter

You are now at the next line, with your cursor blinking under the W of the word WRITE.

On the second line,

> 3. **Type** WRITE "Good ; greeting_time; , LAN FAN"
>
>   **Press** Enter

This will bring your cursor to the third line, under the W of the word WRITE on the second line.

On the third line,

> 4. **Type** FIRE 1
>
>   **Press** Enter

FIRE and FIRE PHASERS will produce an audible tone that is sounded to alert you as you log in.

With your cursor blinking under the F of the word FIRE,

> 5. **Type** PAUSE
>
>   **Press** Enter

PAUSE will cause the *"Strike a key when ready..."* to display on your screen, similar to the DOS PAUSE command.

To save the entries you typed on screen to the LOGINTXT filename in your home directory,

FIRE or **FIRE PHASERS**
Used to execute a sound within a LOGIN Script. Fire will execute a sound from one to nine times.

PAUSE
Breaks or pauses the execution of a LOGIN Script until any key is pressed.

INCLUDE
Used to incorporate another script file that is written in LOGIN Script syntax and read into the LOGIN Script as it executes.

FIGURE 8.3

```
G:\>copy con logintxt
write "This is a file included in my login script."
write "Good "; greeting_time; ", LAN FAN"
fire 1
pause
^Z
        1 file(s) copied

G:\>_
```

6. **Press** *CTRL Z*

   Press Enter

You will see the *"1 file copied"* message display on your screen and your cursor blinking at the G:\> prompt.

To place, use INCLUDE to incorporate these commands to execute as you log in,

7. **Type** *SYSCON*

   Press Enter

From SYSCON, move to your LOGIN Script editing screen, and at the bottom of your LOGIN Script,

   Type *INCLUDE G:LOGINTXT*

   Press Enter

Refer to Figure 8.3 for adding this line to your LOGIN Script.
Now for the test. Save your LOGIN Script.

8. **Press** Esc

   Press Enter (highlighted on Yes to save changes)

USER-RELATED IDENTIFIERS

LOGIN_NAME   Displays the LOGIN name.
FULL_NAME   Displays the user's full name as identified and displayed in SYSCON's User Information window.
USER_ID   Displays the number assigned to each user.

Examples of IF...THEN Statements for LOGIN Scripts
1. IF NDAY_OF_WEEK = "6" THEN WRITE "T.G.I.F."
2. IF MEMBER OF "MARKETING" AND DAY = "15" THEN WRITE "Meeting today at 10 a.m." END

From the User Information window,

    Press Alt F10

    Press Enter (highlighted on Yes to exit SYSCON)

At the F:\LOGIN> prompt,

    9. **Type** *LOGOUT*

    Press Enter

At the F:\LOGIN> prompt, having logged out,

    10. **Type** *LOGIN {your username}*

    Press Enter

Provide your password and you are on your way. Go back and edit your script as necessary.

KEY RELATED POINTS

 INCLUDE does not function as the DISPLAY or FDISPLAY commands.

 DISPLAY is used to list the contents of a text file to the screen as you log in. FDISPLAY is used to filter the formatting of a wordprocessing file to display the text to the screen as the LOGIN Script executes, without showing the control codes.

8.4 SIMULATING THE SYSTEM LOGIN SCRIPT

LOGIN /S
Used to override LOGIN Scripts by redirecting to another path where a text file is written in LOGIN Script syntax.

The LOGIN command can be issued as **LOGIN /S** followed by the path to the LOGIN Script text file. This is useful for testing scripts prior to implementing.

    This exercise assumes that you are already logged in and have a blank, formatted diskette in drive A of your computer. This exercise also assumes you have access to DOS EDIT or another ASCII text file editor.

Hands-On Exercises

Logged in and at your home directory prompt mapped to drive G from the previous exercise, at G:\>,

    1. **Type** *EDIT A:REVIEW.LOG*

    Press Enter

The DOS EDIT screen is displayed.

To begin your script,

2. **Type** *MAP INS S1:=SYS:PUBLIC*

   Press Enter

For the second line,

   Type *MAP S2:=SYS:PUBLIC\%MACHINE\%OS\%OS_VERSION*

   Press Enter

On the third line,

3. **Type** *COMSPEC=S2:COMMAND.COM*

   Press Enter

This will set the command processor to reload DOS to your workstation. On the fourth line,

4. **Type** *WRITE "This is the Review LOGIN Script for %LOGIN_NAME"*

   Press Enter

and then on the next line,

   Type *MAP J:=SYS:USERS\HOME\your home directory name*

   Press Enter

and for the next line,

   Type *MAP*

   Press Enter

and then on the next line,

   Type *PAUSE*

   Press Enter

EXIT
Terminates the execution of a LOGIN Script and exits to the command-line. Anything placed below the EXIT command will not execute. EXIT, placed in a System LOGIN Script, will bypass all User LOGIN Scripts.

To use the **EXIT** command,

5. **Type** *EXIT*

   Press Enter

and then on the next line, under EXIT,

   Type *DRIVE J:*

   Press Enter

Your REVIEW.LOG is complete and should look similar to Figure 8.4. To save your file using DOS EDIT,

6. **Press** Alt

   Type *F* to pull down the File menu

FIGURE 8.4

```
  File  Edit  Search  Options                                        Help
                            REVIEW.LOG
map ins s1:=sys:public
map s2:=sys:public\%machine\%os\%os_version
comspec=s2:command.com
write "This is the review login script for pharris"
map j:\sys:users/home/pharris
pause
exit
drive j:
_




MS-DOS Editor  <F1=Help> Press ALT to activate menus
```

Type S to Save the file under REVIEW.LOG name displayed at the top of the DOS EDIT screen

and then to exit,

>**Press** [Alt]
>
>**Type** F
>
>**Type** X

You have returned to the G:\> drive prompt.
    To test your script,

>7. **Type** *LOGIN/S A:REVIEW.LOG*
>
>**Press** [Enter]

You are at the F:\LOGIN> prompt rather than drive J because the EXIT command is exiting the LOGIN Script before being able to execute the DRIVE command. To correct, you could edit your REVIEW.LOG file to re-mark the EXIT command using REM EXIT and then test the script again.

KEY RELATED POINTS

COMPSEC is an important identifier that is commonly used in the System LOGIN Script to specify the directory that DOS uses to reload the command processor. As a workstation exits an application, it is essential that the transient portion of the COMMAND.COM file reloads properly so the workstation is not halted from operation.

The System LOGIN Script is contained in SYS:PUBLIC and saved as NET$LOG.DAT, and is created in SYSCON, under Supervisor Options.

The System LOGIN Script maps the first search drive to SYS:PUBLIC to provide access for all users to NetWare utilities (e.g., MAP INS S1:=SYS:PUBLIC).

SET PROMPT = "PG" is recommended to be placed in the LOGIN Script for the directory path to be displayed so the current directory location in the directory structure is visible.

8.5 CREATING A SIMPLE MENU WITH NMENU

Netware's built-in menu system allows you to gain access to resources by customizing the interface to the network operating system. Menus, like LOGIN Scripts, function and run like a batch file. In this exercise, you will create a simple menu using NMENU and MAKEMENU.

This exercise assumes you are logged in and at your home directory prompt shown as drive G, which was established in the previous exercises. This exercise also assumes that you have access to DOS EDIT or another text editing utility that will save your menu file as ASCII text.

At the G:\> prompt displayed on your screen (the root mapping to your home directory for the users\home\your home directory location), use DOS EDIT to create your menu.

Hands-On Exercises

1. **Type** *EDIT MYMENU.SRC*

   Press Enter

The menu file name must have an .SRC extension.
   In the DOS EDIT screen, on the first line of your menu,

2. **Type** *MENU 01, Network Utilities*

   Press Enter

The MENU command will identify the beginning of each menu screen.
   To place an option for your menu,

3. **Press** Spacebar twice

   Type *ITEM File Management*

   Press Enter

File Management will be the first option to appear on your screen.

You need an internal command to execute a file management operation when File Management is selected.

4. **Press** [Spacebar] twice

   Type *EXEC FILER*

   Press [Enter]

When the File Management menu option is selected, this will run the
FILER menu utility.

***NOTE:* Title lines are left-justified, options are indented below the
title lines, and executable lines are indented below the title lines.**

Add a menu option to check your drive mappings,

5. **Press** Remaining on the fourth line, [Backspace] or use the Arrow keys that
   will align your cursor on the fourth line under the *I* of *ITEM A.* shown on the
   second line.

   Type *ITEM List Drive Mappings* on the fourth line

   Press [Enter]

and for the executable line for this menu option,

   Press Spacebar twice

   Type *EXEC MAP*

   Press [Enter]

Add a menu option to exit to the command-line,

6. **Press** Remaining on the sixth line, [Backspace] or use the Arrow keys that
   will align your cursor on the sixth line under the *I* of *ITEM B.* shown on the
   fourth line.

   Type *ITEM Exit to Command-Line* on the sixth line

   Press [Enter]

and for the executable line for this menu option,

   Press [Spacebar] twice

   Type *EXEC DOS*

   Press [Enter]

Refer to Figure 8.5.
To save your menu file using DOS EDIT,

7. **Press** [Alt]

   Type *F* to pull down the File menu

FIGURE 8.5

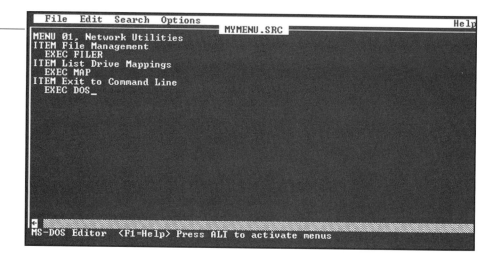

```
 File   Edit   Search   Options                                    Help
                          MYMENU.SRC
MENU 01, Network Utilities
ITEM File Management
   EXEC FILER
ITEM List Drive Mappings
   EXEC MAP
ITEM Exit to Command Line
   EXEC DOS_




MS-DOS Editor  <F1=Help> Press ALT to activate menus
```

Type *S* to Save the file under MYMENU.SRC name displayed at the top of the DOS EDIT screen

and then to exit,

Press Alt

Type *F*

Type *X*

You have returned to the G:\> drive prompt.
To view your file contents,

8. **Type** *TYPE MYMENU.SRC*

Press Enter

The contents of your file should look similar to Figure 8.5.
The next exercise will show you how to run your menu.

OPTIONS FOR THE ITEM COMMAND

BATCH   Used to specify removing the menu program from memory. Approximately 32K of memory are saved by removing NMENU with the BATCH option.

CHDIR   Used to return to the default, original, directory upon completion of the ITEMs.

PAUSE   Used to halt menu execution and display the message, "Strike any key to continue."

SHOW   Used to display DOS commands being executed.

KEY RELATED POINTS

 EXEC will execute any internal or external program. EXEC EXIT, EXEC DOS, EXEC CALL and EXEC LOGOUT are the four options for the EXEC command. EXEC EXIT exits NMENU. EXEC DOS runs a DOS Shell and you type Exit to return to the menu. EXEC CALL starts a batch file running. EXEC LOGOUT exits the menu and logs you out of the network.

 The MENU command is left-justified, followed by a two-digit number, such as 01. The first MENU must be 01.

8.6 COMPILING, RUNNING, AND ADDING YOUR MENU TO YOUR LOGIN SCRIPT

Once the menu file has been created as an ASCII text file, written in menu syntax, and saved with the .SRC filename extension, you are ready to compile and run your menu.

Hands-On Exercises

The MENUMAKE.EXE is stored in the PUBLIC directory and since you have the Read and File Scan rights to PUBLIC, at the G:\> prompt, to compile your menu file,

   I. **Type** *MENUMAKE MYMENU.SRC*

     Press Enter

MENUMAKE
NetWare 3.12 menu compiler, used to convert .SRC files to .DAT files to be used by NMENU.

This will take your file, MYMENU.SRC, and compile it into MYMENU.DAT, making the file much smaller and more flexible to execute. Refer to Figure 8.6.

To run your file, you will use the NMENU.BAT program stored in the PUBLIC directory. To use NMENU,

   2. **Type** *NMENU MYMENU*

     Press Enter

You can test your menu file, or use DOS EDIT to make corrections until your menu is error free.

To add your menu to your LOGIN Script,

   3. **Type** *SYSCON*

     Press Enter

FIGURE 8.6

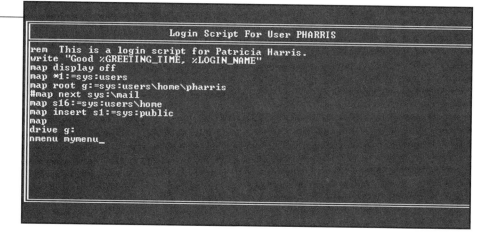

```
F:\USERS\HOME\PHARRIS>menumake mymenu.src
Novell Menu Script Compiler v3.12 (930420)
(c) Copyright 1993, Novell, Inc.  All rights reserved.
F:\USERS\HOME\PHARRIS\MYMENU.SRC:
F:\USERS\HOME\PHARRIS\MYMENU.DAT written.

F:\USERS\HOME\PHARRIS>_
```

FIGURE 8.7

```
═══════════════════ Login Script For User PHARRIS ═══════════════════
rem  This is a login script for Patricia Harris.
write "Good %GREETING_TIME, %LOGIN_NAME"
map display off
map *1:=sys:users
map root g:=sys:users\home\pharris
#map next sys:\mail
map s16:=sys:users\home
map insert s1:=sys:public
map
drive g:
nmenu mymenu_
```

You are at the Available Options menu of SYSCON.

4. Get to the User Information window for your LOGIN name and select LOGIN Script to edit your script.

To execute your menu in your LOGIN Script,

5. Move to the blank line at the end of your LOGIN Script, and

Type EXIT "NMENU MYMENU"

Press [Enter]

Refer to Figure 8.7. Exit SYSCON using [Alt] [F10], log out and log in again to test your changes.

FIGURE 8.8

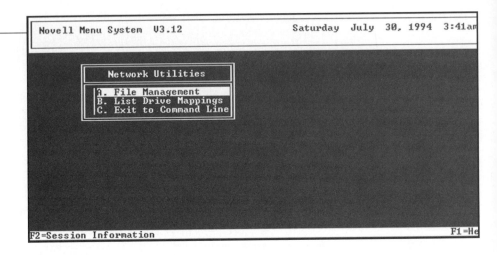

To exit and save your LOGIN Script,

6. **Press** Esc

   Press Enter (highlighted on Yes to Save)

To exit SYSCON,

   Press Alt F10

7. Log out and then log in.

Refer to Figure 8.8. Your menu should look similar.

KEY RELATED POINTS

Compiling is a procedure used to convert programs that are written in human-readable form (source code) into a form that executes more quickly. The .SRC is the source code file and the .DAT file is the compiled file created by running the MAKEMENU utility.

A turnkey system is created by implementing a menu that will execute from a System LOGIN Script. A good menu can be an important security and training device on the network. With limiting the set of options and implementing a menu interface for network workstations, you can lessen both the security and training hazards that are notorious for creating havoc amid network administration.

Inside the menu screen, Pressing F2 gives your session information, such as your LOGIN name, user ID number, how long you have been logged in, etc.

END OF CHAPTER REVIEW

Important Terms

DRIVE	INCLUDE	PAUSE
EXIT	LOGIN /S	WRITE
FIRE or	MENUMAKE	#
FIRE PHASERS		

True/False Questions

1. The three types of LOGIN Scripts are Network, System and User.

2. WRITE "It's %HOUR24:%MINUTE" is a valid LOGIN Script syntax line.

3. The DRIVE command is used to specify your directory location after the LOGIN Script ends.

4. The EXIT command is used to exit the LOGIN Script to begin executing a menu file.

5. WRITE "It's a splendid time to work on the network. It is %hour:%minute:%second AM_PM" is a valid LOGIN Script syntax line.

ON YOUR OWN—HANDS-ON

Using LOGIN/S, create a REVIEW2.LOG file that will:

1. Map drive K to your home directory.

2. Map the next available search drive to the USERS directory.

3. Fire three phasers.

4. Write a greeting message using %GREETING_TIME to display on your screen as you log in.

5. Write the time of day, the day, the month, and the year to display on your screen as you log in.

6. Use the DRIVE command to position you at drive K.

7. Exit the LOGIN Script.

IN YOUR OWN WORDS

1. Write an IF statement that will incorporate a greeting for Friday the 13th.

2. Write another IF statement that will WRITE a message to screen on or after (using >= symbols) the 14th day of the month that will remind you that your rent is due tomorrow (the 15th).

3. Create a text file and use LOGIN/S to test the following LOGIN Script lines. Write what is displayed on your screen on the blank lines below.

   A. WRITE "This is day %DAY."
      What did your screen display?

      _____

      How would this differ from WRITE "Today is the %DAY_OF_WEEK?"

      _____

   B. WRITE "It's %HOUR24:%MINUTE"
      What "type" of time is displayed on your screen?

      _____

4. Under what conditions is the Default LOGIN Script executed?

C H A P T E R   9

Windows and NetWare

OBJECTIVES

- Navigate Windows using a Mouse.

- Use NetWare User Tools to attach to other file servers.

- Obtain a list of active users with NetWare User Tools.

- Map drives with NetWare User Tools.

- Set up Printing with NetWare User Tools.

- Use NetWare User Tools to customize its display settings.

CHAPTER INTRODUCTION

The NetWare User Tools Windows icon is installed when a NetWare 3.12 workstation is installed. The NetWare User Tools window utility enables users to manage their NetWare working environment in a variety of ways, such as logging in and logging out, attaching to servers, mapping drives, changing passwords, and capturing network printers.

Along the top of the NetWare User Tools utility window is a series of buttons in the Button Bar. In Exercise 9.1, you will work with navigating Windows and the NetWare User Tools utility windows.

9.1 NAVIGATING NETWARE USER TOOLS

This exercise is designed to show you how to launch NetWare User Tools utility window. You will learn to navigate in Windows to launch NetWare User Tools.

Once you begin Windows, the Windows Program Manager window is displayed. The mouse is used to select icons in the Program Manager to open other windows where you can run other applications within Windows, such as the NetWare User Tools graphical interface utility for accessing and managing connections with NetWare 3.x servers.

This exercise assumes that you have started Windows on your workstation and are at the Program Manager window. Figure 9.1 is labeled to show you some common elements associated with Windows that you will use as you work through the exercises in Chapter 9.

Figure 9.1 shows the Program Manager window with labels to clarify the Control Menu box, Title Bar, Menu Bar, Program Manager window, NetWare User Tools Application icon, Mouse pointer, Window, pull-down menus, scroll bars, and sizing buttons.

The *first button* in the Button Bar (the open door with the arrow) serves as a quick way to exit the NetWare User Tools utility. Refer to Figure 9.2.

When the *second button* in the Button Bar is selected, the Drive Connections window is displayed. The Drive Connections window is used to map drives, view directory rights, change a drive root map, delete drive mappings, and to display volume and drive information.

The *third button* in the Button Bar is shown as a printer and displays the NetWare Printer Connections window when selected. The NetWare Printer Connections window is used to set printer options such as selecting a print queue and capturing printer(s) to LPT ports.

The *fourth button* in the Button Bar displays the NetWare Connections window, where you can view individual server information, change your LOGIN password, attach and log in to NetWare server(s), and detach network connections.

FIGURE 9.1

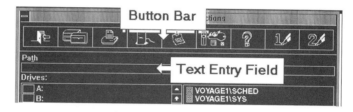

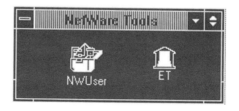

The *fifth button* in the Button Bar is shown as a note held by a push-pin. When this button is selected, the NetWare Send Messages window is displayed. The NetWare Send Messages window is where you can view and select group or user names for sending broadcast screen messages.

The *sixth button* is used to display the NetWare Settings window. The NetWare Settings window provides you with a window to set the working parameters of the NetWare User Tools utility.

The *seventh* and *eighth buttons,* shown as 1 and 2 in the Button Bar, are user defined buttons. These buttons allow you to start other programs by defining the path to the executable file(s) necessary to load the program. You can, for example, use one of these buttons to start the Windows File Manager utility.

The *ninth button* in the Button Bar, shown as a question mark, is used to access NetWare User Tools Help window contents.

As shown in Figure 9.3, the various window(s) of the NetWare User Tools utility are comprised of a button bar, buttons, fields, list boxes, a title bar, and a close box.

Figure 9.3 shows NetWare User Tools utility window with labels to clarify the buttons in the Button box, the Close box, Text entry field, List boxes, and buttons.

To operate the mouse, some basic terminology is used in this chapter. *Point* is used to indicate moving the mouse pointer. *Click* is used to indicate pressing and releasing the mouse button, while *Double-Click* is used to indicate quickly pressing and releasing the mouse button twice. *Drag* is used to indicate holding down the mouse button and moving an item, carried by the mouse pointer, to another location. *Drop* is used to indicate releasing the mouse button to release the "drag" item.

Terminology for describing mouse pointer shapes used in this chapter are shown by the following tables of shapes and descriptions.

PICTORIAL TABLE OF MOUSE POINTER SHAPES

▶	Arrow Shape	Used to highlight or select items, push buttons, or choose commands.
I	I-beam Shape	Used to position an insertion point.
⌶	Insertion Point	Used to mark a text entry point in a text entry field.

FIGURE 9.2

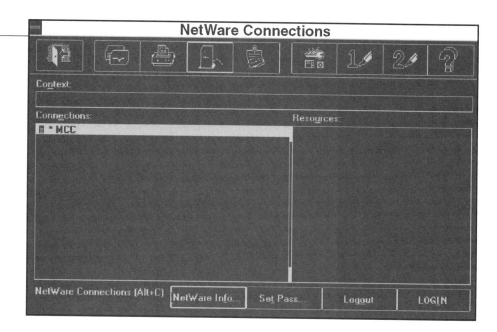

FIGURE 9.3

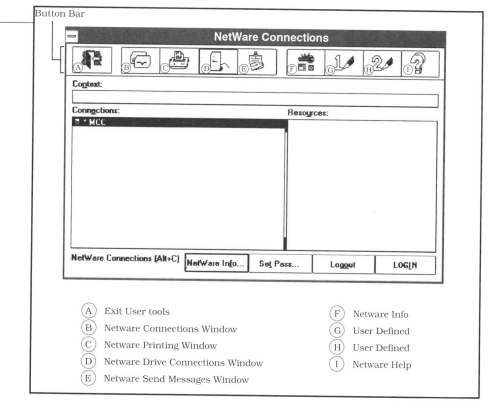

(A)	Exit User tools	(F)	Netware Info
(B)	Netware Connections Window	(G)	User Defined
(C)	Netware Printing Window	(H)	User Defined
(D)	Netware Drive Connections Window	(I)	Netware Help
(E)	Netware Send Messages Window		

PICTORIAL TABLE OF NETWARE USER
TOOLS SHAPES AND ICONS

	NetWare Tools Icon	Used to launch NetWare User Tools, a Graphical User Interface Utility for accessing and managing your connection with NetWare 3.x servers.
	Drive Shape	Used to map drives in the NetWare Drive Connections window.
	Unavailable Drive Shape	Used to indicate no drive mapping possible for the active area in the NetWare Drive Connections window.
	Permanent Drive Icon	Used to indicate a permanent drive mapping in the NetWare Drive Connections window.
	Drive Map Icon	Used to indicate a network drive mapping in the NetWare Drive Connections window.
	Printer Shape	Used to assign a print queue to capture an LPT port in the NetWare Printer Connections window.
	Unavailable Printer Shape	Used to indicate no print queue assignment possible for the active area in the NetWare Printer Connections window.
	Server Shape	Used to log in or log out in the NetWare Connections window.
	Unavailable Server Shape	Used to indicate unable to log in or log out for the active area in the NetWare Connections window.
	User Icon	Used to represent sending a message to a username in the NetWare Send Messages window.
	Group Icon	Used to represent sending a message to the members of a group in the NetWare Send Messages window.

9.2 NETWARE USER TOOLS—NETWARE CONNECTIONS

In this exercise, you will use the NetWare User Tools window utility to log in and log out of the server. You will use the NetWare Info button to gain information about your server and your connection.

This exercise assumes that your workstation has already been installed and configured as a NetWare 3.12 Windows workstation.

Hands-On Exercise

NetWare Connections Window
Lets you view individual server information, change your LOGIN password, and establish a network connection using log in and log out.

To begin, start Windows and click on the NetWare User Tools Windows Icon.

   1. **Double-Click** on *NetWare Tools icon*
      (from the NetWare Tools window—Refer to Figure 9.1)

You are looking at the Connections window.

***NOTE:* To make the NetWare Connections window your active window, you can use the keyboard shortcut, Alt C.**

To log in to your server,

   2. **Double-Click** your server's icon from the Resource box

and then

     Click to push the LOGIN button (at the bottom of the window)

This will open the LOGIN to NetWare window and place your blinking I-beam in the User Name field.

From the User Name field,

   3. **Type** *YOUR USERNAME*

     Press Tab

     Type *YOUR PASSWORD*

***NOTE:* Each character in your preferred password will be displayed as an asterisk (*) in the Password field.**

     Click to push the OK button

Upon a successful log in, your server's icon will be removed from the Resource box and your server will be added to the servers in the Connections window. Refer to Figure 9.4.

To log out of the network, from the Connections box,

   4. **Click** to highlight your file server, and then

     Click to push the Logout button (at the bottom of the window)

You are still highlighted on your file server icon in the Connections box, but notice that your server's icon has less definition and is, in fact, pictured as an outline or shadow of a server. Also, when you are logged out of the server, only the Login button is available at the bottom of the NetWare Connections window.

To log back in to your server,

5. **Double-Click** to highlight and select your file server from the Resources box, and then from the Login to NetWare window,

Type *YOUR USERNAME*

Press (Tab)

Type *YOUR PASSWORD*

Click to push the OK button, or

Press (Enter)

NOTE: **When you are logged in to the server, the icon in the Connections box is pictured as a sharper image and matches the icon in the Resource box at the top of the NetWare Connections window. Notice the icon pictured in the Connections Box of Figure 9.4.**

FIGURE 9.4

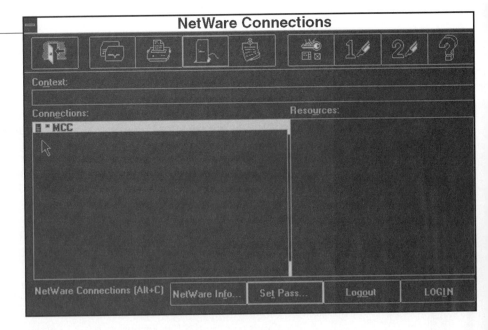

FIGURE 9.5

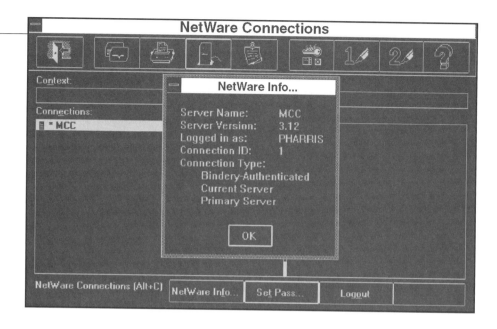

To obtain information about the network,

6. **Double-Click** your server to highlight and select your server from the Connections box

Your screen displays the NetWare Info...window, showing information about the server you are logged in to and information about your connection to the server. Your screen may look similar to Figure 9.5.

After reading the NetWare Info...screen,

7. **Click** to push the OK button in the NetWare Info...window

***NOTE:* Rather than double-click on your server's icon in the Connections box, you could**

Double-Click to highlight your server's icon from the Connections box, and then

Click to push the NetWare Info button

Refer to Figure 9.5.

To set your password,

8. **Click** to push the Set Pass...button (at the bottom of the NetWare Connections window)

Your screen displays the NetWare Set Password window with a blinking I-beam in the Old Password field.

You can see how easy it is to reset your password, so for now,

    9. **Click** *Cancel*

This will take you back to the NetWare Connections window.

    To quickly log out of your file server, you can use the mouse to "drag and drop" your server icon from the Connections box to the Resources box. To use the "drag and drop" method of logging out,

    10. Move the mouse pointer to your server's icon pictured in the Connections box, and,

        Click to select your server's icon and hold down the left mouse button.

        Drag your server's icon toward the Resources box.

FIGURE 9.6

NOTE: **As you drag the server's icon toward the Resources box, an icon similar to Figure 9.6 appears. As you move the icon from the Connections window into the Resources window into the Resources box, the icon changes to closely resemble Figure 9.7.**

Once you drag the server's icon to the Resources box, to log out,

    11. Drop the icon into the Resources box, and release the mouse button.

        The icon has changed back to where you began this exercise, resembling the same grayed outline image of the server's icon pictured in the first step of this exercise.

FIGURE 9.7

KEY RELATED POINTS

 Bindery-Authenticated, shown for the Connection Type in the NetWare Info...window, means you are working from a Bindery Services server. If you were working from NetWare 4.x, the Context field would be important to change how NDS (NetWare Directory Services) views your connection. Since the NetWare Info...window displays your connection as Bindery-Authenticated rather than as NetWare Directory Services, this indicates a NetWare 3.12 server.

NETWARE TOOLS—WINDOW QUICK KEYS

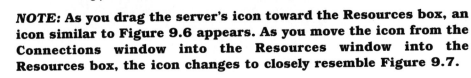

NetWare Connections Window	[Alt] [C]	NetWare Connections [Alt+C]
Drive Connections Window	[Alt] [D]	Drive Connections [Alt+D]
NetWare Help Window	[Alt] [H]	NetWare Help... [Alt+H]
Send Messages Window	[Alt] [M]	Send Messages [Alt+M]
Printer Connections Window	[Alt] [P]	Printer Connections [Alt+P]
NetWare Settings Window	[Alt] [S]	NetWare Settings... [Alt+S]

NOTE: **Each time you use the Quick Keys, the corresponding button in the Resource box will depress automatically. When the mouse pointer is resting over an icon in the Button Bar, the keyboard alternative (shortcut key) is shown in the lower-left corner of the window.**

9.3 NETWARE DRIVE CONNECTIONS

This exercise introduces you to the NetWare Drive Connections window, and assumes that your workstation has already been installed and configured as a NetWare 3.12 Windows workstation. It also assumes that you have started Windows and are active in the NetWare Connections window.

Hands-On Exercise

After logging in from the NetWare Connections window, to view information about your drive connections,

    I. **Press** Alt D

Your screen displays the NetWare Drive Connections window.

NOTE: **To view your drive mappings, you could also click on the Drive Connections icon from the row of icons at the top of the NetWare Connections window.**

To map drive K to your home directory,

    2. **Click** on drive K in the Drives: window and then

        Double-Click on the volume SYS icon in the Resources box.

The directories for volume SYS appear as folders. To open your home directory folder,

        Double-click on the Users Folder and then

        Double-Click on the Users and then on the HOME directory folder.

NOTE: **The Path: field is tracking your selections from the Resources box and displays "\\servername\SYS\USERS\HOME."**

Find your folder in the list of folders under the HOME folder and

        Click once to select your home directory folder.

To finish mapping this drive,

        Click to push the Map button at the bottom of the NetWare Drive Connections window.

Drive K is now showing "*servername*\SYS\USERS\HOME*your home directory name*\" and drive K is now mapped to your home directory. Refer to Figure 9.8.

To obtain information about your home directory, while highlighted on drive K, mapped to your home directory,

3. **Click** to push the Drive Info... button

The Drive Info...window displays your server, path, username, and effective rights to this directory.

Click to push OK (on the Drive Info...window)

You are back at the NetWare Drive Connections window.

To delete the drive mapping, while still highlighted on drive K in the Drives: window,

4. **Click** to push the Map Delete button

Your map for drive K has been deleted and the grayed text labels over the control buttons at the bottom of the window indicate they are no longer available. The Map button is the only button available.

Notice that the path in the Path: field near the top of the window still displays "*servername*\SYS\USERS\HOME*your home directory name*\." To map drive S to your home directory,

5. **Click** the ⬇ in the Drives: box six times to display drive S.

Click to select drive S

Click to push the Map control button.

To collapse the Directory Tree of folders in your Resources box,

6. **Click** to push the ⬆ on the vertical scroll bar of the Resources box until you reach the top of the Directory Tree.

With the Server icon for volume SYS showing,

Double-click on the Server icon for your server.

Your screen displays the Volume SYS without the Directory Tree of folders.

KEY RELATED POINTS

 The Permanent button in the NetWare Drive Connections window stores the location designated in the directory structure to invoke the map setting whenever you start the NetWare Tools, NetWare Windows interface.

FIGURE 9.8

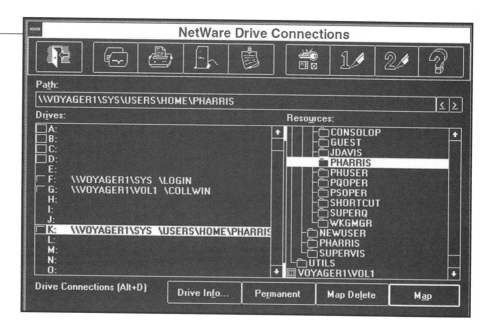

NetWare Drive Connections

Path:
\\VOYAGER1\SYS\USERS\HOME\PHARRIS

Drives:

Resources:

A:
B:
C:
D:
E:
F: \\VOYAGER1\SYS \LOGIN
G: \\VOYAGER1\VOL1 \COLLWIN
H:
I:
J:
K: \\VOYAGER1\SYS \USERS\HOME\PHARRIS
L:
M:
N:
O:

CONSOLOP
GUEST
JDAVIS
PHARRIS
PHUSER
PQOPER
PSOPER
SHORTCUT
SUPERQ
WKGMGR
NEWUSER
PHARRIS
SUPERVIS
UTILS
VOYAGER1\VOL1

Drive Connections (Alt+D)   Drive Info...   Permanent   Map Delete   Map

9.4 NETWARE SEND MESSAGES WINDOW

In this exercise you will work with the **NetWare Send Messages Window**.
This exercise assumes that your workstation has already been installed and configured as a NetWare 3.12 Windows workstation. It also assumes that you have started Windows and are active in the NetWare Connections window.

Hands-On Exercise

To quickly move to the NetWare Send Messages window,

1. **Press** Alt M

You are highlighted on your file server icon in the Connections box. Refer to Figure 9.9.
To view information about your connection,

**NetWare Send
Messages Window**
Lets you show or
hide groups or users,
send messages to a
group or user, and
display information
about the server.

2. **Click** to push the NetWare Info...control button at the bottom of the NetWare Send Messages screen.

Notice this is the same network information displayed for Exercise 9.1, using the NetWare Connections Window's NetWare Info...button.
To hide the users,

3. **Click** to push the Hide Users button at the bottom of the NetWare Send Messages window.

FIGURE 9.9

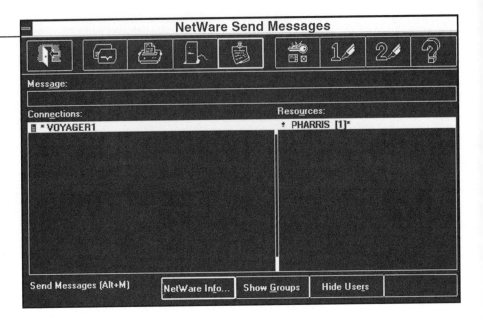

The listing of users logged in disappears.

To show the users logged in (similar to using USERLIST at the command-line),

4. **Click** to push the Show Users button at the bottom of the NetWare Send Messages window.

The listing of users logged in is displayed in the Resources box. The number inside the square brackets ([ ]) listed after your username is your connection number.

To show all the groups for this server,

5. **Click** to push the Show Groups button at the bottom of the NetWare Send Messages window.

This feature is used to send a message to a group, rather than to an individual user.

To select a user and compose a message,

6. **Click** to select your username from the Resources: list box

(Click to push the Show Users button to find your username)

Move the mouse pointer to the Message: field. As you move it, notice that the mouse pointer changes to an I-beam. When the mouse pointer has changed to an I-beam in the Message: field,

Click to activate a blinking Insertion mark in the Message: text entry field, and then

Type *TESTING*

To send your message,

> 7. **Click** to push the Send button at the bottom of the NetWare Send Messages window.

The Send Message Info pop-up window displays the confirmation that your message was sent and shows your username.

> **Click** to push OK

To receive your message, use the MS-DOS Prompt, leaving Windows, for Username PHARRIS, the screen message at the DOS prompt reveals, >>From: PHARRIS[1]: Testing (Press Ctrl Enter). Type EXIT at the prompt to return to windows.

NetWare Printer Connection Window
Lets you set printer options, make a print queue connection permanent, and connect and disconnect a print queue.

NetWare Settings Window
Lets you set permanent connections to restore when loading Windows, set message reception on or off, set the print manager and resource display options, and change the hot key value.

9.5 NETWARE PRINTER CONNECTIONS AND NETWARE SETTINGS WINDOWS

In this exercise you will work with the **NetWare Printer Connections** and **NetWare Settings Windows**.

This exercise assumes that your workstation has already been installed and configured as a NetWare 3.12 Windows workstation. It also assumes that you have started Windows and are active in the NetWare Connections window.

Hands-On Exercise

To quickly move to the NetWare Settings window,

> 1. **Press** Alt S

Your screen displays the NetWare Settings windows.
To turn off messaging for your workstation,

> 2. **Click** to deselect and remove the X from the Broadcast field in the Message Reception box.

You have removed messaging from being broadcast to your screen. Refer to Figure 9.10.
To move to the NetWare Printer,

> 3. **Click** to push OK in the NetWare Settings window

You are back at the NetWare Connections window.

> **Press** Alt P to move to the Printer Connections window

In order to work with this screen, you must select an LPT port and a print queue from the print queues listed in the Resources box.
To select a print queue, move your mouse pointer to the queue name, and

> 4. **Click** on the queue name in the Resources box. Select your Q1*xxx* queue.

Next, select the LPT port from the Ports box and then

5. **Click** to push the Capture button at the bottom of the NetWare Printer Connections window.

Refer to Figure 9.11.

To increase the number of copies to be printed from one to two copies,

6. **Click** to push the LPT Settings...control button at the bottom of the window.

Click ⬆ once in the Copies field

The number 2 now appears in the Copies field.

To change the second Banner name from LST: to print your first name,

7. Move the mouse pointer over the letter S of LST: shown in the second Banner name field.

Double-Click to select the field contents, LST: and then,

Press Del on your keyboard.

This removed the LST: entry in the second Banner name field.

Type *YOUR FIRST NAME*

Click to push the OK button

Refer to Figure 9.11.

FIGURE 9.10

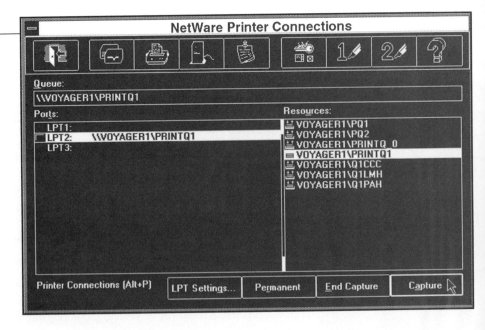

FIGURE 9.11

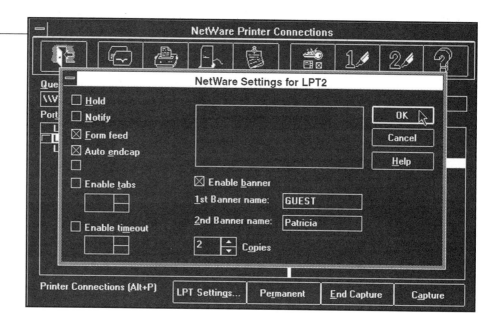

KEY RELATED POINTS

- The Bindery Resource Display Options from the NetWare Settings screen is any entry maintained for a NetWare 3.x in the bindery database files. Objects in the bindery database, such as users, groups, and printers, are checked and granted access as you log in.

- DS Objects are Directory Services objects, associated with NetWare 4.x servers. Each object for a NetWare 4.x Directory Services server are either network resources or objects that reside in the Directory Tree. The DS Container is a container object for other objects in NetWare 4.x.

- LST: indicates a CAPTURE submission into the Print Queue, and a filename indicates an NPRINT submission. Refer to Chapter 6, Exercise 6.2, for more information.

END OF CHAPTER REVIEW

Important Terms

NetWare Connections Window
NetWare Printer Connection Window

NetWare Send Messages Window
NetWare Settings Window

True/False Questions

1. To quickly move to the NetWare Send Messages window, you press Alt S.

2. The NetWare User Tools Windows icon is installed when a NetWare 3.12 workstation is installed.

3. Along the top of the NetWare User Tools utility window is a series of buttons called the Button Bar.

4. When the second button in the Button bar is selected, the NetWare Connections window is displayed.

5. To quickly log out of your file server, you can use the mouse to "drag and drop" your server icon from the Connections box to the Resources box.

ON YOUR OWN

1. Using the NetWare Drive Connections window, map drive M to volume SYS, map drive F to the LOGIN directory, and map drive J to your User ID numbered directory listed in the MAIL directory folder. Make drive F mapping a permanent mapping.

2. Use NetWare User Tools to find out which window matches the specific function.

   1. NetWare Drive Connections
   2. NetWare Server Connections
   3. NetWare Settings
   4. NetWare Printer Connections

   A. Sets Passwords
   B. Customizes NetWare User Tools for Windows display settings.
   C. Maps a drive to a directory.
   D. Captures workstation's printer ports to a network print queue.

3. Use NetWare User Tools to answer the following True/False Questions.

   A. NetWare User Tools is used to manage printer connections and printer setup.
   B. You can assign directory rights with NetWare User Tools.
   C. You can view users and send messages with NetWare User Tools.
   D. Using NetWare User Tools you can create groups.
   E. With the NetWare Settings window you can set connections to network servers.
   F. With the NetWare Settings window you can change the hot key value for NetWare User Tools.
   G. With the NetWare Settings window you can view the drive mappings for your workstation.
   H. With the NetWare Settings window you can allow or block incoming messages.
   I. With the NetWare Settings window you can allow for permanent connections.

Electronic Messages— FirstMail in 3.12

OBJECTIVES

- Address and Send a NetWare FirstMail Message.

- Read, Reply and Forward a NetWare FirstMail Message.

- See Delete a FirstMail Message in your mailbox.

- Explore the Anatomy of a Message Header.

CHAPTER INTRODUCTION

Basic MHS (message handling system) and FirstMail come with NetWare 3.12 as a starter kit for electronic messaging. FirstMail is the electronic mail utility and Basic MHS is used to install FirstMail. Basic MHS provides message delivery among users on the same file server, and can be upgraded to Global MHS for messaging among users at multiple-file servers to allow communication among multiple workgroups.

The Basic MHS database defines the users of FirstMail, or whatever MHS-compatible electronic mail application you use for electronic mail delivery. With Basic MHS, the users are organized into logical groups, called *workgroups*. The default addressing for workgroups is the name of the file server. You are prompted for a long name and a short name for workgroups during installation.

The User Addresses are uniquely identified by MHS during installation. You have the option to use either the full names or LOGIN names for the MHS names upon installation. For example, to send a message to Paul Dixon on the Alfie file server, the address could be given as *"Paul Dixon@Alfie"* if you had chosen the full name option upon installation. If you had chosen to use the LOGIN names, and Paul Dixon's LOGIN name is PDixon, then you would address the message *"PDixon@Alfie."* Since Basic MHS only supports communication within a single-file server, when you send a message, the workgroup address is optional.

Upon installation, the Default subdirectory location for users' mailboxes and the Basic MHS database is located off of volume SYS: in the MHS\MAIL subdirectory. This can be changed to another subdirectory location to allow more space for messaging.

When NetWare users are created, they are assigned to a subdirectory within the SYS:MAIL directory by the User ID number and identified as having this as their mailbox for accessing User LOGIN Scripts each time they log in. This is not to be confused with the Basic MHS mailbox under SYS:MHS\MAIL, where electronic messaging is supported. However, the SYS:MAIL subdirectory can be used by mail programs that are compatible with NetWare.

NetWare contains a database, called the bindery, that defines entities for users, and is designed to organize and secure the operating environment. The members of the bindery object group Everyone can be added automatically as Basic MHS users upon installation of Basic MHS, or you can choose to add users manually to the Basic MHS database. By default, the installation of Basic MHS authorizes the Supervisor and Supervisor Equivalent users to update the MHS database.

The System LOGIN Script can be updated upon installation of Basic MHS to automatically enable MHS for all users. Also, the file server can be set up so Basic MHS is automatically loaded as the file server is booted.

FirstMail is available in both DOS and Macintosh versions. Upon installation, FirstMail for DOS is automatically established in the SYS:PUBLIC subdirectory when Basic MHS is installed. Basic MHS maintains the FirstMail, SMF directory list of users. When you address your message recipient(s), you can use the SMF directory list by pressing F2.

10.1 GETTING STARTED WITH FIRSTMAIL

In this exercise, you will start FirstMail from your workstation. You will compose, address and send a message.

This exercise assumes that MHS and FirstMail have been properly set up on your file server. This exercise also assumes that you are logged in to your NetWare file server.

Hands-On Exercise

After logging in to NetWare, from the F:\LOGIN> prompt, to start FirstMail,

1. **Type** *MAIL*

   Press Enter

The Mail Options menu should appear on your screen. Refer to Figure 10.1.
   To compose a message,

2. **Type** *S* for Send a mail message

The Send Message: Editing Screen appears on your screen. Refer to Figure 10.2.
   To address your message,

3. **Press** F2

You are viewing the Directory List.

   Press ↓ to move the highlight bar to find your name in the list

Once highlighted on your username,

   Press Spacebar to Select

   Press Esc to exit Selecting

You are now back at the Editing screen.
   For the subject line,

4. **Type** *FIRST MESSAGE*

To compose your message from the Send Message screen,

5. **Type** *MY FIRST MAIL MESSAGE.*

   Press Enter

To send your message from the Send Message screen,

    6. **Press** Ctrl Enter

You can see the Options screen.
    To send a copy to yourself, highlight Keep a copy? from the Options screen,

    7. **Type** Y at Keep a copy?

You will be sent a copy of this message.
    To send your message, from the Send Message: Editing Screen,

    8. **Press** Ctrl Enter

FirstMail returns you to the Mail Options, FirstMail's main menu.

KEY RELATED POINTS

Basic MHS maintains the FirstMail, SMF directory list of users. When you address your message recipient(s), you can use the SMF directory list by pressing F2.

The group Everyone can be added automatically as Basic MHS users upon installation of Basic MHS, or you can choose to add users manually to the Basic MHS database.

FIGURE 10.1

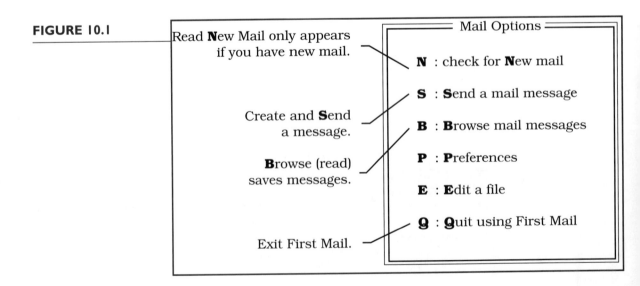

Read **N**ew Mail only appears if you have new mail.

Create and **S**end a message.

Browse (read) saves messages.

Exit First Mail.

Mail Options

N : check for **N**ew mail

S : **S**end a mail message

B : **B**rowse mail messages

P : **P**references

E : **E**dit a file

Q : **Q**uit using First Mail

FIGURE 10.2

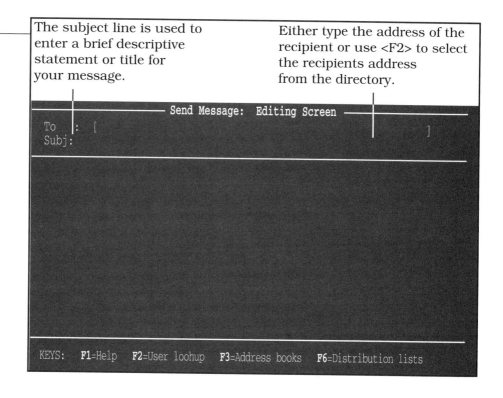

The subject line is used to enter a brief descriptive statement or title for your message.

Either type the address of the recipient or use <F2> to select the recipients address from the directory.

```
─────────────────── Send Message:  Editing Screen ───────────────────
 To  |: [                                                            ]
 Subj:

KEYS:   F1=Help   F2=User loohup   F3=Address books   F6=Distribution lists
```

COMMON KEYS FOR FIRSTMAIL'S
SEND MESSAGE: EDITING SCREEN

F1	Help	F7	File attachments
F2	User lookup	F9	More options
F3	Address books	Alt F10	Quit FirstMail
F5	Mark multiple items	Ctrl Enter	Send the message
F6	Distribution lists		

10.2 READ, REPLY AND FORWARD A FIRSTMAIL MESSAGE

In this exercise, you will learn how to read, reply and forward a FirstMail message. You will also be given information on deleting a message.

This exercise assumes that MHS and FirstMail have been properly established on your file server and that you are logged in to your NetWare file server.

Hands-On Exercise

After logging in to NetWare, from the F:\LOGIN> prompt, and starting FirstMail, from FirstMail's main menu, Mail Options,

 1. **Type** *N* to read your New Mail messages

Displayed on your screen is the New Mail folder showing the New Mail message from Exercise 10.1. Refer to Figure 10.1

With the highlight bar on the message you sent yourself from the previous exercise with the subject title showing *"First message,"*

 2. **Press** Enter

You are now at the screen where you are reading your message. This screen is used for either reading new mail or browsing previously read mail messages with the Browse mail option.

***NOTE:* While reading your message, look at the bottom of the screen at the commands available. Notice that you can read the next message by using the plus (+) key or read the previous message by using the minus (–) key.**

When you are reading your message, you can also forward or reply to the message. While reading your message, to forward this message,

 3. **Type** *F* to select the forward option

Refer to Figure 10.3.

At the Forward Message or file window, with your cursor at To [,

 Press F2

The Distribution List is shown. Move the highlight bar to your name in the list and then,

 Press Enter

To finish forwarding this message, at the Edit before sending? question,

 4. **Type** *Y*

Your message is displayed so you can edit it before sending it.

To add a new line of text to your message,

 5. Move your cursor past the last line of text and on the next line,

 Type *THIS IS A FORWARD, NOT BACKWARD, MESSAGE.*

Then to send the message,

 Press Ctrl Enter

FIGURE 10.3

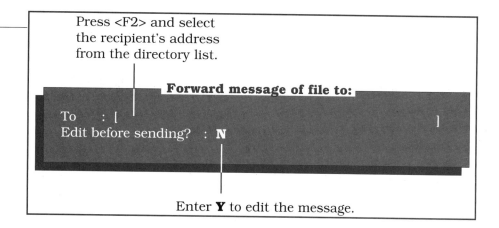

Press <F2> and select
the recipient's address
from the directory list.

Forward message of file to:

To   : [   ]
Edit before sending?   : **N**

Enter **Y** to edit the message.

FirstMail forwards the message and returns you to the New Mail window.

To reply to a message, first

6. **Press** [Esc] to return to Mail Options

From Mail Options,

Type *B* to Browse messages

You are at the Browse mail messages window, similar to the one displayed when you selected the option to read New Mail.

To reply to a message from browse,

7. **Type** *R* to select Reply

When you select the Browse mail option, FirstMail will always open the folder you were in last.

From the Select reply format window,

8. **Type** *N* for all options listed in this window

Refer to Figure 10.4.

When you are finished setting your reply options,

Press [Ctrl] [Enter]

You are now at the Editing window.

At the Editing window, to finish your reply and send your message,

9. **Press** [Ctrl] [Enter]

You are returned to the Browse mail window.

Press [Esc] to exit to the Mail Options window

FIGURE 10.4

To include the original message in the reply, set the Include message option to Y.

To send a copy of this reply to anyone else who received a copy of the original message, set the appropriate fields to Y.

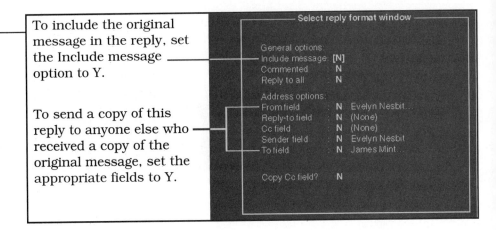

KEY RELATED POINTS

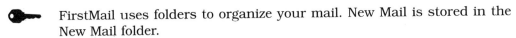 FirstMail uses folders to organize your mail. New Mail is stored in the New Mail folder.

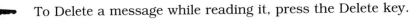 To Delete a message while reading it, press the Delete key.

END OF CHAPTER REVIEW

True/False Questions

1. FirstMail keeps your read mail messages in the New Mail folder.

2. After forwarding a message from the New Mail window, FirstMail forwards the message and returns you to the New Mail window.

3. Alt Enter is used to send a message.

4. When addressing your message, F2 is used to select a recipient from the SMF directory list.

5. By default, Basic MHS mailboxes are created under SYS:MHS\ MAIL where electronic messaging is supported by FirstMail or other MHS mail products.

ON YOUR OWN—HANDS-ON

1. Write (compose) and send a mail message to your instructor about why you are taking this course. Make a copy for yourself before sending the message.

2. Compose a message to a classmate about your favorite feature of FirstMail. Explain how this feature is important or beneficial to enhancing your productivity with electronic messaging. Include a copy for your instructor.

IN YOUR OWN WORDS

1. Send an electronic message to your instructor that explains, in your own words, the relationship between Basic MHS and FirstMail. Cite why both products are necessary.

2. Send an electronic message to your instructor that would explain options you would keep at the Default and ones you might think of changing for a course with high enrollment that teaches strictly electronic messaging. Explain if you think you might create work-groups and, if so, what would the workgroup name(s) be. For this course, would you think teaching mail administration would be an important component or just teaching the "how to's" of operating an electronic messaging package.

Command Summary

ATTACH NetWare command used to open another logical connection with another server. Type ATTACH servername/LOGIN name at the command line. This command depends upon you having access (a valid username and password) for another server.

CAPTURE NetWare's command-line printing utility used to re-route your print jobs to a specified print queue.

CHKDIR Command-line utility for viewing directory and volume disk storage space available and in use.

CHKVOL Command-line utility to show volume information.

DRIVE Specifies your default drive as you exit the LOGIN Script. Used in LOGIN Scripts to set your default drive so you will not have to change your preferred drive specification every time you log in.

DSPACE Menu utility for viewing directory and volume disk storage space available and in use. The System Administrator may use this utility to change disk storage space on a volume or directory.

ENDCAP Used to re-route printing to LPT1, reassigning the captured network printer for LPT1. END-CAP must be used when CAPTURE's NoAutoendcap option is chosen.

EXIT Terminates the execution of a LOGIN Script and exits to the command-line. Anything placed below the EXIT command will not execute. EXIT, placed in a System LOGIN Script, will bypass all User LOGIN Scripts.

FILER NetWare's menu utility for controlling volume, directory, and file information.

FIRE or FIRE PHASERS Used to execute a sound within a LOGIN Script. Fire will execute a sound from one to nine times.

FLAG Used to change or view file attributes. Comparable to DOS ATTRIB command.

INCLUDE Used to incorporate another script file that is written in LOGIN Script syntax and read into the LOGIN Script as it executes.

LISTDIR Command used to view directory structure and rights information.

LOGIN NetWare's Command to activate and open a session (log in) to the Network Operating System (NOS) for a user. The full syntax for the Login command is LOGIN servername/ username. The severname option is only used to specify a particular server, and usually not needed to log in. The LOGIN username option is typically given at the command-line to log in to your workstation's default server. Refer to Exercise 2.1 to see your default server.

LOGIN/S Used to override LOGIN Scripts by redirecting to another path where a text file is written in LOGIN Script syntax.

LOGOUT NetWare's command to terminate a logical connection.

MAP Used to create, change, or view network drive mappings.

MAP .. Remap one level back in the directory structure

MAP ... Remap two levels back in the directory structure.

**MAP ** Remap to the root directory, NetWare's volume level.

MAP *(number):= Used to assign the second network drive letter to a directory path. (e.g., MAP *2:=/USERS).

MAP DEL Used to delete drive mappings. Referred to as NetWare's Map Delete command. Works the same as MAP REM.

MAP DEL drive letter: Commonly used to delete network drive mappings. When used to delete a search mapping, NetWare notifies you of deleting your search map and asks for confirmation.

MAP DEL S(*number*): Used to delete search drive mappings.

MAPS INS Used to create a search drive mapping by inserting a mapping at a specified search numbered location. MAPS INS automatically renumbers and rotates the existing search mapping(s), moving them farther down the search path to make room for the inserted search drive mapping.

MAP NEXT Used to map the next available network drive letter to a directory path specified.

MAP REM Same as MAP DEL. Referred to as NetWare's MAP REMove command.

MAP ROOT Used to create a fake root directory. Can be assigned to any location in the directory structure.

MAP S16 NetWare assigns the next available search drive when using S16 as a way to prevent overwriting existing search drive mappings. Sixteen search drives are possible with NetWare. Defining drive mappings using S16 will map the next available search drive number.

MENUMAKE NetWare 3.12 menu compiler, used to convert .SRC files to .DAT files to be used by NMENU.

NCOPY Used to copy files and retain their attributes. Comparable to DOS COPY command.

NDIR Used for listing file and directory information. NetWare's NDIR command is comparable to DOS DIR.

NPRINT NetWare's command-line utility for printing text files.

PAUSE Breaks or pauses the execution of a LOGIN Script until any key is pressed.

PC Personal Computer. With networks, any personal computer can be called a node.

PCONSOLE Menu utility for controlling network printing.

RENDIR NetWare's command-line utility used to rename a directory.

SALVAGE NetWare's menu utility for recovering or purging deleted files.

SESSION Netware's menu utility to enable users to set up and change their own working environment.

SLIST Command-line utility is used to view information about your physical connection and other available file server(s) on a NetWare LAN. The Status column will display Default for your active physical connection and ATTACHED for other logical connections you establish with other servers.

SYSCON NetWare menu utility used to configure and restrict accounts.

TLIST . GROUPS Used to view the trustee rights granted at a specific directory location resulting from Group membership.

TLIST . USERS Used to view the trustee rights granted at a specific directory location resulting from User assignment.

USERLIST Lists users currently logged in and their connection information.

VOLINFO Menu utility to show volume information.

WHOAMI Lists information about your connection and privileges on the network.

WHOAMI/G Adds a listing of the Groups of which you are a member to the WHOAMI command.

WRITE Used to customize LOGIN Scripts by displaying text or identifier variables to screen as you log in.

Glossary

Used in LOGIN Scripts to call and execute external programs.

Access Method A set of rules determining which workstation has access to the medium at any moment.

ATTACH NetWare command used to open another logical connection with another server. Type ATTACH servername/LOGIN name at the command line. This command depends upon you having access (a valid username and password) for another server.

Attached Resource Computer Network (ARCnet) A network cabling transport system that uses a token-passing access method to connect as many as 255 workstations, using coaxial, twisted-pair, or fiber optic cabling.

Bandwidth The transmission capacity of a network medium, typically stated in megabits per second (Mbps).

Baseband Network transmission used by most LANs which transmits signals as direct current pulses. A single digital signal describes the channel (bandwidth).

Booting Starting or restarting the workstation.

Broadband Network transmission which includes voice, video, and data over the same medium. This transmission divides the channel into several distinct channels that can be used concurrently.

CAPTURE NetWare's command-line printing utility used to re-route your print jobs to a specified print queue.

CAPTURE SH CAPTURE SHow is used to list the current status of your LPT ports and how they are configured if captured.

Carrier Sense Multiple Access (CSMA). Popular baseband protocol where each node listens. CSMA/CD networks transmit only when the line is free, avoiding collisions and detecting when a collision occurs by waiting a random length of time before retrying the transmission.

CD.. DOS command to be avoided in NetWare. Used to move backwards one directory level in the DOS directory tree structure. To be avoided with NetWare unless you want the drive remapped as you go.

CD DOS Command to be avoided in NetWare, unless you want the drive remapped. CD\ is used to change your directory to the Root of a DOS Directory structure. CD\ is to be avoided with NetWare for CD\ remaps your network drive letter.

Centralized Network A computer network in which a single, extremely powerful computer coordinates network-wide services to clients.

CHKDIR Command-line utility for viewing directory and volume disk storage space available and in use.

CHKVOL Command-line utility to show volume information.

Client A PC directly attached (physically attached) to the LAN cabling system installed and running client software to activate its network connection.

Client-Server Network A network architecture where clients request resources from the servers. Servers store data and programs, and coordinate network-wide services to clients. Client-server architecture exploits the power of the network server.

Coaxial Cabling (COAX) A high-capacity cable that contains a solid, inner copper wire acting as a conductor and surrounded by plastic insulation and an outer braided copper or foil shield.

Command-Line Utility NetWare commands issued from the network drive prompt (or command-line prompt). SLIST is an example of one of NetWare's command-line utilities.

Disk Operating System (DOS) The most common local operating system for NetWare client workstations. Macintosh, OS2 and Unix are other operating systems that NetWare will service as clients.

Disk Restrictions Set to limit volume storage space.

Distributed Network A computer network in which processing is performed by several separate computers linked by a communication medium. The processing unit, referred to as the server, completes the task independently and reports the results when completed.

DOS Acronym for Disk Operating System. An operating system typically found on client workstations, known as DOS clients, originally developed by Microsoft for the IBM PC. Novell markets Novell DOS, originally developed by Digital Research and called DR-DOS.

DOS Shell Menu-driven, user interface utilized for processing DOS commands.

Downsizing The redesign of mainframe generation computing to interconnected, desktop PCs (local area networks).

DRIVE Specifies your default drive as you exit the LOGIN Script. Used in LOGIN Scripts to set your default drive so you will not have to change your preferred drive specification every time you log in.

DSPACE Menu utility for viewing directory and volume disk storage space available and in use. The System Administrator may use this utility to change disk storage space on a volume or directory.

ENDCAP Used to re-route printing to LPT1, reassigning the captured network printer for LPT1. END-CAP must be used when CAPTURE's NoAutoendcap option is chosen.

Ethernet Network cabling transport system using CSMA
CD to prevent failures or collisions when two nodes try to access the cabling system at the same time. Ethernet uses coaxial, fiber optic or twisted-pair cabling connected with a bus topology.

EXIT Terminates the execution of a LOGIN Script and exits to the command-line. Anything placed below the EXIT command will not execute. EXIT, placed in a System LOGIN Script, will bypass all User LOGIN Scripts.

Fiber Optic Cabling Cabling that sends pulses of light along optical fibers. Immune to electrical interference and often used as a high-speed transmission medium.

FILER NetWare's menu utility for controlling volume, directory, and file information.

FIRE or FIRE PHASERS Used to execute a sound within a LOGIN Script. Fire will execute a sound from one to nine times.

FLAG Used to change or view file attributes. Comparable to DOS ATTRIB command.

Gigabyte(GB) One GigaByte is equal to approximately 1,000 MegaBytes.

Groupware Software specifically designed to be used by a group working on the same project and needing to share or coordinate data.

IEEE A coordinating body founded in 1963 to develop computing and communications standards. Particularly noted for the IEEE 802-series standards.

INCLUDE Used to incorporate another script file that is written in LOGIN Script syntax and read into the LOGIN Script as it executes.

LISTDIR Command used to view directory structure and rights information.

Local Area Network (LAN) A group of computers and peripheral devices located in a close geographic region and connected by a communications medium. The medium is typically coaxial, twisted-pair or fiber optic cabling and responsible for carrying the communications along the connecting path.

Logical Connection Logging on to the network. Also called network session or user connection.

LOGIN NetWare's Command to activate and open a session (log in) to the Network Operating System (NOS) for a user. The full syntax for the Login command is LOGIN servername/ username. The severname option is only used to specify a particular server, and usually not needed to log in. The LOGIN username option is typically given at the command-line to log in to your workstation's default server. Refer to Exercise 2.1 to see your default server.

LOGIN Directory   Created upon installation of a NetWare file server. Used for logging in to the network. Contains the LOGIN.EXE file.

LOGIN/S   Used to override LOGIN Scripts by redirecting to another path where a text file is written in LOGIN Script syntax.

LOGOUT   NetWare's command to terminate a logical connection.

MAP   Used to create, change, or view network drive mappings.

MAP ..   Remap one level back in the directory structure

MAP ...   Remap two levels back in the directory structure.

**MAP **   Remap to the root directory, NetWare's volume level.

MAP *(number):=   Used to assign the second network drive letter to a directory path. (e.g., MAP *2:=/USERS).

MAP DEL   Used to delete drive mappings. Referred to as NetWare's Map Delete command. Works the same as MAP REM.

MAP DEL drive letter: Commonly used to delete network drive mappings. When used to delete a search mapping, NetWare notifies you of deleting your search map and asks for confirmation.

MAP DEL S(number):   Used to delete search drive mappings.

MAPS INS   Used to create a search drive mapping by inserting a mapping at a specified search numbered location. MAPS INS automatically renumbers and rotates the existing search mapping(s), moving them farther down the search path to make room for the inserted search drive mapping.

MAP NEXT   Used to map the next available network drive letter to a directory path specified.

MAP REM   Same as MAP DEL. Referred to as NetWare's MAP REMove command.

MAP ROOT   Used to create a fake root directory. Can be assigned to any location in the directory structure.

MAP S16   NetWare assigns the next available search drive when using S16 as a way to prevent overwriting existing search drive mappings. Sixteen search drives are possible with NetWare. Defining drive mappings using S16 will map the next available search drive number.

Medium   Used to interconnect computers on a network. Bounded (cabling) medium is more common than unbounded (microwave, laser, etc.).

Megabyte(MB)   One MegaByte is equal to approximately 1-million bytes of information.

MENUMAKE   NetWare 3.12 menu compiler, used to convert .SRC files to .DAT files to be used by NMENU.

Menu Utility   Type of interface used to provide menu options, rather than entering commands to perform network task, SYSCON and FILER are examples of NetWare's menu utilities.

Metropolitan Area Network (MAN)   A high-speed, geographically dispersed network that typically connects LANs across a metropolitan city.

NCOPY   Used to copy files and retain their attributes. Comparable to DOS COPY command.

NDIR   Used for listing file and directory information. NetWare's NDIR command is comparable to DOS DIR.

NetWare   Multi-task network operating systems developed by Novell, Inc.

NetWare Connections Window   Lets you view individual server information, change your LOGIN password, and establish a network connection using log in and log out.

NetWare Printer Connection Window   Lets you set printer options, make a print queue connection permanent, and connect and disconnect a print queue.

NetWare Send Messages Window   Lets you show or hide groups or users, send messages to a group or user, and display information about the server.

NetWare Settings Window   Lets you set permanent connections to restore when loading Windows, set message reception on or off, set the print manager and resource display options, and change the hot key value.

Network Interconnection of computers and devices using various media. Typically established to share and distribute information to computing resources using a high-speed data communication medium.

Network Drive Pointer Defined using the MAP command. Used to assign a single drive letter as an identifier or shorthand notation for a directory path location for a specific server volume.

Network Interface Card (NIC) Also called Network Adapter Board. Expansion component (adapter board) which interconnects workstation(s) and server(s) using the network cabling system.

Network Operating System Software which is installed and configured to coordinate the many functions of computer-to-computer communication. With client-server networks, the NOS is installed and runs on the network server.

Network Server A computer that coordinates access to files, printing, communications, and other resources available on the network. A server typically has a more advanced processor, more memory, and larger disk storage capacity than client workstations.

Network Topology The map of the network. The physical arrangement describes the physical topology. The logical path the message takes to get from one computer to another is the logical topology.

Node Computing device capable of communicating on a network. With NetWare, a workstation is often called a node.

NPRINT NetWare's command-line utility for printing text files.

PAUSE Breaks or pauses the execution of a LOGIN Script until any key is pressed.

PC Personal Computer. With networks, any personal computer can be called a node.

PCONSOLE Menu utility for controlling network printing.

Peers Computers acting as either a client and/or server simultaneously.

Peer-to-Peer A network architecture where two or more nodes communicate directly without the need of an intermediate device. A node can be both a client and/or a server.

Physical Connection Activates the Network Interface Card (NIC) inside the workstation to receive information from the network cabling and file server.

Polling Access Method Network access method where a host device controls communications in a predetermined order between secondary devices.

Protocol A set of specifications defining the procedures to follow for format, timing, sequence, and error checking when a message is transmitted and received.

Public Directory Created upon installation of a NetWare file server. Contains NetWare's utility command files.

Pure Network Applications Programs that must be installed on the network as they are reliant upon simultaneous access, or the connections the network avails.

RENDIR NetWare's command-line utility used to rename a directory.

SALVAGE NetWare's menu utility for recovering or purging deleted files.

Search Drive Pointer Like a Network Drive Pointer, defined using the MAP command, and assigns a drive letter as an identifier. Unlike Network Drives, Search Drives only work to point to executable Files, much as the DOS path command does as it searches in order of the path in memory. The first search drive is drive Z and are lettered in reverse order through the alphabet.

Server A powerful PC configured to load the network operating system and direct resources to network clients.

SESSION Netware's menu utility to enable users to set up and change their own working environment.

SLIST Command-line utility is used to view information about your physical connection and other available file server(s) on a NetWare LAN. The Status column will display Default for your active physical connection and ATTACHED for other logical connections you establish with other servers.

Stand-Alone Applications Programs typically installed on the stand-alone PC. Some stand-alone applications can be adopted for multi-use on a network server, while others cannot.

Standards Establishing connectivity using multiple vendors within an open architecture. Standards, such as the OSI model, are formed by committees, such as the International Standards Organization.

Station Restrictions Set to limit the physical location a user can log in from.

SYSCON NetWare menu utility used to configure and restrict accounts.

Terabyte(TB) One TeraByte is equal to approximately 1,000 GigaBytes.

Terminal Combination keyboard and display devices that do not have distributed processing capability, commonly referred to as dumb terminals.

Terminal Emulation A method of operation or software which turns a PC or networked workstation into a terminal, usually for the purpose of communicating with a mainframe or minicomputer.

Time Restrictions Set to limit the hours of the day users can log in.

TLIST . GROUPS Used to view the trustee rights granted at a specific directory location resulting from Group membership.

TLIST . USERS Used to view the trustee rights granted at a specific directory location resulting from User assignment.

Token Passing Access Method Network access method which uses an electrical signal, called a token. The token passes from node to node, providing access to the medium for the node controlling the token.

Token Ring Cabling transport subsystem which uses a ring structure to pass a token to regulate traffic on the network.

Trustee Directory Assignment The rights which a user or group trustee rights have been granted. The trustee rights are extended to each subdirectory of the directory structure location where they are granted, unless they are changed in a subsequent subdirectory.

Twisted-Pair Cabling (TP) Cable comprised of two or more pairs of insulated wires, twisted together, at six twists per inch. The cable may be shielded or unshielded. In twisted-pair cabling, one wire carries the signal and the other is for grounding.

Upsizing Matching the application requirements to the capabilities of the available hardware and software.

USERLIST Lists users currently logged in and their connection information.

VOLINFO Menu utility to show volume information.

WHOAMI Lists information about your connection and privileges on the network.

WHOAMI/G   Adds a listing of the Groups of which you are a member to the WHOAMI command.

Wide Area Network (WAN) A network dispersed across a large geographic area, often crossing boundaries of cities and states.

Workgroup Manager One of NetWare's system managers. Responsible for adding and deleting users. Can also view, add, and delete User Account managers, but cannot create other workgroup managers.

Workstation Any personal computer (other than the network server) attached to the network. This term also can refer to high-performance computers optimized for scientific or graphic applications. Workstations, in this book, take on the former, rather than the latter, definition.

WRITE   Used to customize LOGIN Scripts by displaying text or identifier variables to screen as you log in.

Index